DATE DUE

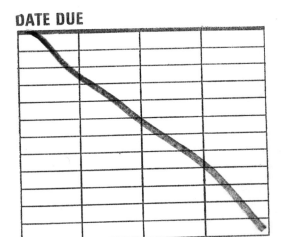

DEMCO

GOOD CONNECTIONS

A CENTURY OF SERVICE BY THE MEN & WOMEN OF SOUTHWESTERN BELL

by David G. Park Jr.

1

CONTENTS

St. Louis, 1927. The St. Louis Plant Department got together for this group photo after restoring tornado damage.

By Zane E. Barnes
*Chairman of the board,
president and chief
executive officer,
Southwestern Bell Corporation;
president and chief
executive officer, Southwestern
Bell Telephone Company*

THIS VOLUME deals with slightly more than a century of telephone history, but it isn't the conventional history text. Instead, it's an attempt to give recognition and honor to the hundreds of thousands of men and women who have worked for Southwestern Bell.

In a book this size, there's hardly room to name all these people, let alone tell something about them. If such records were available, just listing the names would create a volume like a big-city telephone directory. The very idea recalls the old joke that the telephone directory is short on plot but has a whale of a cast of characters.

So instead of naming them all, we've singled out a fair sample of individuals—named or nameless—to stand for the group. These devoted men and women came from varied social backgrounds. They don't fit into a mold any more than any other similar-sized group of Americans.

But, by and large, they have something in common: a zeal to give the customer the best possible communications service at a reasonable price. Few will deny that they've succeeded in doing just that.

Most employees, however, would shy away from being put into the spotlight for the contributions they make. They tend to draw satisfaction from two sources other than public recognition — doing the job well and working with others with similar interests and goals.

I don't think it's just my personal bias speaking when I assert that these people share a comradeship—a sense of "family"—that's found in few other enterprises. Typically, their working relationships are carried over to off-hours social relationships. The fellowship of Telephone Pioneers is just one example of this.

Telephone people care about their work; they care about the public they serve; they care about each other.

All of us at Southwestern Bell have just gone through an enormous change, the breakup of the Bell System. This company is on its own now, wholly independent from AT&T. I would be uneasy about the future if I didn't have the utmost confidence in the people of Southwestern Bell Corporation. They have shown themselves able to meet any challenge in the past. They will meet this challenge, too.

In the next few years the changes in our business will be greater than any that occurred in our first century of existence. But one thing will remain, must remain unchanged: the tradition of caring.

This book is about people who cared. It has a whale of a cast of characters. I hope you enjoy reading it.

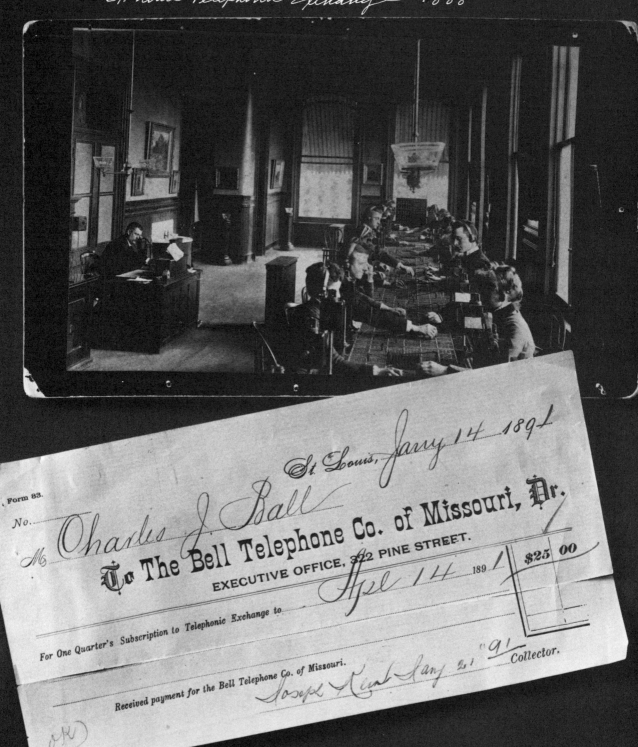

St. Louis Telephonic Exchange — 1888

St. Louis, Jan'y 14 1891

Form 83.

No.

M Charles J. Ball

To The Bell Telephone Co. of Missouri, Dr.

EXECUTIVE OFFICE, 322 PINE STREET.

Apl 14 1891 $25 00

For One Quarter's Subscription to Telephonic Exchange to

Received payment for the Bell Telephone Co. of Missouri.

Joseph Kent Jany 21 '91 Collector.

THE TRAIL BLAZERS

CHAPTER ONE

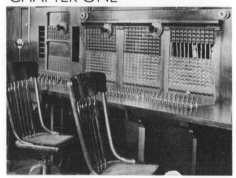

CHARLES W. MCDANIEL got started toward the telephone business while waiting for a barber shop shave.

George Freeland Durant was looking for a better way for people to communicate than by using the facilities of the telegraph exchange he ran in St. Louis.

A. H. Belo wanted to keep in touch with the breaking news at his Galveston newspaper even when he was at home.

There were others—thousands of others: men who were looking for the big breakthrough. Alexander Graham Bell's invention seemed like the answer. Those who could put this invention to use might make their fortunes (but few of them did). Regardless, they would be at the cutting edge of progress, as people say in the 1980s. In the 1870s, they would have said the telephone looked like the Big Chance.

Those were exciting, stimulating times. The nation was still licking its wounds from the War Between the States, but there was an exhilarating feeling of success in the air. Prosperity was indeed just around the corner. The railroads were spanning the continent. So were the telegraph lines. What would be the next innovation?

"I was sitting in a barber shop in Corning, Iowa, one Sunday morning in 1876," McDaniel recalled many years later, "when a man read aloud an article about the invention of the telephone. This was interesting to me, and I went out and bought a copy of the paper. I took it home and read the article to my wife and said I thought it was the greatest invention of the age. I determined to learn all about it."

At the time, McDaniel, a native of Hannibal, Mo., was a tinner in a Corning hardware store. Among the store's customers was one "Professor Marchand of the Icarian community." Marchand, a professor of physics, helped young McDaniel in his attempts to create a working model of the telephone.

"To carry out my experiments, it became necessary for me to have a shop," McDaniel continues. "I had a very good barn in which I kept my cow and pony. I turned the cow out of doors and secured a turning lathe which I set up in the cow's stall. . . . Night after night I worked till after 12 o'clock, and my friends often asked me if I ever went to bed."

McDaniel's tinkering wasn't confined to the telephone; he also worked on phonographs and electric lighting. But his destiny pointed him toward developing Bell's invention. By the year 1878, he had learned enough to build a telephone line a mile and a half long from Corning to the county fair and charged 10 cents for people who wanted to talk over it. "As a profitable venture, this was a failure," he observes ruefully.

Theodore N. Vail

The experience, however, stood McDaniel in good stead. In the philosophy of another inventor and experimenter, Thomas Edison, he had learned something wouldn't work and that meant he could go on to something that would. His opportunity came when a friend, James Reiger, offered to put him in touch with Theodore N. Vail. It turned out that Reiger and Vail had worked together in the Railway Mail Service. Vail was now the guiding force of the National Bell Telephone Company, based in Boston, and was looking for ways to expand the business across the nation.

McDaniel was not one to let grass grow under his feet. He developed what was apparently an intense correspondence with Vail—if Vail replied as promptly to other prospective "agents," one wonders how he found time to run the rest of the business! Two of Vail's letters to McDaniel are dated March 8 and March 17, and apparently they are answers written the day McDaniel's questions were received.

"We have considerable unoccupied territory in St. Joseph, Hannibal and other towns of about the same size, and we wish to make arrangements with parties who will establish the exchange or district system when we arrange for these cities," Vail writes. In a subsequent letter, he tells McDaniel:

"It would take about $3,000 to start a good system in Hannibal and about the same in St. Joseph. We would not care to make contract unless that amount could be raised by you. If you think of trying, it would be well for you to proceed quietly and not let anyone know except those who were furnishing the money until you had made all arrangements to commence."

Three thousand dollars! A substantial sum for a tinner in a hardware store to raise, but obviously McDaniel wasn't daunted, for we soon find B. E. Madden, superintendent of agencies for National Bell, explaining further:

"In establishing an Exchange system, you would have to furnish each subscriber with an electric call bell, costing you $3.25, and one or two telephones costing you $5 per year, each. . . . I enclose an estimate of the cost of construction and expense of operating the system in Rochester, N.Y., which was made up very carefully. . . .

"As to the rates, I think you will have no difficulty in realizing $3 per month where you can furnish one telephone and $4 where you can furnish two, and you might get $1 per month more. . . . You can readily see that there is big money in the business. I don't know of anything which will pay so well, and I sincerely trust you will make up your mind to go into it at once."

Springfield, Mo., 1880.
Operators at work.

The figures Madden submits as samples of what it cost to start a telephone exchange operation in those days are interesting. Construction for the Rochester company, with 200 subscribers, was $2,950, broken down as follows: 25 miles' line material and labor, $1,250; 200 "gravity batteries," $200; connecting materials for subscribers—bell, insulated wire, flexible cord, labor, $1,100; office connections, switchboards, $400.

As for monthly expenses, Madden figured them like this: $12.50 for rent; $70 for "operators, three boys 16 and 18 years old"; $40 for "linemen to make repairs, put up wires"; $50 for superintendent ("which you can fill yourself"); $25 for battery maintenance; and $83.34 for the rental of 200 Bell telephones. Total monthly operating cost, $305.84.

"Bear in mind this is for 200 subscribers, say $3 per month," Madden wound up. "Profit . . . $294.16." Not a bad monthly return on a $3,000 investment.

McDaniel went to Omaha in March 1879 to meet Madden, and the latter told him his previous job was selling sewing machines. He supposed he had obtained his job with the telephone business because of his "gift of gab."

McDaniel wouldn't have needed much persuasion by this time, however. He went back to his home town of Hannibal, enlisted the aid of friends, raised $2,500 from just five of them and organized the Hannibal Telephone Company. After turning back the challenge of the Western Union Telegraph Company to obtain a franchise (McDaniel had thoughtfully arranged to get a member of the city council on his board), the company started operation. Later it established "long distance" service to New London, 10 miles away, and Palmyra, 12 miles away. These were the first long distance lines in Missouri, according to McDaniel, and those who used them were charged 10 cents a call. This time, the enterprise was a success.

McDaniel's telephone career didn't end with the Hannibal Telephone Company. When that company was taken over by the Missouri & Kansas Telephone Company, he came along as a valued employee and rose to the title of general superintendent at the Kansas City headquarters before he retired in 1913.

St. Louis

George Durant didn't have to make connections, like McDaniel, in order to get into the telephone business. He came in on the ground floor. To be specific, he came to St. Louis in 1874 as general manager of the American District Telegraph Company's operations there.

A.D.T. had lines running from its main office to its subscribers' homes and offices, just like a telephone system. Only, of course, there was no voice communication. Instead, customers were furnished with a code system whereby they could signal simple messages—"Have the livery stable send over a rig"; "Get a messenger boy here"; and the like.

With all these circuits available for his use, Durant wanted to experiment with the newfangled telephones. He obtained 41 of the instruments, hooked them up in subscribers' residences and business locations, connected all 41 leads together in the A.D.T. office, and created what was probably the world's biggest party line for the time. In fact, it would be remarkable even today.

Over this party line one evening, a musical concert was "broadcast." There was singing, trumpet playing and other entertainment, while perhaps 100 people took turns listening at the different locations. Even the governor of Missouri witnessed the demonstration that the telephone was practical.

Emboldened by this success, Durant talked his superiors into letting him try

Charles W. McDaniel

Hannibal, Mo., 1889. Workers posed on top of the central office. They are: (1) J. H. Flien; (2) Harry Bellard; (3) Ollie Cole; (4) Ben Reovell; (5) H. W. Crabb.

to organize a telephone system in St. Louis. That wasn't so hard; the hard part came in trying to get the conservative burghers of St. Louis to "subscribe" to such a notion. It was one thing to listen to a novelty concert; it was something else to lay out $300 in cold cash for three years' telephone service—the minimum Durant would accept for a contract term.

We can imagine the conversation when Durant made his first sale, to Judge George A. Madill, lawyer and financier. Judge Madill listened carefully to the proposition. If it worked out, yes, it could prove to be quite worthwhile—a newer, faster, more convenient way of communicating. To be an early subscriber to a successful enterprise like this would be something to talk about at the club. "Telephone service? Why, of course, I've had it from the beginning, when you fellows were still making jokes about it and saying it wouldn't work."

And yet—suppose it *didn't* work? Suppose there was something wrong, something that Durant had overlooked? People would laugh at anyone connected with the failed enterprise. "Hey, there's old Judge Dingaling Madill. You'd think a man like that would be too smart to fall for such a harebrained scheme."

Finally, the judge made up his mind . . . sort of. "Durant," he said, "your proposition sounds interesting. I'll gamble on the idea if some other people go along. Here's a list of 10 other law firms. You go out and sell half the names on that list, and you've got me as your first subscriber."

Durant took the list and went out to hit up the other prospects. But even with Madill's lukewarm backing, he could sign up only 4 of the 10. Judge Madill decided that was close enough and let his name stand on the list.

Durant persisted. Eventually the St. Louis Telephonic Exchange opened April 19, 1878, with 12 subscribers. The rest, of course, is history. Durant became general manager of what was eventually called the Bell Telephone Company of Missouri, and he still held that post when he died in 1909.

George F. Durant

St. Louis, 1884. The building at right housed the city's only local exchange.

Kansas City

In Kansas City's turbulent early telephone history, perhaps the most intriguing character is a man whose name is lost in the mists of history—"the stranger from the East" who spoke to J. D. Cruise. Cruise himself recalled the incident in a report dated April 20, 1908:

"One bright spring morning in 1879, the writer, who at that time represented one of the prominent railroad trunk lines of the West, was approached by a stranger from the East who inquired for a telephone. I informed him that as yet Kansas City had not reached the telephonic age; that my information was that an abortive attempt had been made to establish an exchange for the Edison telephone, but it was a failure, one of the few things that Edison did not make successful.

"The gentleman said, 'By all means, get a Bell telephone; there is no other worth the name. Write Mr. Gleason, manager of the Indianapolis, Ind., exchange. He will give you the proper information to form a stock company and go to work. Kansas City needs an exchange, and unless I am very much mistaken, it will prove an excellent field.' "

Who was the stranger? Cruise said he regretted that he had lost the man's name, as this was some of the best advice he ever received.

To cut a very involved story shorter, Cruise, after an initial failure, succeeded in establishing the "Kansas City Telephonic Exchange" with an authorizing city ordinance dated May 1, 1879.

Y' Gotta Have Heart

A. B. HOMER was a man who might have blazed a telephone trail, but he lost his nerve.

The story of Homer, a Galveston cotton buyer, is recounted by an anonymous historian in a 1929 review of Southwestern Bell's origins. Homer was probably the first person in Texas to secure licenses from the Bell interests to use their patents. He was granted a contract for "all of southern Texas" (no indication of where the line was drawn between north and south).

Homer's first idea, naturally, was to establish a Bell exchange in Galveston. But the powerful Western Union interests were at that time (1879) making a fight to drive the Bell interests to the wall and secure the budding industry for themselves. They sent word to David Hall, their Galveston manager, to stop Homer if he could and, at any rate, to build a Galveston telephone exchange before Homer could get his going.

Hall tried bluffing Homer out, telling him that the Bell patents were invalid and he could be sued if he tried to act on them. Homer didn't accept this idea, but the bluff must have given him second thoughts. While he was having those thoughts, Hall got the Western Union telephone exchange in operation.

Homer felt the Bell management didn't back him up in his fight with Hall, and in anger, he canceled his contract. Within a year, Western Union lost its court battle with Bell and contracted to turn all its exchanges over to the Bell interests.

Homer never got over the fact that he had surrendered his license and consequently was shut out of the telephone business in Galveston. In his later years, he declared that he took a trip to Boston every year to "cuss out" Bell executive Theodore N. Vail for not giving him more encouragement.

The anonymous historian concludes dryly: "Of course, a man who expected encouragement at that state of telephony was apt to wait a long time for it." ∎

Oklahoma Telephone Tales

NOT ALL the stories that have come down to us from early telephone days can be accepted without a grain of salt. For example, this one from Oklahoma's Indian Territory seems apocryphal:

To overcome Indian suspicion that telephones would work only in the white man's language, a demonstration was arranged when an early toll line was built from Tahlequah through Fort Gibson to Muskogee, all territory ruled by the Cherokee Council.

A medicine man at Tahlequah approached suspiciously, struck the telephone pole with his staff, then listened over a test instrument hanging on the pole. He found himself talking to an interpreter at Fort Gibson, who reported that the medicine man's wife had just given birth to twins.

The Indian turned away from the phone to tell the other tribesmen: "Hit pole too hard."

On the other hand, this story seems well authenticated:

John M. Noble and J. N. Coulter raised the capital needed to

"Hit pole too hard."

build a telephone line from Perry to Pawnee (it cost $2,200). Connections were completed on a cold day in October 1897.

Noble and Coulter agreed to test the line in this manner: Noble would be at the instrument in Perry and Coulter at the one in Pawnee. At a specified time, they would try to talk; if they could not hear the conversation, both were to start walking along the line trying to locate the trouble.

When the appointed time came, Noble was so excited that he put the receiver to his deaf ear. Naturally, he heard nothing, so he struck out on the route to Pawnee. Coulter, however, had heard Noble's "hello" and was well pleased with the experiment's success as he sat by the fire in his Pawnee hotel room.

Noble finally completed his 31-mile hike right up to Coulter's room. It took a while to convince him that the circuit was in good order; the only thing wrong was that he had tried to hear with his deaf ear. ∎

It was a race against time. Western Union had organized another telephone company, the Gold & Stock Company, and it opened for business 11 days after that first Cruise ordinance was passed. And, in fact, the Gold & Stock Company bought a controlling interest in Cruise's firm shortly afterward.

Within two years, these events occurred: Both firms were bought out by Bell of Missouri (the St. Louis operation), and the Western Union facilities were abandoned; then Bell, in turn, sold out to Central Union; and in 1882, this group turned over the property to the newly organized Missouri & Kansas Telephone Company. Each time the property changed hands, the price went up, although figures are not exactly comparable because M&K included a number of other exchanges in its $1 million capitalization.

Once bitten by the telephone bug, Cruise and his partners began to dream large dreams of "building exchanges and running connecting lines between towns in Kansas, western Missouri, southern Iowa and Indian Territory (which was the name for Oklahoma before it became a state)." Most of these plans were indeed carried out, but not by Cruise, who disappeared from control amid all the financial wheeling and dealing. One hopes he was adequately compensated for his enterprise.

Kansas City, Mo., 1892. Service demands were so great that these extensions had to be added to the city's original switchboard.

Hot Springs, Ark., 1906. An early construction crew.

Fort Smith, Ark., 1901. An operating room.

Arkansas

The man who brought telephone service to Little Rock had a special mission: "Keep out Bell!!" And for a time, he was successful.

Actually, the wondrous new invention was first demonstrated in the Arkansas capital by a Bell representative, James Hamblet of St. Louis. He came to Little Rock in February 1878 and spent several days displaying the telephone's working. The *Daily Gazette,* reporting on his visit, said Hamblet "desires to establish a state agency in Little Rock." Apparently nothing came of this plan.

But there was a bitter struggle going on at this time between the newly organized National Bell Telephone Company and the firmly established Western Union Telegraph Company. The Bell interests, losing their initial enthusiasm, once offered to sell their patent rights to Western Union. The offer was refused. But when the telephone actually began to win acceptance, the Western Union management had second thoughts. They began to set up competing exchanges, hoping to drive the upstart Bell interests to the wall. Meanwhile they took every legal step they could in order to discredit the Bell patents they had once refused to buy.*

As part of this struggle, the order went out to all important Western Union offices: "Set up a telephone system as soon as you can and keep Bell telephones out of your territory." In Little Rock, this assignment fell to Edward C. Newton, the company's local manager.

Newton knew nothing about telephones, but he knew how to carry out orders. He started calling on local businesses whose telegraph patronage indicated they could also afford to pay $5 a month for telephone service. It took him almost a year to sign up 10 subscribers. But on March 10, 1879, Newton announced he was ready to construct a telephone system. The exchange actually opened for business November 1 of that year. The central office was a small room adjoining the Western Union office.

The *Gazette,* which had been a promoter of the telephone since Hamblet's first demonstration in the newspaper office, triumphantly predicted:

"The telephone exchange was a long stride and one which will meet with appreciation. After a while, it will not be necessary for a businessman to leave his office—only to eat and get out of an unwelcome visitor's way."

Edward Newton's enterprise in stealing a march on Bell probably solidified his tenure at Western Union, but the exchange didn't prosper as the *Gazette* expected. In 1880, the telegraph company got out of the telephone business, selling the exchange to local interests.

The next year a man with bigger dreams than Newton engineered a takeover of many exchanges in the Southwest, including those abandoned by Western Union in Little Rock, Galveston and Houston. This man, by a trivial coincidence, had "Newton" for his middle name—he was, in full, Jasper Newton Keller.

Keller had once been a telegrapher for the Union Pacific Railroad. An enthusiast for the telephone and its potential to link the nation, he started by building an exchange at Ogden, Utah. But Keller wasn't satisfied with an exchange here and another there; what he envisioned was a single telephone network like the railroad network of the day.

Jasper N. Keller

*See page 266. Persons interested in more details of this epic struggle may wish to refer to John Brooks' authoritative history, *Telephone—the First Hundred Years.* Note page 61: "The rival that emerged [in the fall of 1877], and that over the next two years was to come within an ace of putting the Bell interests out of business, was none other than Western Union Telegraph Company . . . [which] had decided to spend millions of dollars challenging the Bell patents." Brooks' summary is supported by many exchange histories, including that of Little Rock.

Logan H. Roots

Having established a connection by correspondence with Colonel Logan H. Roots, Little Rock banker, Keller arrived in the city in January 1881. Roots was a major stockholder in the telephone exchange.

The two hit it off from the first. Roots was a distinguished gentleman, perhaps the leading citizen of the state, well educated and with a keen knowledge of finance. Keller, a comparative youngster in his mid-30s, was described by the colonel as "vigorous in health, fine in physique, engaging in manner, and a most agreeable, companionable, and intelligent personality."

A month later on February 5, 1881, these two men announced they had organized the Southwestern Telegraph & Telephone Company, with headquarters in Little Rock. They had exclusive rights to the use of Bell's telephone patent in both Arkansas and Texas, and they set about developing a unified telephone system for the two states.

Growth was rapid. In 1883, the company had 36 exchanges in the territory and 4,214 telephones. And then—such changes were typical in those early days—Roots and Keller sold the firm they had built to an eastern organization known as the Lowell Syndicate. Apparently they made a healthy profit from their two years at the head of the enterprise.

Keller stayed in the telephone business and later rose to the presidency of the New England Telephone & Telegraph Company, retiring in 1912.

Oklahoma

When the telephone was born in 1876, there wasn't a state of Oklahoma—in fact, it wouldn't come into being for another 31 years. In 1876, there was only "Indian Territory" and a strip of "No Man's Land" cut off from Texas (that strip is now the Oklahoma Panhandle). To a large extent, the whole area was ruled by Indian tribes, although the United States government had the ultimate authority, subject to treaties.

Indians had learned to be wary of white men's innovations, but they weren't completely opposed to progress—only those changes which might destroy their way of life. Thus, members of the Cherokee tribe promoted, built and financed the first commercial telephone line in Indian Territory in 1886. It ran from Tahlequah to Fort Gibson and Muskogee, linking, respectively, the capital of the Cherokee Nation, an Army fort and the Indian Union agency for the Five Civilized Tribes.*

But the council which approved this project also stipulated that the lines should be constructed over a route inaccessible to railroads and that no surveyor's instruments would be used. They had observed that in the white man's country overhead communication lines usually paralleled the railroad right of way, and they reasoned that running such lines up and down the hills and mountains would discourage railroads and protect against sectionalizing of their land.

Three Indian citizens of Tahlequah were the prime movers in this enterprise—Henry Eiffert, J. S. Stapler and D. W. Lipe. The council resolution granting them an exclusive charter for 20 years provided that a small portion of the gross receipts would go to a school fund. It pointed out that construction of such a line would enable the people to get timely reports of the stock and produce markets.

This was hardly the first use of the telephones in Indian Territory, only the first

*As every Oklahoma schoolchild knows, the Five Civilized Tribes were the Cherokees, Choctaws, Seminoles, Chickasaws and Creeks. Their democratic form of government compared favorably with that of the white man and, in fact, their constitution provided the pattern for Oklahoma's state constitution.

commercial enterprise. As early as 1879, telephones were added to an Army telegraph line between Fort Sill and Fort Reno. Correspondence still in existence reflects an amusing battle of wills between Second Lieutenant C. A. Tingle of the Army Signal Service in Denison, Tex., and P. B. Hunt, Indian agent at Anadarko, Okla.

Tingle obviously wanted telephones to be used and Hunt was skeptical of their utility. We read Tingle's letter of October 7, 1879, saying that he has shipped "two call bells and telephones" to Fort Sill to be set up "as soon as practicable." More than a month later, on November 15, a much shorter and curter letter from "Tingle, Lt." to "Mr. Hunt, Indian Agent, Sill, I. T." says, "Please take one call box and one telephone with you to agency or arrange to have it sent up. I shall leave here via Reno either Monday or Tuesday to set it up for you."

On November 25 Hunt writes Tingle: "In view of the fact that the telephone *cannot be used with success* as a means of communication from this point to Ft. Sill, I respectfully ask that a telegraph office be established here. . . ."

But Tingle apparently had the last word November 30: "Would advise you to run telephone line from office to school building with wire I left you and test telephone before building permanent line. Line is open today between Sill and Reno." Add Second Lieutenant Tingle to the list of early trailblazers who brought the telephone to the Southwest!

This list, however, would be quite incomplete if it did not include the name of John M. Noble, one of the organizers in 1897 of the Arkansas Valley Telephone Company. Noble could be considered the "point man" for a consortium which

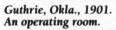

Guthrie, Okla., 1901.
An operating room.

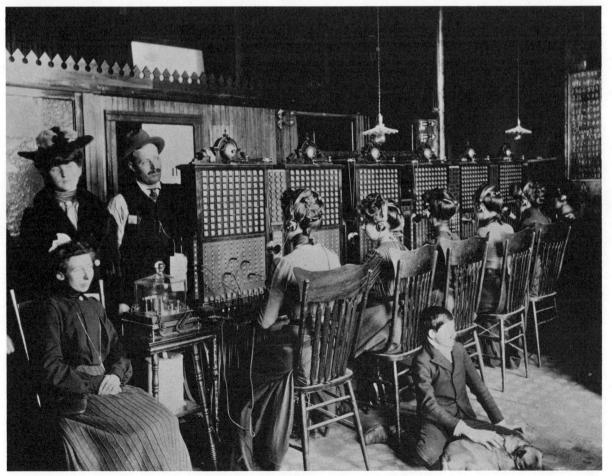

There Were Giants in Those Days

ONE OF THE almost legendary figures of the telephone's early days is Charles A. Sloan. Sloan hardly qualifies as a "trailblazer," since he entered the telephone business only in 1901; but his bulldog tenacity in keeping service going almost single-handedly is reminiscent of the men and women who started and conducted the telephone business in the 1880s.

Sloan, a native of Minnesota, had an intimate knowledge of poles and telegraph line work. In 1887, he supervised the building of the Western Union–Rock Island Telegraph lines from Herington to Liberal, Kan. He left his maintenance assignments with these lines to purchase the Pratt, Kan., exchange in 1901. At that time, the two-year-old exchange had only 90 subscribers, the original owners having neglected it after starting service.

Sloan replaced the switchboard with new central office equipment and developed rural lines and toll lines serving the exchange. His funds, however, wouldn't stretch to rebuilding the outside plant in the city itself. He added open wire to the poles already in use until a practical limit was reached and even exceeded; thereafter, customers had to be content with party lines.

When winter's sleet storms struck western Kansas, Sloan "stayed up all night with his plant like a farmer with a sick horse," says a contemporary account, which continues:

"While the sleet was still forming in a misty atmosphere, Sloan mounted a 30-foot pole on the axle of a two-wheel slop barrel. After midnight, when low temperature had rendered the ice dry and brittle, Sloan and his single helper used the balance pole as a battering ram against supporting poles to shake loose the ice load. The 4 a.m. gale which wrecked other telephone plants found Sloan's heavier leads free from ice and but little damage was done."

Sloan organized the Southwest Long Distance Telephone Company in 1909, keeping his headquarters in Pratt. He remained president of the company until his death in 1921. ■

Sloan and his single helper used the balance pole as a battering ram.

included J. E. Coulter, E. D. Nims, B. S. McGuire and E. E. Westervelt. The Arkansas Valley company was set up to provide some lively competition for the Missouri & Kansas Company. M&K had established exchanges in Oklahoma at Oklahoma City and Guthrie in 1893, then concentrated further expansion efforts in Missouri and Kansas.

Since the telephone business, like nature, abhors a vacuum, a number of competitors to M&K sprang up. The Arkansas Valley Company quickly became M&K's principal challenger, starting by constructing a toll line connecting Perry, Pawnee and Stillwater. Eventually the two companies buried the hatchet. The Arkansas Valley Company had expanded, by exchange growth and acquisition, to a statewide network under the name of Pioneer Telephone & Telegraph Company. This firm exchanged its holdings in Kansas for M&K's holdings in Oklahoma.

Noble continued as general manager of the Pioneer Company until his retirement. Nims, one of his earliest associates, went on to become the second president of Southwestern Bell.

Leavenworth, Kan., 1895.
The central office.

Kansas

Although the first recorded use of telephones in Kansas was at Lawrence, in 1877, real telephone service in the sense we understand it today didn't arrive in the state until two years later.

Earlier telephone conversations were between a pair of instruments. The linkup at Lawrence was between a wholesale grocery house and a packing plant. At Leavenworth, Alexander Calder, a wagon manufacturer, used the telephone to communicate from his downtown office to the penitentiary, where state prison labor made some of his wagons under contract. Telephones were used for classroom demonstrations at Bluemont College in Manhattan and at Washburn College in Topeka.

It was at Topeka, too, that the first Kansas switchboard was installed. June 4, 1879, E. L. Smith, manager of the local Western Union office, announced the opening of a telephone exchange. It began service September 11 of that year with 52 subscribers—44 businesses and 8 residences.

Like other exchanges in those early days, no telephone numbers were assigned and connections had to be made by name. There was no directory; the list of subscribers was published in the daily papers as they were connected.

The Topeka exchange was sold in 1881 to the Merchants Telephone & Telegraph Company, a Kansas City enterprise.

Texas

In the 1870s, Galveston was one of the largest and most important commercial cities in Texas, overshadowing future giants like Houston and Dallas. It was only natural, therefore, that the first commercial use of the telephone in Texas would be at the city on the bay.

A. H. Belo, publisher of the Galveston *News* (as well as the Dallas *Morning News),* had been to the 1876 Philadelphia Exposition and had seen the demonstration of Bell's new invention. Later he brought back two of the instruments from the East and had them hooked up to connect the newspaper office with his home. Newspaper records show that this was accomplished March 18, 1878. Somewhat later that same year, the newspaper was connected by telephone with the United States Signal Corps station on the coast to help get early warnings of rough weather in the Gulf and news of shipwrecks.

Belo, incidentally, established another precedent when he linked his Galveston and Dallas papers by leased-line telegraph, so the city to the north could have the news almost as fast as it came in to Galveston from the rest of the world. Belo was fired with the innovative zeal of the time.

That same desire to be first with the latest must have motivated the two men who set up a telephone line "in 1877 or 1878" over Western Union telegraph lines between Austin and nearby Manchaca. The men had the intriguing names of W. A. Pillow and Sebe Sneed. The records don't reveal Pillow's role at the time, although he afterward became "auditor, superintendent of supplies and cashier" for the Southwestern Telegraph & Telephone Company; he was the brother of Ben Pillow, local Western Union manager. Sebe Sneed was superintendent of Austin schools.

George W. Foster, telephone historian, says flatly that San Antonio's "first telephone line for business purposes was built for George W. Brackenridge . . . from the head of the river to his office downtown. . . . About the same time, a line was built for Jack LaBatt, government contractor, San Antonio, from the *Post* downtown." Unfortunately, Foster gives no date for either hookup.

Similarly lacking is a date for the establishment of a line from the Dallas waterworks pumping station at Browder Springs to the fire chief's office downtown. Almost certainly this was later than the other cases, however. It featured a technological breakthrough—an "intermediate telephone" at the home of Alexander Sanger, department store magnate.

The early days of the telephone in Houston show parallels to what happened in Little Rock. J. W. Stacey, Western Union manager, installed a demonstration line from the city's fairgrounds to a room in the building of the Houston *Telegram*. This was during an encampment of the state militia in June 1878.

"Everybody wishing to have the pleasure of conversing with a friend a mile distant will have an opportunity," the *Telegram* announced.

The first two telephone exchanges (as distinguished from point-to-point hookups) in Texas were established in 1879. Galveston was first, with a date of August 21; the corresponding date for Houston is not available, but it was later that year. Both were established by the Western Union company, and the Galveston central office was located on the northwest corner of Tremont and Strand streets over Brown Hardware Company's store.

In 1881, the two exchanges were purchased from Western Union by Jasper Keller's firm, Southwestern Telegraph & Telephone Company. David Hall,

J. W. Stacey

George W. Foster

W. A. Pillow

A. H. Belo

Western Union manager who established the Galveston exchange, must not have been too happy about the sale. It's reported that at the time of takeover he tossed the exchange records to T. W. Milburn, the Southwestern manager, and growled: "Here, take the damned things."

Keller quickly moved ahead to establish operations throughout Texas. Under his leadership, five new exchanges were opened in the year 1881: Dallas—June 1; San Antonio—June 17; Austin—June 24; Fort Worth—September 1; Waco—October 1. In the following year, Keller opened 13 other Texas exchanges.

A name that should not be overlooked when calling the roll of Texas telephone trailblazers is that of Daniel M. Clower, known in his later years as "the grand old man of the telephone business."

In 1905, at the age of 72, Clower wrote a letter of reminiscence about early telephone days in Dallas which is worth excerpting:

"On April 1, 1881, I left Dallas with a crew of men, wagons and teams with a full camping outfit for the cedar brakes near the mouth of Five Mile Creek between Miller's Switch and Hutchins on the H&TC Railway. I got out 600 poles ranging from 25 feet 4 inches to 35 feet 4 inches. . . .

"I loaded about 400 of these poles and shipped [them] to Dallas and Fort Worth. I then came to Dallas and constructed the telephone exchange. We put the central office over 224 Elm Street on the same floor with the Western Union Telegraph offices. . . .

"We opened the exchange on June 1, 1881, with about 40 subscribers and Miss Jennie E. Thompson as the day operator. I am happy to say that she is still living and looks as young and pretty as any 20-year-old young lady. (Would tell her present name and address, but she is a widow). . . . "

Clower always had an eye for the ladies. A charming anecdote from his retirement relates that when he was touring Valley Forge, Pa., he took time out to visit the nearby Bell exchange in West Chester. He spent an hour talking with the employees and afterward commented: "My, but you have nice girls in your exchange." Perhaps noting his interviewer's lifted eyebrows, he added: "The man who does not like the girls is in his dotage." Clower was 87 at the time. ∎

Daniel M. Clower

San Antonio, Tex., 1887.
The first branch exchange.
The numerals indicate pole
numbers.

GERARD B. ALLEN, President.   HENRY B. LOUDERMAN, Vice-Pres. & Sec'y.

American District Telegraph Co.

(LICENSED UNDER BELL'S PATENTS.)

Executive Office, 214 North Sixth Street.

INSTRUCTIONS

I. Before using the instrument... DICATOR projects above the BELL... use, and the KNOBS must not be to...

II. Each station on your cir... SIGNAL.

III. **TO Call any Station on y...** signal of that station twice on the... a few seconds, then strike your ow... moment for the answer on the Bel... the call in the same way.

CIRCUIT No. 1.

SIGNAL.   STATION.
2   District Office, 506 Leffingwell Ave.
4   Chester H. Krum, 2720 ...
6   ...

...G. Blow, 2635 Washington Ave.
S. M. Dodd, 2311 Locust.
Thos. E. Tutt, 2307 Locust.
Jno. T. Davis, 2123 Locust.
Harrigan & Cullinane, Livery
J. C. Birge, 1027 Clay Ave.

REGULATIONS:—T...
...e is required see if others...

ORDERS and SHORT...
...witching.

Messages sent to the Off...
From 10 P. M. to 7 A. ...
Parties not connected with...
the District Offices.

Should your Bell or Telephon...
Messengers are furnished at...

The Bell Telephone Company of Missouri

St. Louis, July 31, 190...

Received from ____ S. 207a Steinmeyer Hwd.
____ Co.

for Telephone Service du... ____ Broadway. Total $ 9
120 city messages ... quarter ending July 31, 1903,
For Toll Service during the m... ...te of rates named in Contract $8 9 75
...July, $

NOTE: THIS RECEIPT, TO BE VALID, MUST BE COUNTERSIGNED BY THE AGENT THROUGH WHOM THE AMOUNT IS COLLECTED.

COUNTERSIGNED ____ DAY OF ____

LIST OF SUBSCRIBERS
1883

Hot Springs Telephone Exchange

INSURE YOUR DWELLINGS AND STOCKS WITH

W. W. WIGGS,
HOT SPRINGS, ARKANSAS.

Telephone Connection.

ROOM No. 10, GAINES' BLOCK, UP-STAIRS.

McCAFFRAY & GROSS,
UNDERTAKERS

If you Wish to Speak to Us, Call for No. 100.

◄VALLEY STORE►
→Dealers in←

DRY GOODS
FURNISHINGS,
...thing Outfits.

Allard, Cad, res., Central ave.
Arlington Hotel, office, Central ave
Arlington Hotel, storeroom
Avenue Hotel, office, Park ave
Avenue Hotel, storeroom, Park ave
Avenue Hotel Drug Store, Park ave

Barnet, A. L., grocer, Park ave
Bentz Bros., undertakers, Central ave
Beitler, D. A., grocer, Washington ave
Bernardinia, R., French rest., Central ave.
Buchanan, Dr., office, Exchange st.
Buchanan, Dr., res., Exchange st.

Cabell & Newman, druggists, Central ave.
Chambers, Jas. A., m'g'r. Telephone Ex., Ouachita ave.
Chandy, A., Restaurant, Central ave
Chief of Police
Clarendon Hotel, Park ave
Clifton House, Chapel st.
Conger, J. N., res., Benton st
Court Place, private board, Prospect ave

Davies, R. G., res., Central ave.
Delaney, P. J., grocer.

Electric Light Co., light house, Benton st
Ellsworth, Dr., res., Park ave
Eveland, Chas., res., M. V. road.

...grocers... city hall

Keller, Dr. J. M., res., Central ave.
Kentucky Stables, Park ave.
Kling, Frank, gas works, Malvern ave.

Lane, Grace, res., Valley st
Little Grocery, ...
Little Rock, ...
Loughran & ...wood
Lyon, Z., New Valley Store

McCaffray & Gross, undertakers
Mendell Bros., dry goods
Miller, Stearns & Co., hardware, second office.
Mountain Valley Co., office, second, Mountain Valley
Mountain Valley Co., hotel, Mountain Valley
Morse, Mrs. S. B., res., Central ave
Morse, Wm., res., Malvern ave.

News, Daily, office, Central ave.
Nickerson, A. S., plber.

O'Bryan, M. C. & Co., grocers, Central ave.
O'Neil, Thos., palace market.
O. K. Meat Market.

Plateau Hotel, Central ave.
Polhaus' ice Co., depot.
Polhamus ice Co., factory, Benton road
Pollard & Co., Live and Let Live drug store

Rector, E. W., res., S. Central ave.
Rector, E. W., office

Sentinel, daily, office, Central ave.
Shield's Hotel, court house.
Shield's Hotel, Malvern ave.
Stephen & Dow, planing mill, Valley st
Smith, Miss Minnie, res., Central ave.
Street Car Co., office, Central ave.
Street Car Co., stables, Park ave.
Stitt, S. H., res., Park ave.
Sumpter House, office
Sulphur Springs.

OUT OF MANY, ONE

CHAPTER TWO

THERE'S AN ANECDOTE (probably apocryphal) about the United States visitor to a Latin American metropolis who found it hard to make business contacts—because the city was served by two competing telephone companies.

"I can't understand how you can be satisfied with service from two telephone companies," the American told one of the local businessmen.

"Yes, I know what you mean," was the reply. "You would think that a city this large would have at least five telephone companies!"

The idea of two or more local telephone companies seems bizarre to most Americans today. But all the way into the 1920s, such a situation existed in some United States cities. If Mrs. Jones wanted to talk to Mrs. Smith down the street and Mrs. Smith had "the other company's phone," Mrs. Jones would just have to walk to Mrs. Smith's house.

Well, there was another possibility: If Mrs. Smith had a neighbor who was served by the same phone company as Mrs. Jones, then Mrs. Jones could call Mrs. Smith's neighbor and ask her to summon Mrs. Smith to the phone. Such an arrangement was an annoyance to all three ladies but especially to the unfortunate neighbor whose phone was tied up on a call that didn't even concern her.

Business people, just learning to rely on their telephone service to reach customers, found the situation was more than annoying; it was expensive. To reach everyone, they had to have service from each company serving their trade area. Newspaper advertisements of the period often announced proudly, "We have both phones," and listed the two different numbers that could be rung up.

Fort Worth, Tex., 1887. Southwestern's telephone poles are on the left, while Pan-Electric Telephone Company poles are on the right.

St. Louis, 1913. The phone lines of the Kinloch Telephone System, a major Southwestern competitor of the day.

John M. Noble, a founder of Oklahoma's Pioneer Telephone Company (he retired in 1932 as a Southwestern Bell vice president), summed up the situation in these words: "In the days of the dual exchange, most business houses were annoyed with two bells, two books, two bills. Too bad."

When a company established a second central office in a community, the original office was almost certain to be called "Central." And if it was, then the competing company, in a display of one-upmanship, would call *its* first central office "Main." These venerable name prefixes hung on in many cities until the advent of All-Number Calling, the modern system of using only digits (no letters) for a telephone number.

Many citizens, and especially many political leaders, felt that competing telephone companies were a good thing. After all, didn't competition keep prices down? And as a matter of fact, that did occur. The price wars in the early days were waged unto business death; one company would finally go bankrupt. Then the survivor, badly crippled by the struggle, would try to regain financial health by jacking up the rates again. The resultant uproar by the citizenry forced city councils to get involved.

It took many years before it was generally recognized that a franchise run by a *regulated monopoly* was the best method to provide everybody with utility service at reasonable rates. And because a city's telephones must all be interconnected to be of maximum value, the principle applies even more strongly to telephone service than to a city's other utilities.

John M. Noble

"Competition" died hard, however. Even in the 20th century, major cities like Dallas, Kansas City and St. Louis had two telephone companies for a while; in residential areas, one company's lines might run along poles beside the street while the other's pole lines were in the alleys.

Incidentally, it was not always the Bell interests—the enterprise that developed from the original Alexander Graham Bell patents—which won these power struggles. Other financial behemoths were in the battle for franchises, too. Their shrewdness in manipulating public opinion was shown by the way they rallied newspaper editorial pages to their cause, portraying the Bell group as interlopers from the effete East with no local ties.

Glossed over was the fact that in practically all these cases the competition's "local ties" consisted of a few prominent citizens who were cut in for shares of stock in exchange for the use of their names on the letterhead.

But even while these battles were going on, other telephone people were realizing that the future of the business depended upon cooperation. Cooperation in buying could create economies which helped hold down rates; lower rates would bring more customers, which in turn meant benefits to existing customers. Cooperation in sharing operating techniques meant that service improvements developed in one location could be applied to all; again, customers benefited.

And obviously every time the customer benefited, the business enterprise benefited too, creating more and better jobs for employees and better profits for the owners.

Considerations like this—economy, efficiency, service improvement, profit— all worked toward the idea of consolidating telephone operations. And as a result of this consolidation, where there had been a multitude of single-town companies there finally arose four Bell-affiliated companies in the five states where Southwestern Bell operates today.

These four were the Bell Telephone Company of Missouri, whose principal territory was St. Louis and a cluster of communities surrounding the city on both sides of the Mississippi; the Missouri & Kansas Telephone Company, whose base of operations was Kansas City; the Southwestern Telegraph & Telephone Company, initially an Arkansas operation which eventually included a large part of Texas as well; and the Pioneer Telephone & Telegraph Company, serving much of Oklahoma.

Then, as today, there were also many small and not-so-small companies not included in Bell operations; they are treated at greater length in Chapter 12, which discusses the "independent" companies.

Many of these have become parts of other chains, like General Telephone, United Telephone, Continental Telephone. Other "indies" remain one-city enterprises, and all are linked to the long distance network so that today any telephone user can call any other, anywhere in the country.

The family tree of Southwestern Bell is highly complex, as detailed by an item on page 262. When the M&K Company was incorporated in 1882, it linked 12 enterprises operating in 21 cities, stretching from Hannibal, Mo., to Wichita. When the Pioneer Telephone & Telegraph Company was organized, it embraced 16 separate telephone properties previously acquired by the Arkansas Valley Telephone Company. A similarly tangled web illustrates the development of the Arkansas/Texas Company, and even Bell of Missouri owned and operated several other Missouri exchanges outside its principal territory.

Kansas City, Mo., 1893. The July 4 employee picnic of the Missouri & Kansas Telephone Company.

By the second decade of this century, however, territorial boundaries had become more firmly established among the four Bell companies. It was time to take the final steps in a consolidation process that must have been foreseen decades before but was announced by the Bell System only in 1911.

As early as 1912, the four Bell companies discussed above were operating with a single general staff and were known as the "Southwestern Bell Telephone System." (Even today, it's possible to encounter retirees who speak of the "Southwestern System," a term that became obsolete in 1920.)

For reasons comprehensible to lawyers, the Kansas City operation—M&K—

was chosen as the parent company for a formal merger. M&K first absorbed Bell of Missouri, the St. Louis–based operation. A number of name changes ensued. Finally the three surviving companies—one operating in Missouri, Kansas and Arkansas, another in Oklahoma, and the third in Texas—were formally united in April 1920 as "Southwestern Bell Telephone Company" with headquarters in St. Louis.

Since that era, the changes have been less striking though not insignificant. The new company absorbed several of its subsidiaries, such as Southeastern Missouri Telephone Company and Ozark Central Telephone Company; it acquired exchanges and divested itself of others in accordance with the wishes of regulatory commissions. The final step was to straighten its boundaries to conform with those of states. Illinois properties in two counties were sold to Illinois Bell January 1, 1975; and in January 1982, Southwestern Bell bought Mountain Bell's El Paso operations in the far western tip of Texas.

The economic soundness of the resulting structure has been confirmed by recent developments: When the Bell System was broken up on January 1, 1984, Southwestern Bell stood as an independent company, with the same boundaries it attained in January 1982.

After AT&T's financial shelter was removed, other Bell companies were associated into "regions" for operating efficiencies. But Southwestern Bell, which had constituted approximately 10 percent of the Bell System, became a "region" all to itself. ■

The Dallas Telephone Company, 1920.

In the early days there were only two departments—operating and mechanical.

THE AGE OF SPECIALIZATION

CHAPTER THREE

WHEN WILLIAM C. MAAS was made the telephone company's manager at Eagle Pass, Tex., it was supposed to be a promotion. Maas didn't see it that way. In his reminiscences he says: "I was doomed to take further punishment (after a series of mishaps while working in the supply room and as a pole-climbing lineman)."

That was in the fall of 1892. Maas had progressed to the job of "inspector" in Fort Worth. Now he would be a boss—of sorts. He found when he got to Eagle Pass that the manager was also "the bookkeeper, cashier, lineman, night operator and janitor."

The young man (too young to vote) did so well at restoring good relations with customers, improving service and especially at getting collections up to par that he was moved to the manager's job at a much larger exchange. How was he notified? "Mr. Farnsworth, the auditor, stepped into the office and ordered: 'William, pack your grip, we are going over to Corpus Christi.' "

The incident is illuminating. The men who got ahead in the business (no woman could ever aspire to a higher post than chief operator until a considerably later period) were expected to be able to handle any problem that came up. As another Texas old-timer, William H. Walker, observed:

"Those men were all good, all-around telephone men, generally able to land on their feet wherever they found themselves."

Take note that the order for the transfer of Eagle Pass manager Maas came from the company's Auditor (with a capital "A"). In the words of a popular American philosopher of the time, "Responsibility gravitates to the man who knows how." It never occurred to young Maas to wonder where the auditor got the authority to transfer him.

A casual relationship like this was natural for a business just entering its adolescence, so to speak. The boss was whoever could exercise control, at least until a bigger boss came along. It may be fact or only a myth, but it was said that the indispensable quality for a line crew boss in the early days was the ability to whip any man in his crew—and the readiness to do so when the occasion demanded.

Inevitably, though, such a rough-and-ready organization would have to change as the business became more specialized. Advanced technology required more know-how than any individual could acquire in a lifetime; people had to concentrate on building plant or handling calls or dealing with customers or keeping

Waurika, Okla., 1917. The operating room and the terminal room were one and the same.

the books straight . . . the list goes on and becomes increasingly complex with the passage of years.

And so the departments came into existence.

Apparently, Bell companies at the turn of the century made do with two basic departments—one was called the "Operating Department" and the other, the "Mechanical Department."* The great change took place toward the end of the 20th century's first decade. The Bell System official chronology does not mention it, curiously; but it must have been part of the transformation instituted by Theodore Vail when he was elected president of AT&T for the second time in 1907.

We know from a report in the Dallas *Times-Herald* that Southwestern Tel & Tel was reorganized on a functional basis October 1, 1909. We also know that SWT&T was not the first to institute the change. Year-by-year records of the Oklahoma City exchange include this passage:

"Soon after the occupation of the building (at the northwest corner of Third and Broadway Streets in 1908), the American Telephone & Telegraph Company secured full ownership of the Pioneer Telephone & Telegraph Company and began to place into effect their operating methods and practices. In February 1909, the 'three column' type of organization was placed into effect. . . . The department heads reported to the general manager, John M. Noble."

The voluminous memoirs of Mima Blanchard, an Oklahoma City operator, indicate that when she was hired in 1903 there was no "Traffic Department." Later in her narrative—setting the year at 1907, but this must be faulty memory—she writes:

"We now have a Traffic Department, which has been functioning after a fashion, with E. V. Adams at the head of it. Edwards is his assistant. [Then] Mr. Adams takes other work and Mr. Barnes becomes Mr. Edwards' assistant. All three of these men have had experience in other places. . . ."

The change was not a painless one—what change ever is? To quote Mima Blanchard further:

"We are growing too fast for our equipment. . . . We get service complaints, out-of-order complaints, in fact every kind of a complaint known in the telephone business. Earl Wall and T. Golay join Mr. Edwards and Mr. Barnes in the Traffic Department—bright young men who know nothing about telephone work. Personally we, of the operating force, regard them as a pain in the neck. They run up and down the switchboard trying to correct phraseology—what do they know about it when they don't know how to set up a connection? We have no book of instructions and everyone has a different idea as to what should be done. We are bewildered. . . ."

It requires no crystal ball to guess that similar problems arose in the other new departments—plant and commercial. (Engineering, at this time, would have been a headquarters staff function.) And the Bell System practice, which later tied it all together, still would have been in the developmental stage.

At any rate, the organization finally settled into a pattern familiar to today's telephone old-timers. There was plant (including construction), which put the equipment together and kept it in working condition. There was traffic, which handled the customers' calls. There was commercial, which dealt with the cus-

*Payroll records still extant show a report, for instance, of the Lindell Avenue (St. Louis) "Operating Department" for November 1897. The first name is that of the night manager, Joe Byrnes, followed by the chief operator, Mollie Sommers, and 22 others. All appear to be operators except for "M. Potts, Janitress."

How To Succeed in Business, Etc.

J. C. MABEN, who retired as Fort Worth district manager, began his telephone career as an 11-year-old messenger boy. The title covered a wide assortment of activities, and as he describes them, one gets the impression that he could have modeled as the original Peck's Bad Boy.

"On a cold and frosty morning, February 27, 1888, at 6 a.m., I started my labors with the telephone company. The duties of a messenger boy were to do all the janitor work, collect the charges on toll calls made by the subscribers on the previous day, notify people who did not have a telephone that they were wanted on long distance and relieve at the switchboard when one of the operators was sick or wanted to go to the matinee.

"Any spare time was used in entertaining myself by dropping sacks of water from the third-story window onto the sidewalk in front of some pedestrian, shooting pins across the street at persons or animals and in the winter time carrying our supply of coal up three flights of stairs.

"All one needed for this job was a strong back and a weak mind, and the pay was $10 per month. For a boy from the farm, it was easy work and big pay."

Maben had to be versatile because the staff was rather skimpy, even for a mere 285 customers. Besides the manager, W. B. Elliott, there was one other man employee—"Charlie Goodson was inspector, lineman and installer"—and there were five operators. When one of the operators got sick, Maben was called in to relieve, an experience he apparently enjoyed:

"Sometimes this meant a week or 10 days, but as my voice had not changed from soprano to the bass tone of today, the subscribers did not know the difference,

especially the men who sent me boxes of candy or flowers, trying to make a date.

"One of our operators eloped with [an important citizen], and I had to work until another operator could be broken in. [The citizen] being a married man, and his family very prominent socially, the elopement caused quite a bit of newspaper publicity and talk about town"—a juicy bit of scandal that obviously made an impression on a boy of tender years.

In 1890, J. F. Henderson succeeded Elliott as manager. Henderson, we're told, was "nationally known and loved by all telephone employees whose good fortune it was to come in contact with him." However, he wasn't much good at book work, a fact that benefited his teenage messenger boy.

The manager was supposed to keep a rental ledger of all subscribers in alphabetical order. In addition to maintaining a monthly debit and credit record of the customer's account, the ledger also showed "the number of his receiver and transmitter"— the instruments were the property of the AT&T and leased to the operating company.

One day a traveling auditor arrived to check the books, and after spending about three weeks (ordinarily two days was enough) and calling in the chief auditor from Dallas to help, "They, at Mr. Henderson's suggestion, turned the books over to me in addition to my duties as collector, with the enormous increase

of $15 per month, making my salary $30."

Young Maben was surprisingly well qualified for his new assignment; he had taken a course in bookkeeping at night while working as collector during the day. In three months, he was able to reclaim about $600 which Henderson had "over-remitted" (to Dallas, presumably) while the manager had struggled with the books. And as the business was rapidly increasing, Maben asked for more money or additional help.

Henderson couldn't get the suggested $15-a-month increase approved, but he got permission to hire a collector at $35 a month. This left Maben with only the books to keep, which took him only about two hours a day. Then the next month, the increase was approved after all.

"The next time, instead of an increase in salary, they gave me a title—cashier—which sounded big but did not buy any bacon," he recalls. A little later, in 1900, "The company had an economical fit." Word came down from the general office in Dallas that all cashiers and bookkeepers were to be let out and the local manager would have to do this work.

But Henderson, remembering his previous experience at this assignment, "reared up on his hind legs" and threatened to quit. The general superintendent backed down. "Thus ended another business bubble," Maben reflected; "Mr. Henderson and I had agreed to open up an insurance business should the company accept his resignation. Henderson and Maben Insurance—who knows what financial heights we might have attained? But the fates decreed that we should stay in the telephone game, and I have never regretted the decision." ∎

tomers' problems and handled billing and collections. There was engineering, whose most important responsibility was to see that service was provided as economically as possible.

Accounting, which kept the company's books and other records, became a separate department in 1926.

In addition there were the small departments with few members but vital to the scheme of things—legal, personnel, treasury.

Commercial tended to be the catch-all department, and as it grew, some of its functions were split off or partly allocated to specialists. Thus the Public Relations Department became an important staff function. Sales, originally just one aspect of the commercial (and plant) activities, became a department of its own under the name marketing. The directory function got to be so complex that it required a veritable army of sales and production specialists and evolved as a quasi-department.

Cleburne, Tex., 1913. Three of these men were the whole Plant Department for Cleburne. The fourth, at right, was a prospective employee who didn't sign on with the company.

For many years the hierarchy ran straight to the top—company headquarters. After 1920, the Mima Blanchards of Southwestern Bell could find, if they cared to inquire, that the chain of authority began at their switchboards and ended at the desk of the general traffic manager in St. Louis. This person in turn reported to the vice president-operations, who was beholden only to the president.

On this stairway to the stars there were landings of authority at the "area" operating headquarters, but there was no ultimate boss there. The head of Commercial Department operations for Oklahoma had no power over his counterpart in Oklahoma plant, and vice versa. If a dispute arose between the two and they couldn't settle it amicably, the appeal was to St. Louis, where the general commercial manager and general plant manager might, as a last resort, appeal to the vice president-operations.

As a practical matter, of course, very few disputes got that far. Career advancement in any large organization has always depended upon getting the job done without "making waves" unnecessarily. There was a fair amount of who-blinks-first jockeying for position at area levels instead.

*Great Bend, Kan., 1912.
The auditing office.*

*Great Bend, Kan., 1912.
The auditing office.*

*Fayetteville, Ark., 1912. The
Traffic Department handled
customers' calls.*

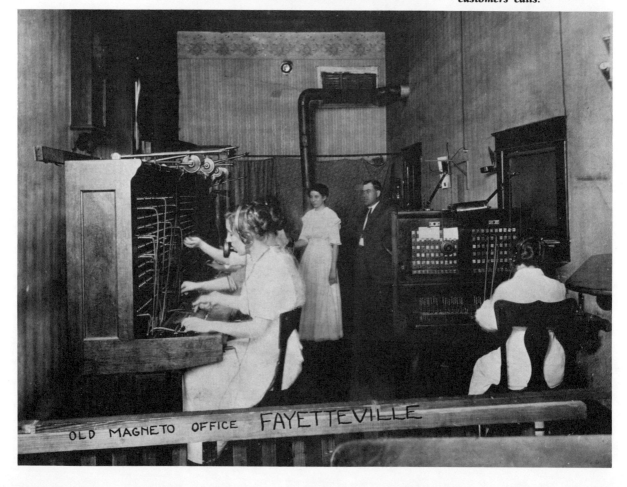

Dallas, circa 1910. Officials of the Commerical Department, the "catch-all" organization that handled everything from sales to directories.

During most of this period, the first half of the century, Southwestern Bell and its predecessors got along with just four operating areas, roughly coinciding with the boundaries of the companies from which Southwestern Bell was created. Texas comprised one of these operating areas, Oklahoma another. The Western Missouri–Kansas Area was the former operating territory of the Missouri & Kansas Telephone Company. The Eastern Missouri–Arkansas Area was heir to the territory of the Bell Telephone Company of Missouri, plus the Arkansas portion of what had been the Southwestern Telegraph & Telephone Company.

In 1950 the company's growth necessitated a new set of changes. Five operating areas were created in place of four. Kansas became an area of its own, as did Arkansas. Western Missouri and Eastern Missouri were combined into a single area (which also included a sliver of Illinois).

A general manager, later titled "vice president and general manager," was installed in each of these new state-area operating headquarters. The Commercial, Plant, Traffic and Engineering department heads reported to this individual, and the general manager in turn reported to the operating vice president at St. Louis headquarters.

The number of these areas grew eventually to eight, with three in Texas and two in Missouri, but there was no significant change in the basic pattern until the first century of telephony was almost complete. Had the telephone business remained totally a regulated monopoly, there might not have been a change even today. But this was not to be.

In the late 1970s, Southwestern Bell and indeed the whole Bell System were restructured once more to meet the challenge of competition. Federal courts and commissions, not to mention the Department of Justice, had torn away parts of what the System had considered its special function in public service.

Up to 1968, before the Carterfone decision in June of that year, the System had maintained that no one had the right to connect his or her own equipment to System facilities. Yes, there were cases where it was done, but only with the System's consent. Thus, independent (non-Bell) companies hooked up their circuits to System facilities . . . but under the System's rules.

When the Federal Communications Commission struck down existing interstate tariffs relating to interconnection, a door was opened a crack; in a few short years the door had been thrown wide open. And the old departmental structure, those running the Bell System decided, was too codified—not flexible enough—to meet the new challenge of competition. And so the telephone world turned upside down, or so it seemed to the veterans.

The three "core" departments—plant, traffic and commercial—as well as the Engineering and Marketing departments, were abolished. In the place of these five came three new "segments" whose domains have been repeatedly revised. They are network, comprising most of the old traffic organization and much of engineering; and business and residence, which apportion the functions of the old Commercial, Marketing and Plant departments according to the type of customer to be served.

The operations of the new segmented telephone business are largely subjects for future histories, however. In the current discussion we'll take a look at the departments and their subdepartments as they were for most of the telephone's first century—plant, traffic, commercial, engineering, accounting, directory and sales. The people who worked in those units are the people this history acclaims as the builders of the business. ∎

Fort Worth, Tex., 1918.
A heavy construction gang.

Calling a Bluff

J. R. Peterson retired in 1962 as Southwestern Bell's vice president-personnel, but he spent most of his career in the Traffic Department in Texas, Arkansas and Missouri, later serving as general manager for the Missouri-Illinois area. His memoirs are worthy of reprinting in full; here is a sample concerning interdepartmental rivalry, from the period when he was a district traffic superintendent.

THE 1927 sleet storm had demolished the recently purchased Kinloch Company rural line plant in north St. Louis County. It was decided to establish a new office of the agency type* near Spanish Lake, rather than to rebuild the lines all the way into Ferguson. The work of establishing the new Spanish Lake office moved rather slowly—so slowly that Mr. Elias, the operating vice president, sent word down the pipe that something had better be done quickly.

The division plant superintendent, Mr. Bookout, decided to get his department off the hook and announced that he was ready to cut the first line into the new office. Actually, there was much work yet to be done, but "Booker" figured that we in the Traffic Department were not ready to operate the new office and that by rushing in one line, he would get the monkey on traffic's back.

Ben Cravens called me about noon on the day that he learned of Booker's ruse and told me that I would have to get an agent on the job that afternoon, so I drove out to Spanish Lake through a driving snowstorm to try to find someone to employ.

In those days Spanish Lake was only a farming area— no town, not even a village. I dropped in at a general store on Bellefontaine Road and asked the old German storekeeper for help in locating an agent. The old Dutchman couldn't think of anyone, but referred me to a nursery that, he said, had several families living on the premises. The nursery owner, after hearing my story, sent for one of his workmen and discussed the job with him. He said he thought his wife would be interested in the job, but then timidly asked: "Would she have to speak English? She's just come from Poland." Obviously, that wouldn't work very well.

I checked at the little house where the agency office was to be located, not knowing just what I was going to do if the plant people had a line ready to connect to the magneto switchboard. Sure enough, the foreman said they would be ready with that one line in about an hour.

I went back to the little store to get a bite to eat, as it appeared I would have to man the switchboard myself that night. The old German, however, volunteered the suggestion that maybe his stepson could be the operator until I could locate someone else, and I gratefully went after him. I discovered that the stepson was a "halfwit," but nevertheless I took him back to the little office and showed him what to do if the little magneto drop fell.

I went back to the store to get him an oil stove, as it was bitter cold, and then I proudly told the plant foreman we were ready to "cut over." Actually, it was two or three days before the plant really did get a line ready to cut in, and by that time I had located and moved in an agent. ∎

*In an "agency" operation, a traffic center was supplied with Bell equipment and connected to Bell lines, but was run by a private individual under contract — usually a housewife who had the central office in her living room.

"Would she have to speak English?..."

Ed West, the old Supt.
said you're not supposed
to do that.

THEY PUT IT ALL TOGETHER

CHAPTER FOUR

WHAT MAKES a plant man?* From the beginning, the most important single characteristic seems to have been "ruggedness." Plant men usually began their careers in the full vigor of youth, and they were expected to start producing their first day on the job.

In fact, "job" wasn't the operative word in the eyes of those who did the hiring. The key word was "work." E. M. "Cap" Cummings recalled how he approached the foreman of a line gang working near his home at Violet Springs (in what is now Oklahoma) July 4, 1904.

"I asked Mr. Annis for a job, and he said, 'You want work or a job?' Real quick I answered, 'I want work,' and that must have been the right answer because Mr. Annis said, 'Well, if you want a job, I don't have any. But I got plenty of work!' " And within five minutes young Cummings was busy digging holes in the Indian Territory hardpan where poles would be set.

Physical qualifications may not have been spelled out in the practice, but they were pretty clearly understood by the men doing the hiring. Henry Altepeter, veteran plant man and engineer, tells of observing this process in the late twenties:

"The construction superintendent questioned them as to their age, height, weight and looked to see if they had two hands, two feet and ten fingers. Also he checked

---

*Yes, there were women in the Plant Department in the later years, and there are far more of them performing such functions today. But most of the early "plant women" worked at desks, behind the scenes, taking customer trouble reports. More on this subject later.

whether they could see and hear well. He then said to those who passed this test, 'Turn around and take all the stuff out of your pockets.' He was interested to see whether their posterior development was such as to hold up a safety belt full of tools."

There also was a generally understood requirement that a plant man should be above average height, so he could reach far out along the crossarms of a pole or on the higher shelves of a distributing frame in a central office. But there were men of lesser stature in the plant group, too—as long as they could handle the work.

One such was J. C. Phillips of Fort Worth, who began work with a line gang in January 1895. ("I started on a Friday, the day they hang men," Phillips observed. But he loved the life of a lineman.)

Phillips' crew was stringing wire in August 1895 when two young, broad-shouldered farmhands asked the foreman for jobs. They thought stringing wire looked easy and said they didn't believe a man could do a day's work in a mere 10 hours, the typical workday in 1895. They were hired and started the following morning—"The boss told one of them to buck the reel with 'that little skinny man,' which was me."

Phillips may have been diminutive, but he was used to the work and could stand the heat. The young farmer didn't know that and told the boss, "That man can't stand up to work with me." The boss replied that he should go down the line with Phillips until Phillips couldn't keep up any longer. "Then come back and tell me," the boss said, "and I'll give you a box of fine cigars."

That day is recalled by Phillips with special relish. In the morning the farmhand would exhort him, "Partner, let's go; time is money." But by the noonday meal he had fallen silent, and about 2:30 in the afternoon he was staggering. He set the reel down and said, "I'm all in."

Phillips had been waiting for this. With a straight face he told his erstwhile tormentor, "Partner, let's go; time is money." And then he added: "You can't all the time judge a man by his looks." The farmhand never got to collect that box of cigars.

Pride in one's ability to get things accomplished regardless of the odds was characteristic then and still is today. But the other side of the coin was a spirit of derring-do, a willingness to take chances, that caused real concern among the older, wiser heads in the business.

Before Bell System safety practices took firm hold in the 1920s, it was common for linemen to pose for pictures as they stood on a crossarm atop a 30-foot pole. Accidents were virtually an everyday affair, and little attention was paid to them. F. E. Pace recalled a few incidents before 1914, when "education to prevent accidents was started."

At El Paso, a lineman was using an eight-foot drill bar to cut through concrete and, "being rather careless," drove the bar through his shoe and big toe. In those days the sovereign remedy for wounds was kerosene, so this was poured right on the shoe, which wasn't removed from the wounded foot.

The lineman worked until quitting time. That night the shoe had to be cut off his foot. The next morning he reported for work as usual, the wounded foot tied up in a burlap sack. Pace's account stops here; we aren't told how or whether the man recovered.

In an incident at San Antonio, a double carload of poles was being unloaded

Edmond, Okla., 1912. Obviously, safety practices hadn't taken hold.

El Reno, Okla., 1916.
A terminal room.

when "W. F. Hendricks in some way allowed his thumb to get between the anchor and rope." The first joint of Hendricks' thumb was cut off. Still he finished his job, then trimmed up the bloody stump with his pocket knife and wrapped it in rubber tape to stop the bleeding. Finally came the old standby, kerosene. Hendricks, too, showed up for work as usual the next morning and when asked whether the injury had caused him pain, growled, "Hell, no."

Safety training? Pace recalled that "the method of education by the regular men was ridicule. No reports were made except in the case of broken legs, broken arms or death."

Another byproduct of pride in one's ruggedness was a zest for horseplay, which sometimes could have dangerous consequences. Ralph Louis of Topeka, who began in the Plant Department and finished in engineering, has a wealth of anecdotes about shenanigans in the switchroom.

Some of these stunts were harmless, if annoying: soldering a fellow worker's toolbox shut; smearing graphite oil on a telephone earpiece, then calling someone to the phone; putting a string-leash around a live mouse's neck and "walking" the critter through the operating room while the ladies shrieked; dangling a dead herring down the tube through which "permanent report" tickets were sent from the switchroom to the test desk. (No one at the test board could figure out what was causing that stench until it was noticed that something was stopping the tickets from coming through.)

Ever Have One of Those Days . . . ?

WHEREVER PLANT MEN congregated in the early days, someone was sure to come up with a new tale of woe. Somehow they never seemed very funny at the time to the person involved, but in later years, even the victims could laugh, and the stories took their place in a litany of anecdotes which could fill a library. Here are a couple of samples reported in 1926:

Little Rock lineman Horace Sykes was sent out on a June day to locate and clear a case of trouble. Sykes discovered the problem was caused by a colony of bees, which had set up housekeeping inside an equipment box on a pole.

There was nothing in the System practices to cover this, but Sykes was resourceful—if injudicious. He got a newspaper and some matches and climbed the pole to smoke out the bees. The bees came out and began to sting Sykes, who dropped the blazing newspaper. It fell into a pool of oil, which had been poured around the foot of the pole to kill the high grass.

Flames leaped up. Sykes couldn't get down the pole, a fact that suited the bees just fine. By the time the fire department reached the scene and rescued Sykes, he was half baked and thoroughly stung. His boss told him to take the rest of the day off.

At Lawton, Okla., repairman A. M. Oliphant was caught in a torrential downpour while he was retransposing some open wire. Discretion might have suggested returning to his work center, but Oliphant was the stubborn type and kept on. Eventually water was standing on the road in "puddles" as much as 3 feet deep.

In midafternoon, Oliphant's truck ran into one of these puddles and stuck. Instead of trying immediately to rescue the truck, Oliphant got out, waded to a nearby pole and went on with his work. When he got back to the truck, it couldn't be budged, let alone started.

Oliphant slogged through the mud to a nearby farmhouse and hired the farmer's team of mules to pull out the truck. Then one of the mules got stuck, too. It took all the strength of Oliphant, the farmer and the other mule to get the trapped animal up to firmer ground.

Oliphant left the truck where it was until the next morning. He finished off his workday by walking six miles through the mud back to his work center. ∎

A practical joke that could have had more serious consequences was the compressed-air caper. A switchman observed that the cardboard cylinders in which switch shafts were shipped would fit nicely over the air gun at the work bench. (The air gun was used to blow dust off switch contacts.) The next step was to add a weight to a cylinder and presto! a handy, supposedly harmless dart gun.

At this point one of the switchmen stepped into the aisle where the gun was being pointed. Phhtt! The unpointed "dart" struck him in the forehead, and he fell like a pole-axed steer.

"It scared the socks off us," Louis recalled. "We thought, 'Oh, boy! If the chief switchman finds out about this, we'll be in real trouble.' We weren't worried about the guy who was hit; we were worried about our own skins!" Fortunately, the victim, although dazed, wasn't seriously hurt, and apparently the chief switchman never heard of the incident.

The same spirit of tomfoolery animated the test board at Kansas City, Kan., during the years 1905-1906, when the M&K Company was expanding its facilities rapidly and doing everything it could to make demand for service keep pace.

A crew of salesmen had been hired to canvass all business establishments with an offer to install telephones on a 90-day free trial. One of these salesmen per-

Near Dallas, 1912. Linemen hoisting a pole come up with a new definition of "water logged."

1923. Linemen prepare a fresh load of telephone poles for planting.

Above: A cook waits for "chow time" at a linemen's construction camp. Top right: The Houston-to-New Orleans toll line construction crew. Middle right: A toll line camp outfit ready to hit the road. Bottom right: Near Rockey, Okla., 1911. A line crew posing for posterity.

suaded a Chinese laundryman to sign up; another was successful in talking a German groceryman into taking trial service, too. Neither businessman was fluent in English. The situation was made to order for pranksters.

Whenever there was idle time at the test board, someone would call up the two lines on test, ring both telephones and let the Chinese and the German talk to each other. Neither could understand the conversation, but they were thoroughly sold on the idea that the telephone would bring them business. So they would keep talking for as long as five minutes before hanging up in disgust.

When the salesman went back to the German at the end of the trial period, hoping to sign him to a regular contract, the groceryman said he had got "lots of business" over the telephone but hadn't sold anything because he couldn't understand the orders. And a similar visit to the laundry showed it had been vacated,

St. Louis, 1914. This test room was home base for telephone trouble shooters.

Dallas, 1919. Records of customer line trouble were kept in files like these in wire chiefs' offices.

"Phantom" Circuit

Establishing the first coast-to-coast radio network was a momentous achievement. It also created the environment for the first coast-to-coast embarrassing moment.

The city where the following incident occurred must remain unidentified, but it was in the Southwest. An unlocated cable splicer had been sent there to put more pairs in use. The cable he would work on had some pairs for local service and others for long distance or special facilities, like the radio network.

Needing a helper to identify the pairs he was going to splice, the visitor hired a young fellow off the street. This worthy's job was to stay inside the central office, clip a test set to the pairs where they appeared on the frame and talk to the splicer, who was busily at work outside the building.

Although there were large red tags hanging everywhere with the warning "Special Circuit Radio," the neophyte clipped onto the special coast-to-coast radio pair. The network program of the moment was a selection of hymns, played by the famous organist Jesse Crawford. Over the organ music, a coast-to-coast audience suddenly heard a plaintive voice:

"J---- C------! There's music on this ------ pair!"

Radio stations instantly cut out of the network, and a search for the source of this interference began. The search was fruitless, of course, because no one would own up. But telephone company officials had the difficult task of persuading the radio network—and the FCC—that it would never happen again. ■

You Never Know What You Can Do....

Courage, determination, an idea and $1.30 in cash—these were the assets Zora Tinsley brought from Fort Worth to Muskogee, Okla. With these assets, Tinsley, a black man who was almost totally blind, built and operated a telephone company. He was never an employee of any Southwestern Bell affiliate, but his story is reported here to show how telephony can bring out the best in people.

Tinsley lost most of his sight when his eyes were accidentally burned by quicklime while he was working as a hod carrier. When he came to Muskogee, there were no telephones in the rural area where he lived. Tinsley conceived the idea of starting his own telephone company.

He went to Harry Lyons, manager of the Southwestern Bell exchange, and proposed that he set up a rural line connected to the Bell circuits. It wasn't an unusual arrangement at the time. What was unusual was the fact that Tinsley was blind and broke. Besides his $1.30, all he could show to persuade Lyons were three contracts signed by neigh-

bors who wanted phone service.

Lyons had his doubts, but he felt anyone with so much courage should have a chance. The manager leased Tinsley five old telephones and a six-line switchboard. Next, Tinsley went to a Muskogee hardware man and bought three miles of wire—on credit—showing his agreement with Lyons and promising to pay $9.30 when he got the money.

Now Tinsley borrowed a team from a neighbor and, although barely able to tell darkness from light, cut trees for his first poles. Unaided, he dug holes, set the poles, hooked up his switchboard and installed his first pair

of telephones for his customers.

There was still the slight technicality of paying the first monthly connection charge of $10. This hurdle was overcome, too, when Lyons lent Tinsley the ten-spot.

The enterprise was a success from the start. The six-line switchboard couldn't handle the demand for service. Tinsley bought a larger board and worked night and day expanding his plant. By 1921, when this story was reported in the daily press, the Tinsley Telephone Company had 49 subscribers, white and black, who were served by 45 miles of wire in a 20-square-mile area. ■

Vehicles have always been vital to Southwestern Bell business, and the company tries hard to buy from a wide assortment of suppliers, at the same time making sure the company gets the most value for the dollar. That's part of being a good corporate citizen.

A Day To Remember

The trip from Fisher to Tulsa was rather unpleasant . . .

THE RIGHT-OF-WAY man in the plant group had a job few would envy. It was his assignment to persuade landowners to let the telephone company build its lines across their property. In days before microwave transmission, a pole line (or, later, buried cable) was the only way to get from point A to point B. And in between, there would be protective dogs, aggressive bulls and irate humans wielding shotguns. The task called for utmost patience, diplomacy and not a small amount of courage. The tale of L. M. Jones, recalled 26 years after the events took place in 1906, is instructive. (Jones became secretary of the Oklahoma employee benefit committee.)

The telephone company was building a toll line from Tulsa to Cleveland, Okla., along the Frisco railroad tracks. There was no road leading along the route. Tools and materials had to be brought to the work sites by handcars, and horses or mules were used to drag the poles, often through heavy timber or other obstacles.

W. C. Shull was the construction foreman on the job. Shull got permission to build from all but three owners. Now let's hear what happened, as we listen to L. M. Jones' own words:

"There were two places where Mr. Shull was not even permitted to enter upon the land and was told that if an attempt was made to do so the man would be shot. One of the places was between the flag stop of Fisher and Tulsa. The other was near Keystone and was owned by the mother of the famous outlaw, Henry Starr.

"After Shull had failed to get permission, Mr. Noble and Mr. Westervelt (owners of the Tulsa exchange) instructed Mr. Piatt to negotiate for the privilege. Unfortunately, Mr. Piatt was indisposed and thought that I was the proper person to make the negotiations.

"My first attempt was with the mother of Henry Starr. After spending about one-half day there and being given my dinner by Mrs. Starr, I received verbal permission for the line to be built across the property provided that I was personally responsible for it and that old man Shull did not come on the place. This was easy.

"After riding a freight back to Fisher, I walked from there back to the second place in the timber, a walk of about six miles along the railroad. After being rescued from the tree by the owner of this land, where I had taken refuge from his pack of dogs, I succeeded in getting the same privilege from him. I was successful in this by my story about the permission from Mrs. Starr. This man only asked that he be paid for clearing the right of way and be given the wood for his own use. As I recall it, the total cost of this was $25.

"On the road back to Fisher to catch the passenger train that night, I ran afoul of a civet cat and, as a result, could not eat supper at Mr. Fisher's place. His hounds would hardly let me in the yard long enough to get my overcoat and lantern to flag the train.

"The trip from Fisher to Tulsa was rather unpleasant for the reason that I could not remain in the smoker car very long on account of the odor of the civet cat. After I remained on the platform for a little while, the brakeman or conductor would run me back into the car.

"It was customary for the deputy United States marshal to search everybody coming into this section of the state on account of the embargo on bringing liquor into the Indian Territory. One whiff of this civet cat caused them to defer their search of me and my belongings." ∎

with the door standing ajar. On the telephone was a large sign with Chinese characters on it. The puzzled salesman took the sign to another Chinese laundryman for translation. He was told that, in effect, the sign said: "This thing's no good for doing business. Take it out!"

The horseplay, the striving for a rugged image, the pride in one's ability to carry on where lesser men would fall by the wayside—all these characteristics added up then, and add up even today, to an intangible called "morale." Perhaps people's ideas of bravery and humor have become more refined over the last hundred years, but the zeal to get the job done, to bring the customer service, seems to be as strong as ever.

Stories illustrating the "Spirit of Service" come from all locations. Some deal with all-out efforts after a disaster, natural or man-made. Others concern single individuals or small groups on more routine assignments. A reminiscence by T. J. Handy about his days as a telephone man in Dallas is perhaps not sensational, but it is typical; the incident occurred in 1891, but attitudes would be much the same today.

Handy had been involved in the installation of "a few hundred feet" of a new 100-conductor lead-sheathed cable. He recalls, "The wires were insulated with some kind of black gumbo compound which was very affectionate to the hands on a warm sunny day. I know about this as it fell my job to work up the cables, and I was proud of this honor, since it was claimed at the time to be the first lead sheath cable job in the country."

Handy's self-esteem was less evident, however, a few months later when a fire broke out in downtown Dallas at the same time there was a "typical Texas Blue Norther roaring down." G. W. Foster, the superintendent for North Texas, roused

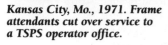

Kansas City, Mo., 1971. Frame attendants cut over service to a TSPS operator office.

Hop Gets the Jump on the Cable Splicing Job

Among the legendary characters of the telephone's early days is a cable splicer named John Hopkins Flynn, known to everyone but the payroll clerk as "Hop."

HOP WAS THE only splicer working for the Missouri & Kansas Telephone Company at the time a large plant expansion project was under way in Kansas City. To handle the job, a splicing crew was borrowed from Western Electric, and Hop was assigned to work with them.

This got Hop hot under the collar. He went directly to headquarters and declared that if the M&K thought it had more splicing to do than he could handle, he wanted to resign. It took some fast diplomacy to soothe Hop's ruffled feathers and persuade him to work with the Western Electric crew.

About noon on the first day he was working with them, Hop came into the foreman's office and said, "I want some more work." The astonished foreman said, "What's the matter with the job I gave you this morning?" Hop replied, "I finished that up."

The foreman, who knew that any of his splicers would need at least two days for the job, went to see for himself. Sure enough, the splice was all "wiped up" (closed and sealed with lead) and every circuit in the cable tested okay.

The foreman assigned Hop another job. But still baffled

about what was going on, he went to the manhole to watch. He signaled Hop's helper not to give any sign that someone was looking on. At last he broke the silence himself to exclaim, "Say, you can't splice those wires that way!"

Hop looked up in surprise, then retorted: "What's the reason I can't? I always do."

A shouting argument ensued because the foreman was positive that both hands had to be used for an operation that Hop was doing with just one hand. Eventually the foreman realized that Hop had stumbled on something new: a method for cutting splicing time at least in half.

Finally convinced, the Western Electric foreman started a school the next day to teach all his splicers to do their jobs the Hop Flynn way. The "pigtail-crank handle" technique was soon introduced throughout the Bell System. ■

It Sounded Too Good To Be True

The unlocated lineman's saga is a colorful part of an earlier epoch in American history; today the job has been largely turned over to contract workers instead of telephone company employees. In essence, most of the job of pole-setting and line-stringing over large areas of open country has been completed. New routes can be handled more easily by microwave equipment.

But until the 1960s it was routine for crews of linemen under a foreman's supervision to leave their home base on a Monday and not return until Friday night. While "on the road" their paychecks included an allowance for B&L— board and lodging—and more than one newcomer thought this meant a virtually unlimited expense account.

But the rude awakening came quickly, as Ray M. Elmore Sr. recounts in this incident reprinted from SCENE magazine.

I RAN A small telephone company in east central Missouri until December 7, 1924, when an ice storm destroyed the outside plant. So I put on denim overalls and a jacket over my suit and, wearing a pair of patent leather slippers, headed for "Ma Bell" in St. Louis.

On Highway 40 near St. Peters, I came across a Bell crew from Arkansas that was placing crossarms on new poles. I asked the foreman for a job, and since I had lineman's tools, he obliged.

The patent leather slippers

I was wearing weren't made for pole climbing, so by the end of the day I could hardly walk.

When we reached the hotel where the crew was staying, the foreman told me the job paid 30 cents an hour and board and lodging. We sat down to supper, and I ordered a T-bone steak.

When the foreman picked up the check, he turned to me and said, "Young man, you owe me $2.50."

I countered with, "You told me I would get board and lodging."

The foreman said, "You're allowed $1.60 a day, or 40 cents a meal and 40 cents for lodging."

I paid the $2.50 and stayed with Bell until I retired on January 1, 1963. ■

Handy from bed to tell him "the fire had burned down a span of our precious cable." Foster ordered Handy to get help and a piece of cable and get the cable up and working as quickly as possible.

"Right then I did not think so much of myself for being the cableman," Handy recalled, "but I backed my ears and bucked the blizzard, and by 8 o'clock the next morning had everything working." Foster was both surprised and pleased and bought the whole crew breakfast in a nearby saloon.

Tales of working through bitter cold wind, snow, ice and rain are so numerous they become repetitious. Henry Altepeter tells a story with a somewhat different twist. It concerns an Arkansas toll repairman who completed a job on a copper wire circuit near Memphis under difficult circumstances—the line ran along a railroad track on a high fill, and the poles themselves stood in about six feet of water.

Instructions were that a workman in such a situation was to get help and reach the trouble location by boat, but the repairman hadn't done this. He explained to Altepeter that he swam out to the pole. Altepeter found this explanation hard to credit because the man's clothes were dry. The repairman then admitted that he had left all his clothes on the fill and swum to the pole *au naturel*. He climbed the pole, made the repairs and swam back to the fill to put his clothes back on.

For the moment Altepeter ignored the safety violations involved but asked the man what he would have done if he had been up on the pole, stark naked, when a passenger train came along on the nearby track. The repairman obviously hadn't even thought of this possibility. He pondered a moment and then said:

"Well, about all I could have done was to beat my head against the pole and pretend I was a woodpecker." ∎

The changing of the guard: A new outside plant technician reports for duty.

The telephone operator—
late forties

			DATE		
3			FROM		
Tulsa					
No.	RI7	5283			OKLA 405
PERS.			SPEC. INST.		
Houston			TO		Texas
					T & C
NO.	WA3	9108			
COL.	PERS.				
YES					
NO	ADD. NAME				
OPR 19					
FILING 4 25 p		MINS.		CLASS	
TERM. VIA					
ROUTE		CHARGE		TAX	

THE VOICES WITH THE SMILES

CHAPTER FIVE

WHEN ALEXANDER GRAHAM BELL spilled acid on his trousers and made history's first telephone call—a call for help*—he didn't need an operator's services. Nor, for that matter, did he "dial up" his assistant, Thomas Watson. Since there was just one working telephone line in the world March 10, 1876, all Bell had to do was speak.

Service like this (two instruments, one line) remained the norm for almost two years, until the world's first "telephone exchange" was established at New Haven, Conn., January 28, 1878. Until that time, a telephone could be used only to talk to one other specific telephone. Exchange operations made it possible to talk to any other telephone which had a line to the "switchboard." Demand for service boomed; so did the need for someone to make the connections. A new job— telephone operator—was created almost overnight.

*There are two official versions of Bell's message. Bell said he exclaimed, "Mr. Watson, come here. I want to see you." Watson's version of what he heard was: "Mr. Watson, come here, I want you." Of course neither wrote down the words at that instant, but each jotted his version in his notebook that night. Under the circumstances, it's remarkable that Bell didn't use more forceful language.

When the first exchange in the Southwest opened at St. Louis on April 19, 1878, the operators were boys. Their training consisted of a few minutes of being shown how to insert connecting cords in "jackknife switches." (This was the origin of the familiar term "jack," the opening where a cord plug is inserted in a more modern type of switchboard.) When a customer tried to place a call, he or she would be challenged with a gruff "What do you want?" And the conversation might very well go downhill from there.

The first telephone operators were boys. The ones shown here are working a "Law board," which was abandoned in 1898.

An oft-told tale of early days in St. Louis goes like this: "One Sunday, one of the boy operators engaged in some lively profanity with a South Side livery stable proprietor—and a liveryman was a citizen of wealth and prominence in this period. He announced he was coming over with a horsewhip to instill some manners in the insolent boy.

"The telephone office was located on the seventh floor, reached by a cast-iron stairway surrounding an airshaft. One of the boys looked over the railing and, running back into the office, shouted: 'The old man is coming up with a buggy whip.' "

The office chairs in those days were equipped with small round cushions. Each boy armed himself with one of these, and as the liveryman entered the door, he was faced with a barrage of flying pillows. The bombardment took him so by surprise that he fled down the stairway.

"One of the operators picked up a bucket full of coal that was standing by the stove and flung it, bucket and all, down the iron stairs, echoing and re-echoing after the subscriber."

In Little Rock, a prominent saloonkeeper rang up and told one of the boy operators, 15-year-old Ashley Peay, "Connect me with my telephone at home. I want to talk to my wife." Ashley replied: "Your wife is talking to someone else."

"Information operators" for the Dallas Telephone Company used books like this to find phone numbers.

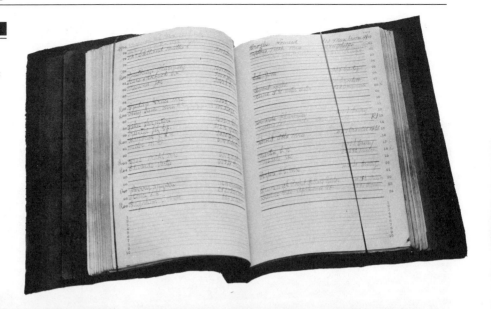

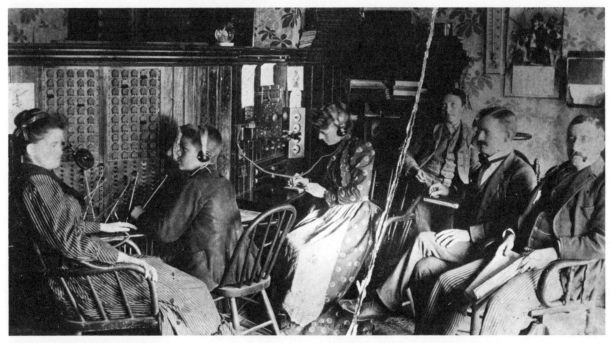

Sherman, Tex., 1890. An early operating room.

"What do you mean, my wife is talking to someone else?" the saloonkeeper growled. "I mean your line at home is busy," Ashley snapped.

The saloonkeeper wasn't accustomed to being turned down by 15-year-old boys. "Get my wife on the line right now!" he shouted. Young Peay's reaction was to say "Aw, shut up," or words to that effect, and yank the connection.

The boy went on to handle other calls. Suddenly he was seized from behind, lifted from the floor and shaken up and down by a furious saloonkeeper. Just as the man was about to fling Peay through a glass window onto the street below, a friend in the office came to the operator's rescue.

Incidents like these occurred not just in the Southwest but throughout the country. Management decided to try a daring experiment: Use females instead of males to handle the connections. Seldom has an experiment been such an instant success.

Little Rock, 1920. This was the main switchboard for the town.

Records indicate that the first female operator was Miss Emma Nutt of Boston, Mass., but she established the mark by only a few months. Apparently the first of her sex to become a "hello girl" in what is now Southwestern Bell territory got such a job in Little Rock, the scene of Austin Peay's close brush with disaster.

Manager Edward Newton decided after that incident that boys just weren't suited to the switchboard task, and he discharged them all late in 1879. To take over the assignment, he hired a grownup man, Arthur Adams. Adams was crippled, and the job proved too much for him to handle alone, so Newton hired Adams' young sister, Kate, to help him. The customers were delighted to hear her voice when they rang up Central.

We are told that Kate was a young girl, not yet 20. She had "big blue eyes, dark brown hair, intriguing freckles and an infectious smile," according to a description in the Little Rock *Gazette* a good many years later. She also had a beautiful singing voice, which was an asset of her church choir. She became so expert at the switchboard that her brother was able to leave all those duties to her and concentrate on collecting customers' payments and doing the bookkeeping.

When the Little Rock telephone exchange went to 24-hour operations, a man named Beauregard Morrison was hired to serve as night operator after Kate went off duty. With their mutual interest in a still-unusual occupation, it's hardly surprising that the two became fast friends. Later, after Morrison had left the telephone business to work for a hardware firm, they were married. As was customary in those days, Kate resigned her job in order to become a housewife, but she didn't lose her interest in the telephone, we're told.

Late in the century, when the first long distance line was opened between Little Rock and Dallas, it was Kate's voice that was first carried over the wire. To commemorate the occasion, she sang a song while enraptured subscribers at each end of the line listened over their telephones.

Besides a pleasant voice, what were the desirable attributes of an operator in those days? We can get an idea from the Topeka *Daily Capital* of February 9, 1900:

Pie in the Sky, Er, Lap

IT HAPPENED some 60 years before, but when Faye Landis Oldham of Rockdale, Tex., told about it, it seemed like only yesterday: the incident of the forbidden switchboard pie.

"We were supposed to be strictly business when we were on switchboard duty, of course," she recalled. "No eating or drinking in the operating room. But when the doors were shut at 9 o'clock so the public couldn't see, the girls would usually call across the street to Hill's Jewelry and Confectionery Store and order some snacks. One girl would have to watch the signals while the others ate in the cloakroom, and then when they came back, she'd get up and go eat her share of the tasty treats.

"Well, this one night when I was the girl who had to wait, they ordered some pie and they left my piece beside me at the board. They had just finished when we heard footsteps coming up the stairs. They hollered, 'Oh, there comes Ruby!' That was Ruby McMillan, the chief operator. Well, they rushed back to the board and sat there, all business, of course. But there wasn't time for me to get rid of my pie, so I dropped it in the lap of my dress and clapped my knees together to hide it.

"When Ruby walked in, I was making out to be busy, just as busy as I could be. But you couldn't fool Ruby; she could tell I was nervous about something.

And she comes up behind me and says, 'Faye, what have you got in your lap?' I sort of screamed, *'Nothin'!'* She says, 'Open up and let me see.' And I opened my knees and that pie was *all over* my dress!"

The chief let Faye off with a reprimand; she probably felt the girl had been punished enough already. ∎

"Now Hear This . . ."

IN THE EARLY days, the operator was far more than a person who switched the calls between customers; to borrow a term from today's TV culture, she was truly a "News Central." Clock stopped; need to know the time? Call the operator. Need the weather report? Call the operator. Is the 12:30 train on time? And so forth, and so forth, and so forth.

Central didn't always wait to be asked but called people and delivered messages. In some cases when it was obvious that everybody needed the news right away, there was a special method to get the word out: the "general line call."

This could be a means of summoning the volunteer firefighters or locating the town marshal when his services were needed in a hurry. It also could be a revenue-raising measure.

The manager of the local opera house would place a "general" call on all lines to advertise the current show. Local dealers who got in a train carload of coal, apples or potatoes would pay to have Central help them move the goods. Each operator would put four long rings on a party line, wait until she heard all the receivers come down and make the announcement. Then she would plug in on the next party line and repeat the process.

Hilda Olson, who became the first telephone operator at Marysville, Kan., in 1906, heartily disliked these general line calls when they were used for advertising. One evening, a clerk at Thompson Brothers Store ordered a general line call to announce the arrival of a carload of watermelons. In appreciation for their efforts, the clerk, whose name was Arthur Kuoni, brought in a large melon for the operators. A few nights later, when Hilda was leaving her job at 9 p.m., young Kuoni "happened" to leave his club at the same time and offered to walk her home. Not long after that, Hilda Olson became Mrs. Arthur Kuoni . . . which shows what a well-timed watermelon can accomplish. ∎

"The physical requirements in girls who are given positions in the telephone exchange are almost as stringent as those insisted upon in men enlisting in the Army. To become a 'hello' girl, the applicant must be not more than 30 years old [and] not less than 5 feet 6 inches tall. Her sight must be good, her hearing excellent, her voice soft, her perception quick and her temper angelic.

"With all these qualifications, a girl might secure a position answering the calls of telephone subscribers and will be enabled to earn from $1.10 to 1.50 a day.

"Every girl's sight and hearing is tested and her height is measured before she is hired. Tall, slim girls with long arms are preferred for work on the switchboards. Fat, short girls occupy too much room and are not able to reach all of the six feet of space allotted to each operator.

"With regard to nationality, it is said that girls of Irish parentage make the best operators."

St. Louis, circa 1915. Women received training at operators' school.

No, that is not a typographical error—the figure quoted for an operator's daily wage. In fact, the going rate hardly changed for the next two decades.

Mrs. Elsa McGary, who retired from service with Southwestern Bell in 1950 with 31 years' service (and later was a hospital PBX operator for another 12 years), recalls very clearly what she was paid when she was hired in April 1919. The base pay for a six-day week was $9, but Mrs. McGary got $1.50 a week differential because she worked night shifts. There was no provision for vacations, paid or otherwise.

Things soon improved somewhat. In June 1919 an unsuccessful attempt was made to organize the operators into a union, and some of them staged a short-lived strike. Mrs. McGary, newly widowed with four children to support, kept on working. (Management promised those who didn't walk out that they would have a "lifetime job" at the switchboards.)

After the strike failed, operators' wages were raised, and Mrs. McGary's base weekly pay went up to $14, with time and a half for any Sundays or holidays she worked. She made do with this and the income from another job she held down during the daylight hours. The term "moonlighting" had not yet come into vogue, but the idea was no novelty.

Working the switchboard in those early days meant living under a benevolent despotism, to hear Mrs. McGary describe it. On the one hand she feels the company treated her well financially, which gives some idea of what women's wages were like at the time. She had a steady job all during the Depression and usually got to work a full week even though the operators generally were on a part-time schedule to spread the work. Her secret? She worked all her assigned days and also substituted for other operators who wanted to take a day off.

"They were real good for paying you when your were sick, too," she says. "Some of the operators really took advantage of the company on this, getting months of sick pay, then coming back to work just long enough to clear the record and then quitting." However, she recalls, if you were sick, you were docked for the first week you were off before benefits began.

Aside from pay and other benefits, though, the on-job atmosphere was strictly business . . . with a vengeance. Operators were forbidden to speak to each other while at the board; away from the board, but still in the operating room, the rule was that everyone must be addressed by the last name. She might be your best friend Mamie, but in the presence of the chief operator, you'd better address Mamie as "Miss Schultz"!

"You could never be friendly in the operating room," Mrs. McGary recalls.

Wichita, Kan., 1911. A toll switchboard.

Another example of the bizarre restrictions she mentions is that wristwatches were forbidden. If an operator came to work wearing one, she had to turn it in until she went off duty.

It may well be that such rigidity was not typical of all the company offices, but just St. Louis. And of course even St. Louis bosses learned to bend somewhat as the years rolled by.

Away from St. Louis and in Oklahoma City, at any rate, the chief operators do not seem to have been such sticklers for discipline. The delightful memoirs of Mima Blanchard about her experiences from 1903 (she was hired at age 15) until 1933 bear out the idea that switchboard work could be fun when the bosses were more relaxed.

An excerpt from her account of her first day on the job: "[I answer a call] for a party living in the 800 block on West Eighth Street. I already know the answer but I'd better make sure, so I call across the room to Miss Emma (Chief Operator Emily Hanson). She gives me a disapproving look and bids me ring her on the trunk on her desk. This I do, and she gets out the directory and informs me, just as I thought, 'There is no telephone for this party.' I go back and tell the waiting party, failing to add this particular block is nothing but a field as I pass it nearly every day.

"I look down the board. Three positions away sits Clara Miller, one of my best friends. She tells the girl next to her something, and this girl relays me an invitation to go home with Clara to dinner. I explain I have brought something to eat with me and some other time would suit me fine. In between times I answer calls—nothing of importance: someone wanting to know the time, or asking about the trains, or perhaps how to spell a word, or the day of the month. . .

"The girl next to me whispers, 'See that girl on Position 0, Nana Van Nort? She's Earl Jennings' girl, and he thinks no one else can put up his test cords for him.' Miss Emma comes over asking, 'Are you girls talking?' We look innocent and try to think of a good answer when some girl from the far end of the switchboard calls, 'Miss Emma, come quick, I have a fire call.'

"Away rushes Miss Emma. Getting the address, she dashes to the fire telephone which hangs on a post in the middle of the room. One long ring and the fire department knows immediately we have a fire call (if it were merely a test call it would be three short rings). Miss Emma is excited, and we are all in the same state. The fire whistle blows, and we hear the fire department going by the office. I'll bet those horses are making at least 15 miles an hour . . .

"Laura Tyson, six positions away, looks toward me and lifts an eyebrow. This could mean several things, but I get her meaning. Bob Snyder, my beau, is over at the water cooler getting a drink out of our one tin cup. He is a lineman and is all of 17 years old . . .

"Suddenly it is 10 o'clock. 'Standing relief,' announces Miss Emma, and we all push back our chairs and stand, except one girl who begs to be excused. Miss Emma consents, and we all stretch tired muscles for 15 minutes.

"Finally it is 12 o'clock and the relief girls come on. We have 30 minutes' relaxation as Miss Emma has gone to lunch at 11:30 and Anna Sanders, the relief chief operator, does not make us behave so well. We talk over the board, visit with each other, listen in on connections [this violation of privacy could cause an operator to be disciplined or discharged!] and, in general, break all the rules laid down for good conduct."

Mima eats her newspaper-wrapped lunch, which she finds totally inadequate—a baked bean sandwich with plenty of sweet relish, a meat sandwich and a huge piece of pie. She promises herself she'll hurry home after work so she can "really get me something to eat." But as it turns out, she and a fellow operator, while walking home from work at 5 o'clock, buy a couple of pies to stave off the hunger pangs until supper.

Incidentally, the fact that Mima went to work at the age of 15 was not unusual. A few years later she tells how some of the operators would roughhouse and break out into giggles during their relief periods. One of Mima's friends comments that they ought to be in kindergarten, and Mima agrees with her—"I am 20 years old and have some dignity, while most of these girls are from 13 to 15 years of age. Their payroll record cards would show them several years older, as we have some restrictions in regard to age, [but] no one asks for their birth certificates when they are employed, merely accepting their word."

Real discipline came to the Oklahoma City switchboard in 1910. Mima reports

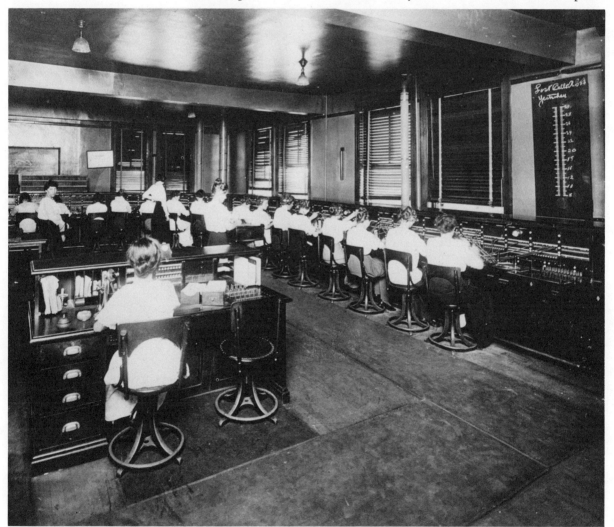

Oklahoma City, 1914. The tally board at right kept track of "Lost Calls Yesterday."

Now, Just Hand Me That Bobby Pin...

SWITCHBOARD operators' ingenuity sometimes made up for technological shortcomings in the early days of telephone service. H. M. Altepeter cites a couple of experiences from his travels as a plant man in Arkansas during the twenties.

"I was in a little manual exchange at Yellville (Ark.)," he relates. "The switchboard there had connections with a number of other small manually operated exchanges. Some of these connections were iron wire and were not quite up to good transmission standards. When two or more such circuits were connected in tandem, the resulting transmission was pretty gruesome.

"However, someone had developed a simple process which at least got the message through. The ends of these circuits had been equipped with a key or switch which, when operated one way or another, permitted the operator to connect herself to each circuit as she wished.

"The operator would get the message from the calling party

and relay this message verbally to the called party and then handle the response in a like manner. In a sense, the operator acted as a *'voice frequency repeater'*! ...

"One morning, I went to the telephone exchange in a small town where a one-position manual switchboard was located on the second floor above a drugstore across the street from the courthouse. The operator told me she was glad to see me because none of the signals on her board was working, and as a result customers could not

get her attention with a signal.

"While I stood there, she suddenly plugged her cord into a jack, said 'Number, please' and completed a call. I asked her how she knew that a customer wanted service, since there had been no signal. She said: 'Oh! I can see across the street into Judge Smith's office, and I saw him take his receiver off the hook.' "

Operator resourcefulness took many forms and for many reasons. Oklahoma City operator Mima Blanchard tells how, in the fall of 1905, she and three other young women had all-night assignments. They used to order coffee from a nearby restaurant, but one night, they found the telephone service had been cut off for non-payment of the bill.

A trifle like that couldn't stop a group of savvy operators. They went to the back of the switchboard and found where the "heat coils" (a type of fuse) had been removed to cut off the circuit. They would put back the heat coils, order their coffee, then disconnect the service again so no one would be the wiser. ∎

Hot Line to Heaven?

IT WAS BACK around the turn of the century that some Tin Pan Alley genius composed *Hello Central, Give Me Heaven*—a tear-jerker about a little girl who wants to talk to Mommy, and her Daddy has told her that Mommy has gone to Heaven. Well, it can happen in real life, too, or something like that.

Loquita Celastine, Wichita operator, reported to Southwestern Bell's *SCENE* magazine that she answered a signal one afternoon and heard a tiny voice say:

"Hello, may I please have God's telephone number?"

The startled operator told the child she was sorry, but she didn't have a listing for God.

The voice persisted: "You mean

God has an unlisted number?"

No, said the operator, God just doesn't have a telephone.

"Well, how can I get in touch with him? I've really got something important to talk about."

The operator attempted to explain that there are more direct ways to talk to God than using a telephone, but the child interrupted her to say:

"Thank you anyway. I'll call back later—maybe you'll have his phone number by then."

If the youngster did call back, Loquita Celastine didn't get to pick up that signal, so she never knew what happened next. ∎

that Jessie Lynn replaced Maude McKinley as chief—"Miss Emma" had quit earlier in a dudgeon because another woman was brought into the organization to be her boss. Mima comments:

"Jessie has real ability; she can get us all to work and do the job well without doing a thing herself. She is mean and doesn't hesitate to thoroughly bawl us out, but we need it. I learn a lot from her about handling people.

"In later years I was criticized for hard-boiled methods in handling people— I learned from Jessie Lynn and she got the job done. With the exception of Miss Emma, she was the best chief operator we ever had. She was a real executive and had the courage of her convictions. When she left in the spring of 1914 [to straighten out the problems of the Tulsa office], she left a perfectly organized force and almost perfect service."

Mima's subsequent career brought her to the post of chief operator at two central offices simultaneously, with 500 operators on the two rosters. It appears that the strain was too much for her; she says:

Kansas City, Mo., 1917. A school for training toll operators.

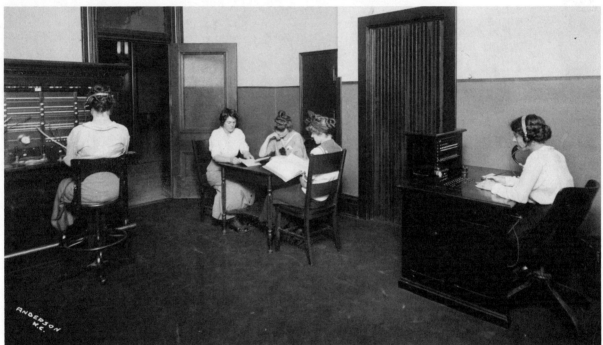

"I am worn out. I go to bed tired and get up tired. I feel I shall never be rested. I want a furlough and tell all my traffic bosses. Mr. Armstrong tells me he has worked for 25 years without a furlough and he isn't tired. I feel worse and worse; my furlough is granted. After being relieved from the strain of work, a reaction sets in, and five weeks later I am in St. Anthony's Hospital. I have five doctors, and each one gives a different diagnosis. At this rate I will soon have every known disease. I go to Dr. Edwards and he tells me I will have to help myself as no medicine can do anything for me.

"After nine months' absence, I return to the office to find my name off the door as chief operator, and I don't care as I feel that operating is a nightmare. I hope to be assigned to some nice clerical position. Instead I am given charge of the cafeteria. I shed tears all over the place. Why wish this job on me when I can't tell beef from pork?"

However, all turned out well. Mima, who didn't know how to make a cup of coffee when she was 30, became something of an expert on food preparation and dietetics, at least by her self-appraisals. By 1933, when her account ends, she seems to be well adjusted to her situation but "appalled" by the way the younger generation is turning out.

Mima Blanchard's account deals largely with people and contains very little about the ever-changing nature of the operator's job. It's not difficult to reconstruct this, however, from a multitude of reminiscences the operators have bequeathed us and pictures of early central offices.

When Mima went to work, the magneto telephone was just about universal. The operator, wearing earphones and supporting an awkward box in front of her face, would dodge around this contraption as she watched for "drops"—metal signals which were normally vertical against the jack array in front of her, but which dropped to a horizontal position when a customer "rang up Central."

Dallas, early 1900s. Information operators used thick books to find telephone numbers.

The operator, thus summoned, would select one of a pair of cords on her key-shelf and insert the plug-end of the cord into the jack underneath the "drop." She would answer the customer, obtain the number wanted, locate that number on the jack array and plug in the other cord of the pair. Then she would turn a handcrank to call the other party, unless she was fortunate enough to be in an office that had some homemade source of ringing current.

As years went by, the clumsy box gave way to a somewhat less cumbersome breastplate, from which the mouthpiece curved up toward the operator's lips. Some earlier models using this principle had the transmitter fixed to the top of the switchboard, which meant that the operator had to duck around it while making connections.

By the thirties, however, a much more comfortable headset had been developed which used a single earpiece, held across the head with an adjustable lightweight spring clamp. From the earpiece a thin metal tube curved around with a small mouthpiece that could be adjusted to the operator's comfort.

This was a quantum leap forward, but its successor, essentially the model used

*Above: Tulsa, 1927. An opera-
tors' lounge. Right: San
Antonio, 1911. A similar
lounge.*

today by operators, comes as close as possible to being nothing at all and still functional. It is made of plastic except for some light circuitry; the earpiece has dwindled to a small plug that fits in either ear, and the transmitter portion is a tube little larger than a soda straw. The heaviest part of the whole array is the cord that plugs in below the keyshelf.

The switchboard itself, of course, has changed dramatically. The common-battery switchboard dispensed with the magneto "drops," replacing them with tiny signal lamps. At the same time this improvement was taking place, however, operators were finding the job more intellectually demanding. The growth of long distance usage meant that they had to learn a new set of routines for handling these calls.

In the early twenties, when a customer (say, in St. Louis) wanted to call out of town, he would say "long distance" when the operator answered his signal. The local operator would connect the call to a "recording" long distance operator, and she would get the information from the customer.

This information was written on a paper ticket. A girl using roller skates would

How To Lose Friends and Alienate Operators

SERVICE MEASUREMENTS are an old story in the telephone business. Work groups and their supervisors win plaudits when the "indexes" are outstanding. But measurement can be a two-edged sword, recalls J. R. Peterson, who retired as vice president-personnel after spending most of his telephone years in the Traffic Department. He joined the department in late June 1920 when the service in Dallas must have been the absolute worst in any telephone company's history. Here's how Peterson tells the story:

"The Texas traffic organization was headed by an Englishman of great personal charm but with little knowledge of the details of traffic operations. The four division heads were strong leaders but, like the top man, not well versed in furnishing high-grade telephone service while controlling the costs.

"Consequently, the performance of the traffic organization at the time I entered it was about as poor as it could possibly be. The situation at Dallas was especially bad. Due to a wage rate for operators far below the community level, coupled with the inherent disadvantages of evening and Sunday work, operating forces at Dallas were 35 percent short of requirements.

"A couple of hundred operators had been imported from San Antonio and Fort Worth and were housed in three dormitories. Naturally, the local girls were envious of the fact that these importees had all living expenses paid.

"The result of all these conditions was that the local service at Dallas was atrocious. The first month of my employment—July 1920—the Dallas local manual

service index was 6 out of a possible 100 points.

"It was a splendid time for a young man to enter the Traffic Department . . . it was practically impossible for the performance to go any way but *up*."

When Peterson comments, "Naturally, the local girls were envious," he is guilty of gross understatement, unless human nature has changed radically in the last 60 years. Wilma Farris (*nee* King) was one of the "importees," and the way she describes their kid-glove treatment it's a wonder that all the local operators didn't quit. Mrs. Farris, who retired at Orange, Tex., in 1961, was 19 years old and living in San Antonio when the telephone company sought her out and asked if she'd like to go to Dallas. Wilma had been an operator in San Antonio but quit because of illness.

"I enlisted and took the train to Dallas," she says. "The pay was good at $18 a week." All the girls from out of town were furnished living quarters and food. I was placed in 'Burrbauer Dorm,' named after two chief operators, Burr of Galveston and Bauer of San Antonio.

"As I remember, there were three dorms in Dallas then. Each dorm housed about 50 girls and had a chaperon, matron, maids, chefs and waiters."

The amenities for an importee went far beyond free room and board. Maids kept beds made and changed linens. Clothes cleaning and pressing were free. Streetcar fare between the dorm and the job was furnished. Every few weeks the girls would be sent back home for a short visit (free roundtrip train fare, including meals in the diner), so they wouldn't get homesick and quit.

To drive the local operators' morale even lower, the district traffic superintendent, who was supposed to handle such basic paperwork as signing payrolls, went on disability leave. Wage payments were often late.

Peterson boosted his standing, especially with chief operators, when he took it upon himself to collect the payrolls each week and take them to the division superintendent to be signed. Shortly, the division man realized a lot of time could be saved by giving Peterson a title and authorizing him to sign for the absent district chief.

"Before long, I was making out for my missing boss," Peterson recalls. "It's really surprising how much an untrained man can do if he's forced to try his wings. . . . The modest success I had during those early months at Dallas (the index improved from 6 to 30) greatly improved my prospects for promotion and my self-confidence."

But telephone service in Dallas didn't really get straightened out until early 1921. "A general traffic manager, A. C. Stannard, was imported and the beginnings of a capable general headquarters staff inaugurated," Peterson recalls. Stannard (who later became Southwestern Bell president) increased operators' wage rates substantially; money differentials for unpopular evening and Sunday work were more than doubled; and clean and attractive quarters were given deserved attention.

Finally, with the cutover of much of Dallas service to dial, it was no longer necessary to use "importees." Wilma King and the others packed up and went back home. The improvement in the local operators' morale can't be imagined! ∎

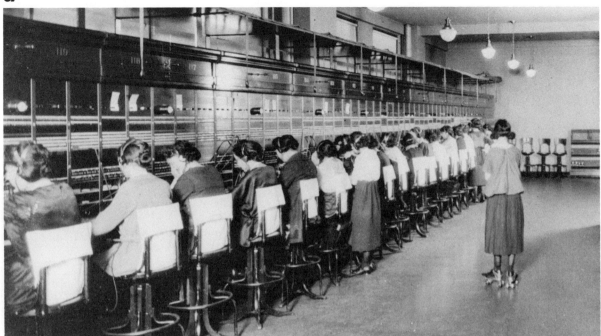

Kansas City, Mo., 1920. In a toll operating room, girls on roller skates were vital links in completing long distance calls.

come whizzing past, grab the ticket and deliver it to a long distance "line operator" at another St. Louis switchboard. The line operator would ring the distant city—say, Chicago.

The Chicago operator who handled incoming long distance calls would contact a "B" operator at the Chicago central office required and tell that operator to ring the desired number.

When the St. Louis "line operator" heard the Chicago customer answer, she would plug into a St. Louis incoming toll trunk, thus reaching a "local trunk operator." The "originating line operator" would say to the "local trunk operator," for example, "1-2-3-4 without." This meant "Plug this line in on jack 1234 without testing to see whether the number is busy." (The line, of course, would probably be busy because the customer was waiting patiently for this call to go through. Then again, the customer could have hung up, which would complicate matters a little more, but not much.)

St. Louis, 1943. The equipment had improved, but information operators still used thick directories for finding numbers.

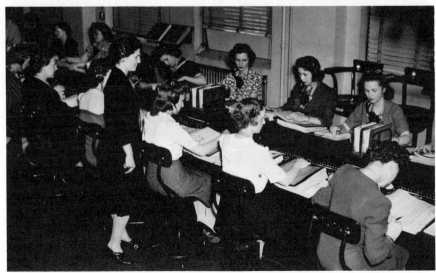

Thus it could take five or more operators to complete one long distance call. More, if additional cities were involved in making the connection.

It was considered a great leap forward when the CLR—combined line and recording—practice was instituted. This combined the functions of two operators in the originating office, but it was still a far cry from today's situation.

Today, with modern TSPS (traffic service position system) circuitry, the vast majority of customers dial their own long distance calls directly; but if they need

Right: Supervisors stand ready to advise, admonish and help. Below: Modern directory assistance operators use computer terminals to find numbers.

an operator's help, there will normally be just one operator involved. (Overseas calls sometimes require two or three operators, depending upon the circumstances.)

The advent of dial systems in the twenties created problems for operators to handle, too. Callers from dial to manual telephones would sometimes go directly to operators for assistance and sometimes, using special circuitry, could dial a manual number; in such a case, however, the distant telephone would not be rung until a "B" operator read the number off a display and completed the call in the traditional manner.

In larger cities a mix of manual and dial service existed from the 1920s into the 1950s, and this necessitated, first, a multitude of special trunking arrangements and second, constant retraining of operators to handle the new circuit layouts as they went into use.

The advent of the TSP—traffic service position, an arrangement that made it possible for customers to dial collect, person-to-person and other types of calls— again created an entirely new working environment for the operator.

Up to this time central offices had been constantly more user-friendly for the operator. The "multiple" (an array of jacks on the switchboard face where numbers appeared repeatedly, typically at every third operator position) became lower and easier to reach; its coloration, instead of stodgy dark varnished oak, went to pastel shades; the keyshelf was easier to handle; dials, and later keypads, made it possible for operators actually to ring distant cities.

But the TSP is something else again. Operators sit before push buttons, many of which are illuminated. They hear signals come in on their headsets and see lighted displays in front of them. At the touch of the proper button, they can tell the number calling, the number called or the rate or total charge of the call.

There are no cords, no plugs, no jacks. Operation is so effortless that the operator can concentrate on projecting a pleasing personality to the customer. To maintain a pleasant mood, the rooms are brightly but not glaringly lighted, and floors are carpeted. Background music may play quietly.

The operator's working conditions today are a dramatic improvement over what Mima Blanchard encountered when she went to work that day in August 1903, and an even greater advance over what was encountered by pioneering operators like Kate Adams.

Yet, as with most of life's improvements, there had to be a tradeoff. The TSP equipment* is faster, more efficient and drastically more expensive than what it has supplanted. Its economic justification, aside from better service, is that it makes it possible for considerably fewer operators to handle the ever-growing flood of calls.

As central offices have been closed in recent years, Southwestern Bell has done its utmost to make the transition a gentle one. There has always been a large turn-over in operating forces, and as vacancies occur they are filled with temporary operators who have the clear understanding that their jobs will last only a month or so. When the offices finally close, veteran operators have a variety of choices. If they qualify, they can retire on pension. They are offered transfers to operator jobs in other cities. Where possible, they are given preference for transfers to other parts of the business. If none of these is satisfactory, the operator is released with severance pay in proportion to length of service.

It would be fruitless to deny that these changes have caused some unhappi-ness among operators who expected to finish out their careers at a switchboard. But surprisingly, some of the operators most willing to take up new jobs have been veterans who value their company service regardless of readjustments.

And the operators who remain at their posts carry on a proud tradition. The "Voice with a Smile"—a slogan coined by Howard Stokes in January 1912—con-tinues to serve customers as it has since Kate Adams of Little Rock, with her church-choir soprano, set a standard in 1879. "Central" still cares. ∎

A modern TSPS board.

*TSPS, a technological advance, resembles TSP but makes it possible for one office to handle a territory several hundred miles across.

THE PUBLIC'S PROBLEM SOLVERS

CHAPTER SIX

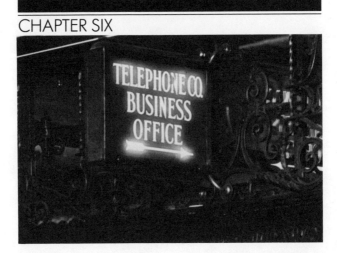

THERE ARE A FEW—just a few—jobs which say "telephone company" to the average customer. There is the operator, of course; and the telephone installer or the lineman (nowadays called "installation technician" and "construction technician"); perhaps the cable splicer . . . now the cable splicing technician. As the business matures, customers hear the operator's voice less frequently, and seldom see the plant people.

But if the customer needs any kind of help other than placing a phone call—from getting a telephone installed to ordering new services and clearing up billing problems—one telephone company employee suddenly moves to center stage.

It was no accident that when the Bell System commissioned artists to depict three typical telephone workers, the selections were an operator, a lineman—and a service representative.

What *is* curious is that for the first two dozen years the Commercial Department existed, there were no service representatives. Although the department was organized in 1909 to make customer contacts more helpful and efficient, the job of service representative wasn't created until 1933.

Of course the function was there from the beginning. Someone had to accept bill payments and arrange for new or changed service and handle complaints—the multitude of problems and services that are involved when dealing with customers.

*Great Bend, Kan., 1912.
Customers paid bills at the
commercial office.*

*Dallas, circa 1910. Customers
applied for new service at the
contract window on the left.*

Some of these chores would be handled as a sideline by the chief operator; if an equipment problem was involved, she would get in touch with the local plant man; if it was a matter of how to administer company policy, she passed the question to the manager for a decision. And even after there was a Commercial Department, this arrangement continued in many small communities without dial service.

But in the larger towns and cities, the clerks in the Commercial Department became the front-line troops to handle all these contacts. Originally the duties were split up. There were counter clerks—most of these were men; there were "girl" order clerks and "girl" collection clerks. (In those days a mature woman, even one about to retire, was commonly referred to as a "girl.")

In imitation of the banks of that period, the lobby of a telephone company public office had rows of waist-high marble counters down each side. Atop the counters was iron grillwork, with gates called "windows" which would be pulled open when a counter clerk was ready to wait on customers.

If a customer came in to make a payment, this would be accepted by a counter clerk and placed in a metal carrier hanging from a "trolley wire" (given this name because it resembled the wire that carried the power for the trolley cars outside). If a request to start service was involved, the signed application would be enclosed in the carrier too.

The clerk would reach up and pull a chain, and the carrier would run along the wire to a cashier. The cashier put the change in the carrier and pulled the chain again, and back came the carrier to the counter window. The procedure

Weatherford, Tex., 1910.
Another commercial office.

The Quality of Mercy Is Not Strained...

TODAY a "collector" in the telephone business would have to be someone who visits pay stations on a regular schedule, removes the full coin boxes and replaces them with empties. But that wasn't the job of W. R. Faught when he was hired as collector in the Dallas exchange in 1892. Instead, his duty was to visit customers' homes and places of business and obtain payment of their monthly bills.

Young Faught was expected to cover his routes on foot—there were only 500 subscribers in all Dallas at the time, so the collecting chore wasn't even a full-time job. He spent five days a month helping to get out the office's monthly reports.

Still, there were some long walks on his routes, and Faught found that using the mule-drawn streetcars saved him many a weary step. They traveled so slowly that he was often able to jump off, make a collection and jump back on the same car without being charged a second fare.

One day the company's general auditor, J. E. Farnsworth, made a routine check of Faught's books and found one of the customers was shown as not having paid his bill, even though the customer had a receipt. In fact, he recalled having paid the bill with a $5 gold piece.

Faught was called in and confronted with the evidence. He admitted that he had made the collection, but the gold piece was missing when he came back to the office, so he left that record blank until he could figure out a way to balance the books. He thought that he must have mistaken the quarter-eagle for a nickel and dropped it in the streetcar cash box. At any rate, he didn't have $5 to make the shortage good.

Nowadays this would be called defalcation and would be grounds for immediate dismissal. But a surprisingly different view was taken in Faught's case. Perhaps the first consideration was how to balance the books, rather than what to do about a collector who didn't turn in what he collected.

Putting their heads together, the general auditor and the general superintendent came up with a tidy solution. They gave Faught a $5-a-month raise in pay! Then they held out the first month's raise and applied it to the customer's account.

The incident must have been completely forgiven, since Faught stayed with the company and eventually rose to the responsible jobs of general cashier, assistant treasurer and paymaster. One assumes he never again mishandled company funds. ∎

Getting Off to a Good Start

PEOPLE HAVE their individual ways of relieving tension and summoning their best efforts. The job of service representative can be stress-producing, especially for a newcomer. So it's not surprising that a representative in St. Louis found it helped to start off each day with a quiet prayer.

She was praying one morning when the signal for an incoming call purred in her headset. She threw the answering key automatically, but instead of using the standard phrase, "This is the business office, Miss Blank speaking," she heard herself saying: "Holy Mary, Mother of God. . . ." She gasped, then gave the routine business office salutation.

A woman's warm voice responded: "I'm so pleased to hear those words. The Holy Mother bless you, dear." The "contact" (conversation) went swimmingly from then on, and the representative reports she had a most pleasant workday. ∎

must have amused children who tagged along when their mothers came in to pay a bill.

The male clerks were expected to stand at their posts, but when it was necessary to detach a "girl" from her regular assignment to help out during a rush, she was provided with a chair. As customers came in, a floor manager would greet them, learn their address and telephone number (if they already had one) and then direct them to the set of windows where their business could be transacted.

If a customer preferred not to come into the office, he or she could call in and would reach one of the order clerks who were seated at desks behind the counters. The information would be jotted down on a scratch pad and later transferred to a service order. (The traditional S-8888 report blank was not introduced until about 1924.)

The collection clerks, meanwhile, were busy on the telephones contacting customers whose bill payments were overdue.

This office arrangement began to disappear in 1930. In January of that year two significant changes occurred. First, Dallas opened Southwestern Bell's first branch business office to accommodate subscribers in suburban Oak Cliff. Then, a few days later, Kansas City became the first large city in the company to have the "counterless" type of business office.

In such offices, the bank-lobby arrangement was abolished and the order clerks were placed at desks, where customers could sit and discuss their business in a relaxed atmosphere.

When the clerk had analyzed the customer's needs, she would call up to the district office in the same building; the district office was where the records were kept. Thus every contact in the public office involved two employees—one to talk to the customer, and one to check the records.

In 1933-34 the functions of order clerk and collection clerk were combined and the title of "service representative" came into existence. Each service representative had access to all information—billing, service records, toll tickets and the like—on a certain group of accounts. Within a two-year period the system was put into effect in all the large cities of Southwestern Bell.

Records were kept at this time and for many years thereafter in "tubs"—deep bins which were located between two service representatives' desks. Each would have access to the same record files. (Such a pair of representatives was unofficially referred to as "tub mates.")

Another change in the forties eliminated the desks where the public could face a telephone employee. The service representatives became invisible voices. A customer who came into the public office would be directed to a cubicle, where he or she would talk over a house telephone with the service representative handling the account. This person might be only a few steps away in a nearby room, or up on another floor.

St. Louis, 1952. A service representative handles customer requests over the phone.

Not all the smiling faces were relegated to back rooms, however. There still had to be someone to accept bill payments, and these people were known as "tellers." Essentially, their job was a reinstatement of the old-time window clerk . . . but without the overhead "trolley lines."

Regardless of where they were seated, the service representatives by necessity became the most widely informed of all company employees. It was a rare day indeed when the routine was not interrupted by a first-time question or request. The public expected (and still expects) the representatives to be authorities on the entire company, to know all the answers. Being only human, they're sometimes stumped, but only for a time; their job calls for them to get that answer and call the customer back. Every time a company practice changes, they are given training in how to handle the new situation. This training can vary from a printed notice to several days away from the job if the change is a complex one.

Although the physical layout of the offices changed, the techniques of handling customer requests remained essentially the same for decades. Then came micro-fiche—a system in which all the records that had been kept on account cards in the "tubs" were transferred to photographic film. Each service representative's desk had a few sheets of such film, as well as a viewer. To the naked eye, the records

Kansas City, Mo., 1971. Service representatives like Karen Fenderson, left, and Wanda Thomson were called "tub mates" because they shared a tub filled with customer information.

were barely visible dots on the film, but the viewer enlarged them so they could be read.

Every evening the records were updated and new films produced in the Accounting Department, so that when the service representatives came to work the next morning, all records were current.

But even microfiche, hailed as a great advance when it was introduced, is bowing out in favor of the computer. Today service representatives—the title is one of the few that have not been changed in recent years—are learning to work with "PreBOSS" and "PREMIS"—information systems that are provided through Dataspeed 4540 terminals. Where the change is in effect, the service representative has access to needed information by touching a few buttons on a keyboard and reading a TV-like screen.

In the Commerical Department as it was constituted until a few years ago, the service representatives were part of a complex establishment that included business office supervisors, managers and unit managers, leading up to district managers. But this organization handled only part of the department's functions. There were also the coin telephone collection group and the group that compiled and issued directories.

The coin collector has a job that keeps him or her constantly on the go, driving a specially equipped company vehicle around town, removing the receptacles from pay stations, replacing them with empty receptacles and taking the full canisters back to the office. There the coins are mechanically sorted, counted, wrapped and tallied for deposit.

For the first 12 years of the telephone's history, there were no coin telephones. Although the telephone companies of the time frowned on the practice and told their subscribers how to prevent it, it was apparently common to "borrow a phone" when a person wanted to make a call.

Since all local service was flat rate at the time, no one lost out by this except the phone company, which would naturally prefer to lease a telephone to the non-customer.*

William Gray achieved a breakthrough in 1888 when he brought out the first nickel-in-the-slot pay telephone for local calls. The first public installation of one of these devices was in the lobby of a Hartford, Conn., bank.

The coin telephone moved quickly from the status of novelty to necessity. It seems to have taken a while to reach the Southwest, however. The earliest record of a coin phone in this territory was in Little Rock's Capitol Hotel. This was in 1894.

These early pay stations accepted only a 5-cent piece, since that was the charge for a local call and they were not connected to the long distance network. It was around 1912 that the first multislot instruments were introduced, with one slot for nickels, another for dimes and a third for quarters.

In 1976, a microfiche system was used to store customer records. Computer technology made this method short-lived.

*Long distance calls were another matter. For a good many years local service could not be connected to long distance lines. People who wanted to call outside the local exchange area would go to a company pay station, where an attendant would take their money, set up the circuit and direct them to a booth to carry on the conversation. A few business customers had "direct loop" circuits installed on their premises to connect them with the long distance office.

The three-slot instruments, which were once found in every public place, survive today largely as novelty table lamps. They have been succeeded by a single-slot telephone (history has a way of repeating itself) that accepts all three coins and distinguishes between them electronically. Incidentally, the single-slot instruments were first manufactured at the Western Electric works in Oklahoma City; and the first one was installed on an Oklahoma City street April 1, 1966—another first for Southwestern Bell.

And in some locations today, public telephones don't accept coins at all. They are engineered to handle only traffic one doesn't pay for in advance, such as credit card and collect calls.

Responsibility for these public conveniences, until departmental structures were realigned, was divided between employees of the Commerical and Plant departments. If any installation, removal or repair was involved, a plant employee would handle the job. But the routine collection of the coins, which might occur once a month or several times a day (depending on usage at that location), was the function of the coin collector, who was a Commercial Department employee after the department was created.

H. P. Bridges, who served all his 41 telephone years from 1929 to 1970 in the metropolitan Dallas commercial engineering section, recalls that during the Depression he was one of several employees on loan to the coin section—Southwestern Bell has always been zealous to avoid layoffs when possible.

San Antonio, 1977. Coin office clerk Laura Valdez demonstrates that modern technology makes it easy to count public telephone collections.

"I was one of the first to install sealed, self-closing, self-locking coin boxes in Dallas pay stations," Bridges reports. "We had to *sell* the customer on the fact that he no longer would see the money counted at his place of business. Also, we had to watch to be sure the customer didn't play with, or try to test, the self-locking mechanism. If that happened, the box would lock itself and couldn't be reset without breaking the seal."

Bridges also remembers the advent of the first "short-proof" coin instruments, which defied efforts to dial a number without a coin in the relay. (Various techniques, such as banging on the side of the box after dropping in a coin, had been discovered to provide both a call *and* a returned coin.) There were some enlightening results from such installations.

Be My Guest

ALTHOUGH the departmental organization of Bell and large independent companies was well established by the 1920s, smaller independents didn't enjoy the luxury of teams of specialists. Instead, they tended to turn out well-rounded jacks-of-all-trades.

In 1950-51, Bill Wimsatt had the title of "manager" for the Liberal, Kan., office of the Southwest Telephone Company, which operated small exchanges in Kansas and Oklahoma. The job entailed the usual responsibilities of customer contacts but also got him involved in things like collecting from coin telephones, helping out on plant problems and taking responsibility for traffic operations.

Then in 1952, Southwestern Bell (with state regulators' approval, of course) incorporated the independent into its operations. It had held a financial interest in the Southwest Telephone Company for some years. Wimsatt's boss broke the news to him, explaining that "of course" he could not expect to be shifted over as a manager with a Bell company; his experience and training didn't qualify him for such a lofty post. However, he would be taken care of. The proposition offered was this:
☐ He would be transferred to Dodge City, a Bell town.
☐ He would be given the title of "outside representative" in the Commercial Department there.
☐ His salary would be boosted $55 a month.

Wimsatt jumped at the offer. "I was in the Bell System for 15 years before I got as good a raise as that one," he chuckles. "And to boot, my boss was one of the finest fellows I've ever met— Gene Arnold. I had a lot to learn and, to some extent, so did he; so we learned together."

An early example of this learn-ing process came when Arnold asked Wimsatt if he could help in a new Southwestern Bell pro-gram to upgrade rural service. At that time, the company con-nected with a good many "ser-vice lines"—farmer built and farmer owned—which were in a sorry state.

To completely rebuild these lines would cost an incredible amount of money—and who was going to come up with this money? The answer seemed eminently reasonable to Bell people . . . but we're getting ahead of the story.

Arnold called Wimsatt into his office one morning and told him, "Bill, I'm talking to a group of farmers in your old territory tonight, and I'm a little uneasy about it. I'm really not familiar with their situation. Would you come along for moral support?"

"Sure," said Wimsatt. By the time they reached the rural schoolhouse where the meeting was to take place, a plan was worked out. Arnold would sit in the back of the room, and Wimsatt would "break the ice," putting the audience at ease and then outlining the company's proposal.

Then Arnold would make his appearance, get the crowd's reaction and discuss the matter further. A formal proposal would be made by mail at a later date.

"I can still see Gene almost doubled up, sitting there at a fourth-grader's desk," Wimsatt recalls. "You know he's well over six feet tall.

"Well, I introduced myself and launched into our proposition. We all agreed, I said, that their service wasn't much good. And there was no hope of making it any better unless the plant was rebuilt, using standard poles and wire and cutting down the number of parties on the line. But we could hardly be expected to pay to rebuild all the farmer lines in Kansas, so we had this suggestion.

"We would obtain the poles and wire and sell them to the farmers at our cost. They would do the manual labor of putting in the new lines—it wouldn't be too hard, especially since we would provide complete instruc-tions and as much supervision as they wanted. When the line was ready, we would buy it back from them for $1.

"And then we'd provide excel-lent Bell service for just 75 cents a month. . . .

"I had hardly finished before one of these gentlemen had climbed out of his desk seat. 'Now just a minute, Mister,' he growled. 'Let me see if I heard you right. We're to buy the poles and wire from you, build the line, and then sell the whole thing back to you for $1 and you're going to charge 75 cents a month to use it?'

" 'That's the idea,' I said.

" 'That idea is a (expletive deleted),' the farmer said. 'I'm going to write the Kansas Corporation Commission and raise hell.'

" 'Go ahead,' I said, still keep-ing my cool. 'They're in Topeka and the street address is . . .' and I told him where to write.

'About this time, there was a commotion in the back of the room. It was Gene scrambling out of his desk seat. 'Now wait a minute, fellows,' he pleaded as he came up the aisle. 'Let's not make any hasty decisions.'

"Things calmed down a little then; but for a while, my big mouth almost sponsored a com-mission complaint against us.

"On the way home, Gene patiently explained to me that a telephone company just does *not* encourage its customers to complain to the commission. Shucks, I didn't know that." ■

Rules Are Rules Are Rules...

IN THESE DAYS, when it seems that everybody is selling telephones, it's a little hard to remember that during World War II they were scarce. The supplies being produced by Western Electric and other manufacturers were earmarked for the armed services. Special government approval was required before a non-military request could be honored.

The late Stuart Symington, president of Emerson Electric, knew all about wartime shortages, but he may not have been prepared for the news that he couldn't get an extension for his home telephone just by calling up and asking for it. At any rate, he felt he knew how to get around this restriction. He wrote a letter to his friend, the president of Southwestern Bell.

"If Mr. Symington had written

to me, I could have cut through the red tape for him," says Bob Hollocher, who was the unit manager in charge of the Symington residence account at that time. "He certainly had good reason for an extension; he might get business calls at night connected with the war effort, and he lived in a pretty big house.

"But he didn't write to me, he

wrote to Mr. Stannard. I suppose our president got several letters like this every day, and the routine was to send them straight down the pipe for the appropriate action. When the Symington letter was routed to me, I couldn't use my own judgment; this was already on the record and I had to adhere to the strict government regulations for such cases.

"We sent the forms to the Symington residence, and when they came back properly filled out, they were routed to the War Production Board for review; and the WPB refused the application!

"But not long afterward, Symington left Emerson Electric when he was appointed U.S. Secretary of Defense. That put him over the War Production Board, and he got his residence extension telephone with no more fuss." ∎

Psychology Pays Off

TELEPHONE COMPANIES feel they lean over backward to be fair to the customers. There is a tiny minority of the public which takes advantage of this attitude.

In the 1930s, the word got around among a group of St. Louis customers that reports of service outage often could bring a reduction in the bill. So they would complain repeatedly about difficulties in using the telephone, even though nothing was wrong. The test desk would check the line, find no problem and file the report as "test okay."

When the customer received the bill, he or she would come in to the public office and complain to the teller that service had been poor that month and some allowance should be made. The teller would check with the test desk, get a report of all the trouble

complaints and make an adjustment.

This petty chicanery was getting to be an epidemic, causing an overload on the test desk and, of course, cutting into company revenues. The chief deskman hit upon a simple but

ingenious way of stopping the chiselers.

Calling one of the chronic complainers, he would ask whether the trouble developed while the telephone was in use or when it was not in use. "Why, when I'm using it, of course," was the unsuspecting response.

"Well, that's why I haven't located the trouble, then," the chief would say. "I've been running all the tests when you weren't using the phone. From now on, I'll check the line every time you talk on the phone until I can find what's wrong."

"You'll do no such thing!" the alarmed customer would exclaim. And, of course, the chief had no intention of doing that. (Against regulations.) But the mere suggestion quickly stopped the false complaints of trouble and the monthly demands for an adjustment on the bill. ∎

"We selected some of the worst cases, such as a tailoring and cleaning business that we suspected was a front for a bookie," Bridges recalls. "After the new instrument was installed, the coin box filled up and jammed the relay, causing a busy signal on all calls, in or out. It was a 5-cent call rate, but the coin box had never before had over $2 in a 30-day collection period." (The implication is that the bookie and his customers had been cheating on the coin telephone.)

"The tailor shop owner demanded that we service the telephone to clear up the busy condition or change the instrument. We informed him that we would gladly sell him full flat-rate business service but would have to change his telephone number to do so. He refused, and since there was nothing wrong with the new telephone, he had to put up with the inconvenience of paying for making calls after that."

Bridges relates how, before the advent of mechanical counting machines, the collectors had to hand-count and roll the coins in colored wrappers stamped "S. W. Bell Tel. Co." Each collector had an individual wrapper color assigned to him so collections could be distinguished.

"There were only two local community banks in Dallas at this time," Bridges says. "The auditor didn't like for us to go to these two banks [to leave collections for safekeeping]. But after you collected all morning, with a locked ring of 90 keys, a fiber-backed route book, wrappers, bad coins, slugs and money, you were very happy to be relieved of all this weight."

The "locked ring" Bridges mentions held keys arranged in numerical order, plus a brass tag showing the route number. The collector was required to make all stops in the sequence in which the keys were arranged. All collections had to be noted on route sheets showing the name and location of the business, its telephone number and the key number of the instrument. When the boxes were brought back to the office, opened and their contents counted, the collector had to fill out a report of the amount obtained and the slugs encountered . . . always a problem.

"All the above had to be in the local cashier's cage by 5 p.m.—written up, balanced, etc.—all without air conditioning or individual fans," he concludes ruefully. ■

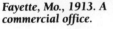

Fayette, Mo., 1913. A commercial office.

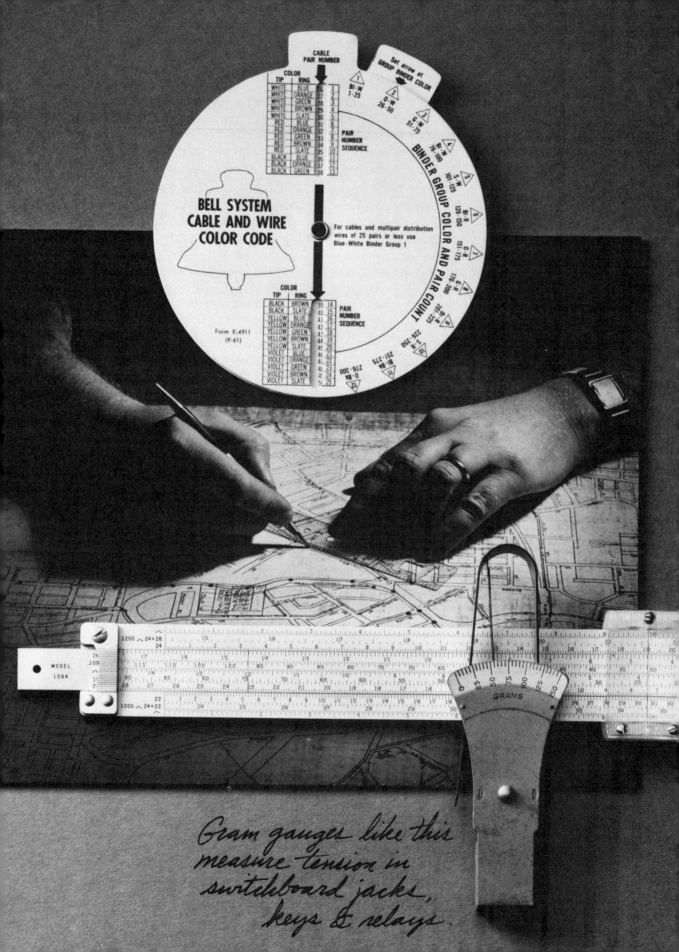

Gram gauges like this
measure tension in
switchboard jacks,
keys & relays.

THE HIDDEN WIZARDS

CHAPTER SEVEN

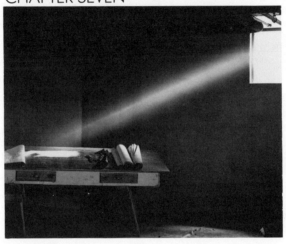

"ONE OF THE THINGS you learn as an engineer," says Si Dietz, who retired from general engineering at St. Louis headquarters, "is that you'd better get your pleasure out of the work itself. You don't want to count on praise from your superiors; they figure you're expected to turn in a top-notch performance. And sometimes it seems that the people further down the chain of command see you as just a bottleneck in getting the job done."

Dietz recites a couple of anecdotes to make his point. One involves the time he received an urgent late-night call to his Kansas City hotel room. Spring floods were about to inundate the central office at suburban Smithville; could Si help the plant people locate emergency equipment?

Fortunately Si could. He knew where there were a temporary switchboard and an emergency power generator. By making a few calls to people he knew in the area office at St. Louis, he soon had the relief on its way. By the time the flood had completely filled the building's first floor, the relief equipment was on site and plant personnel had finished emergency rewiring. So service went on almost uninterrupted.

Dietz was justifiably proud of the work they had done and of his own contribution to the enterprise. When his top boss came over from St. Louis the next day to inspect the job, Si stood ready to answer questions and accept the praise due him with becoming modesty.

Hot Springs, Ark., 1953. Exchange engineer John Bonner uses hand level and tape to measure distance between lines on a telephone pole.

Neither questions nor praise came the frustrated engineer's way, until he finally cornered the boss to ask: "Do you see anything I should have done that I didn't do, or anything I did do that I shouldn't have done?" His boss gave him a fleeting glance and grunted, "No, everything seems to be all right." That was Si's pat on the back for three days of worry, resourcefulness and telephone calls around the state to arrange emergency shipments.

As for the engineer's "bottleneck" role, he relates an incident that took place after he had been moved to general engineering at headquarters. The personnel here, chosen for experience and all-around know-how, had one principal job: They reviewed every construction estimate sent up from the areas to be sure it was in proper form for executive approval. Even though they passed it, of course, it might not be approved if money wasn't available.

Dietz tells about an estimate that was sent to him for a major toll switchboard rearrangement. Something about the proposal didn't look right to him; he couldn't understand how the change was to be accomplished.

"I called the engineer who submitted the estimate and asked him, 'How are you going to do this?'" he relates. "And the fellow says, 'Well, we don't know. We're going to let Western handle it.'" (Western Electric employees routinely installed central office equipment for the operating companies.)

Getting no satisfaction from his talks with the area man, Dietz sent the estimate request across the hall to the staff of general traffic. Back it came, routinely initialed to indicate they had seen it and found nothing wrong. But Dietz still wasn't convinced, so he continued to "sit on it."

Eventually the area's chief engineer called the vice president-engineering at headquarters and said: "Karl, Si is holding up one of our estimates. We've got to get that thing moving. We've got an order due."

The vice president called his next-in-command to ask: "Why is Si holding up that estimate request?"

"He's not satisfied with the answers he's getting from the area when he asks for explanations."

"Well, get him down there and get the damn thing resolved." The next morning, not only Si but the general plant extension engineer and a general traffic spokesman were "down there."

Si found himself on the spot when the meeting got under way. "I had to take a lot of guff from the division traffic man who formulated this plan in the first place." But he stood his ground.

"You say you did this before. I want to see how it was done—because I don't think it *can* be done. If you did it, fine. I'll release the estimate request immediately."

The group went out to the toll office to show this Doubting Thomas. "Here's the switchboard we split two years ago. Now we want to do the same thing on the switchboard upstairs."

"Okay, where was the split made here?"

"Right between these two positions."

Si walked around the back, took one look and announced: "This switchboard has never been split."

Thirty years later, Dietz still chuckles as he tells the story, "Boy, that division traffic engineer's face was really a sight to behold!"

The postscript is that the area withdrew its request, revised it, resubmitted it and finally cancelled the project altogether.

"I know that in that one case I saved the company $1.2 million," Dietz says proudly. "That was the amount on the face sheet for the total estimated cost."

Incidents like these might sometimes give telephone engineers a bad case of the Rodney Dangerfield syndrome—"They don't get no respect," at any rate, not all they're entitled to. But as Si Dietz says, a good telephone engineer learns to get his satisfaction from the work itself.

This attitude shines through a 1977 estimate request signed by W. B. Snyder, Dallas engineering project supervisor. The report reviews a city program for revitalizing the downtown area and urges that the telephone company tailor its own improvement plans to mesh with this program. An excerpt:

"Expensive outside plant rearrangements [will] have to be made to accommodate future underground pedestrian ways, truck tunnels and rapid transit systems. The cost of these city improvements is conservatively estimated at $25 million.

"The answer to the question, 'Who pays for these rearrangements?' is 'The telephone customers and taxpayers'—who are one and the same. Therefore, to do our part to fight inflation, we should plan our plant extensions to eliminate as many conflicts with city improvement projects as we can." Then the report goes on to detail how this can be achieved.

Engineering people become accustomed to thinking in terms of the big picture—that is, spending millions of dollars, but spending them judiciously. Earl Toepperwein, another Dallas engineering retiree, recalls the time the plant extensions people had worked out a proposal for wide-scope calling involving the sister cities of Dallas and Fort Worth. The proposal involved setting aside a group of equipment for customers who wanted to be able to call both cities at a flat rate, i.e., without long distance charges. Extensive retrunking would be required to accommodate the expected demand, even though the rate was originally to be set at $75 a month.

"We went up to St. Louis to discuss our recommendation," Toepperwein reminisces. "We sat down with Dick Goodson, the president, and Ed Greber, the operating vice president. And their first question was the one you'd expect: 'How much is it going to cost?'

"We said, 'Twenty-seven million dollars . . . to begin with.' Well, there was a deathly silence. Then we talked for a half an hour or 45 minutes. Finally, Dick

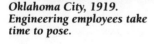

Oklahoma City, 1919. Engineering employees take time to pose.

said to Ed, 'Well, it sounds good to me,' and the two of them signed the thing.

"We came back with a blanket check for $27 million and had the feeling, 'What have we got ourselves into?' "

Despite Toepperwein's attack of stomach butterflies, the program turned out to be a smash success. It was popular with the customers and slashed maintenance costs. Today the cost of this special two-city service is only a few dollars a month more than regular local service. "It's cheap service if you need it," Toepperwein sums up in satisfaction.

Southwestern Bell's Engineering Department was apparently established at the same time as the Big Three—plant, traffic and commercial—even though, at first, engineering was entirely a headquarters function. W. B. Stephenson, retired Oklahoma City chief engineer, remembers that the department existed when he joined the Southwestern Bell Telephone System (not yet fully merged) in 1913. Stephenson, a native of Plymouth, Indiana, was a mechanical engineering graduate at Purdue. He recalls:

"Edgar Bloom, operating vice president, came to Purdue to look for recruits, and I was one he picked. I was hired at a pay rate of $60 a month. For a guy just getting out of engineering school, that was a pretty fair salary. I believe it was the best offer I got, although that wasn't the reason I took the job; it just sounded like an outfit with lots of opportunity."

Stephenson's career, both with the telephone company and subsequently, shows that his appraisal of the opportunity was right on the mark. He started out in St. Louis, was transferred to Kansas City and then back to St. Louis, and went to Oklahoma City about 1936 as chief engineer. There he finished his Bell System career, and in effect, started out again.

"I got a chance to go to France as a communications engineer for the U.S. government. My wife and I lived in Paris for something over two years, and I traveled through the NATO countries. I was assigned to Headquarters, European

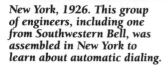

New York, 1926. This group of engineers, including one from Southwestern Bell, was assembled in New York to learn about automatic dialing.

Nobody Knows the Trouble They've Seen

IN THESE DAYS of air conditioning, it would be considered cruel and inhuman treatment to subject telephone office workers to the conditions that were accepted as inevitable as recently as the 1950s. Joe Flath, who retired as general manager-network for the Arkansas area, has amusing memories of the days when he joined the newly created engineering department in Dallas.

Summer daytime temperatures, then as now, were in the high 90s, but the work had to go ahead. Windows were kept open, ceiling fans swished, and pedestal and floor fans whirred.

The drafting section, especially, relied on hundreds of glass paperweights to keep their work from blowing away. Their job was to transcribe wiring diagrams to linen tracings; these diagrams represented the circuitry in Southwestern Bell central offices in Texas. (Later these records were entrusted to Western Electric, but in the 1950s telephone company people kept them and updated them as needed. The records left the office only when Western Electric installers made the indicated changes and were returned when the job was done.)

"One year, somebody decided to build the Life of America building on a parking lot across the street," Flath remembers. "All the steel framework was put together with rivets. You'd be talking on the phone or just sitting there working and somebody would start driving a rivet gun right across the street from the open windows.

"That caused a lot of griping and a lot of 'sidewalk superintending' from our 8th floor offices, but somehow it didn't slow down the work one iota—it kept right on going. This proved that you don't have to be able to hear to be an engineer.

"Another hazard of the open windows was birds. More than once I saw a bird fly in the window and flutter up and down the bullpen. Somebody would take it on himself to catch that bird and put it back out the window while everyone else tended to his job. If that happened on the 8th floor of a building today, I imagine it would cause quite a bit of consternation. . . .

"About 1954, the plant extension portion of the engineering department was on the 13th floor of the building. Les Burns, the extension engineer, had a private office in an area that obviously was not planned as office space. Running right through his office was a pneumatic tube used for sending messages back and forth to different locations in some other department—I don't know what department it was.

"The felt had worn off one of the brass cylinders that traveled through this pneumatic tube. You'd be sitting in Les' office and you'd hear the thing coming like an express train. And as it got closer to his office, you couldn't carry on a conversation. You'd just shut up and sit until it was past. It would thump through the office and then you could hear it racing on to its destination somewhere. Then you could talk again.

"After a couple of years of this, Les got so used to it that it was just automatic with him to stop until the thing had gone past. He'd be looking you right in the eye, stop talking for the necessary few seconds and then pick up right in the middle of his sentence.

"One time, some people from St. Louis came in to see Les and here came this brass canister through the tube. They looked around in bewilderment. As usual, Les just quit talking; as soon as it roared on through, he resumed the conversation as if nothing had happened. But one of the St. Louis visitors stopped him and said: 'Wait a minute; what was *that*?' Les just looked puzzled and said: 'What was what?' He didn't even realize the thing had gone through."

Outside Burns' office, steam pipes ran overhead just beneath the ceiling—which was actually the concrete slab forming the floor 14 feet above; there was no drop ceiling. One of these steam pipes ran over the desk of a man named Francis Edwards. A small leak had developed in this pipe, and the insulation had fallen off. Every few minutes during the heating season, a drop of hot water would splash on the floor in front of the desk . . . but not enough to create a warning puddle that might make an outsider suspicious.

"Eddie" knew about this, of course, and so did the others in the department, who all made a point of not standing underneath the drip. But when visitors came to talk to him, Edwards would sit at his desk and give them no warning; neither would anyone else, but everybody would be watching and waiting for the action to begin.

"Pretty soon a drop of the scalding water would land right on the visitor, and he'd really do quite a dance around there," Flath recalls fondly.

"And Eddie, too, would keep right on talking as if nothing had happened."

Engineers just don't ever seem to overreact. ∎

Command. They had all the branches of the military there, and I worked with them all.

"After that I went to the Pentagon in Washington as a communications engineer and stayed there some two years in the Department of Defense. Then I had a chance to go to Brazil as a consultant to the Brazilian Telephone Company and spent another two years there.

"After Brazil, I 'retired' in Dallas and was there for a year or two when I got a call from an engineering company in Washington. They wanted me to go to South America for a feasibility study for a satellite system. So I worked in Brazil, Uruguay and Argentina.

"Finally I retired for good. I settled in Dallas because my son was working there and my wife was a native Texan. I wanted to retire to Indiana, but we took a family vote, and I lost out," he says with a chuckle.

Stephenson's post-Bell career is impressive but hardly unique. Many of the technically trained graduates of Bell companies find their know-how much in demand after they retire, and a second career of a decade or more is available if they want it. And long before retirement, Southwestern Bell engineering and plant employees have received overseas assignments to help establish communications systems in Third World countries.

The engineering function in Southwestern Bell has grown as the company has grown and as technology has become more and more complex. To draw once more upon Si Dietz's memories, in 1926 the department—*all* of it—was located on the 10th and 11th floors of the old Boatmen's Bank Building in St. Louis; there was a small group of engineering clerical personnel on the 19th floor of that building. (Today there are major engineering staffs in seven cities besides St. Louis.)

In 1926 the engineering staff was divided into two organizations depending on the types of facilities they oversaw. On the 10th floor was the dial group, which handled step-by-step and panel dial equipment. Engineering for manual local switching (common battery and magneto), long distance switchboards and toll terminals was the responsibility of the 11th-floor group.

Dietz came in just as the engineering function was being partially dispersed to the four operating areas, with offices in Dallas, Oklahoma City, Kansas City and St. Louis. In addition to the personnel assigned to the Engineering Department, it should be understood that the company had others with engineering titles in the operating departments.

The *commercial* engineers were responsible for forecasting the growth within the areas. *Traffic* engineers gathered operating data (call volumes, telephone growth and so on) which they converted into facility requirements. And *plant* engineers handled outside plant design and construction, such as pole lines and distribution systems within exchanges.

The chain of communication went like this: Commercial engineers sent their growth forecasts to traffic engineers—who figured out how much additional circuitry would be necessary to handle this growth, and informed plant engineers—who projected what facilities would be needed to provide that circuitry. The area engineering group then summarized this study in the form of a precise recommendation . . . an "estimate request." When this was finally approved, it underwent a name-change to "estimate." General engineering would review each request before it went to company officers and, in some cases, the board of directors.

Before the breakup into area organizations, however, all these processes were

Houston, 1971. In the days before hand-held calculators, Division Plant Engineer Bob Womack used a slide rule to help his forecasting.

handled at the general level. A member of the manual-switchboard organization in St. Louis might be assigned to handle a situation somewhere in West Texas, and when he had finished this, he might work on Topeka growth requirements next.

The same was true of dial engineers. They were principally concerned with Texas and Oklahoma, which became involved with dial switching earlier than the rest of the company. Missouri was one of the last to go to dial; this meant that Missouri exchanges were provided with the "last word" in equipment.

Unfortunately, this was a case where the "last word" wasn't as good as the "previous word."

The "last word" in switching in the 1920s was "common-control," expected to be a big advance over step-by-step. The only common-control switching available in the Bell System at that time was the panel system—"a very grotesque electromechanical arrangement," in Si Dietz's words . . . and those words could have been echoed by anyone else who had the care of these monsters.

The group of headquarters people assigned to panel engineering grew as manual offices were replaced in St. Louis and Kansas City, Mo., the only two Southwestern Bell locations that ever used panel. All other areas used step-by-step when they converted to dial.

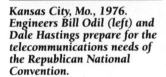

Kansas City, Mo., 1976. Engineers Bill Odil (left) and Dale Hastings prepare for the telecommunications needs of the Republican National Convention.

He Brought His Know-How with Him

DOC (M. L.) ZEIDERS came into Southwestern Bell's newly created Oklahoma Engineering Department from Western Electric in 1927. His job title was toll terminal engineer. (He retired with the title of building and equipment engineer.)

One of Doc's first challenges was to correct a "backward" carrier system. The three-channel system had been installed between Oklahoma City and Wichita, Kan., but somehow the terminal equipment had been put in the wrong places; that is, the Oklahoma City portion was in Wichita and the Wichita portion was in Oklahoma City. This meant that the system wouldn't interact with other carrier systems on the toll line. Emergency!

"Carrier at that time was something of a mystery to telephone engineers," Zeiders explains. "When a mistake like this was made, nobody bothered with components; they just changed out full units and things like that. But the scheduled service date was immediately on

us. We couldn't spend a lot of time undoing the whole thing."

Zeiders' boss asked him if he could figure out anything to do that would make it possible to meet the service date. Zeiders studied the situation for a bit, then told the boss he wasn't sure but he'd like to try.

He took some components out of the Oklahoma City carrier terminal and drove up to Wichita with them. There he swapped those parts for the ones that were in the Wichita terminal and tested the changed equipment to be sure it was working properly. Then he drove back to Oklahoma City and put the parts salvaged from Wichita in the Oklahoma City terminal.

"And to everybody's amazement, the system worked," he recalls with satisfaction. "Nowadays that wouldn't be considered any great accomplishment, but in those days when no one knew what to do, that was something!

"It didn't take a telephone engineer to handle the problem. It just took a qualified installer—and I hadn't forgotten what I had learned at Western Electric." ∎

A panel switching system, "a very grotesque electro-mechanical arrangement" no longer in use.

"Of course, the panel system was ultimately replaced with the 'final word in switching'—the crossbar system," Dietz says wryly. And *this* "final word" has since been largely supplanted by electronic switching systems (ESS). An ESS has a lot of superlatives going for it: It's faster, more flexible, more cost-efficient and provides services unavailable with the older systems.

However, there is still some sturdy step-by-step equipment clacking and snapping away in smaller Southwestern Bell central offices, and not all the excellent crossbar switches have been phased out, either. Only the "grotesque" panel systems have been given an unceremonious heave-ho.

When the first area engineering organization was established in Dallas, people were sent down from headquarters to form a nucleus, but not enough could be spared to bring the Dallas office to full strength. So people were brought in from the area Plant Department, and college engineering graduates were hired, too.

With headquarters ranks depleted by the move to Dallas, the group that would handle engineering for the Eastern Missouri–Arkansas area was about to consolidate its offices in the new headquarters building at 1010 Pine Street, on the 18th floor. The Oklahoma area group moved in there temporarily, too, awaiting completion of Oklahoma's new administration building.

The staff in charge of engineering for the Western Missouri–Kansas area remained in the Boatmen's Bank Building until the new Kansas City administration building was completed. The moves to Oklahoma City and Kansas City took place in late 1927.

The revision of area boundaries in 1950 meant another set of moves, with new engineering groups established at Topeka and Little Rock; and of course subsequent proliferation of areas in Texas and Missouri expanded the total number of area engineering groups to eight. But the major change was in 1926-1927, when general engineering was reduced to what was essentially a skeleton staff.

Curiously, the rebuilding operation at GHQ engineering got under way in the Great Depression. This was because the Bell System was concerned about the effects of economic stagnation on Western Electric.

To avoid layoffs of large numbers of engineers, AT&T appealed to the operating companies (not so hard hit as Western, a manufacturing organization) to take on additional employees. Southwestern Bell accepted a few such transfers.

After World War II, more than a decade of pent-up demand for telephone service had to be satisfied, and the engineering organization, both at area and general levels, expanded to help meet that demand.

Everyone wanted everything and right now—no matter that telephone companies, like other utilities, had limited financial resources to provide that "everything." It took another 10 years before the held-order lists finally dwindled and same-day service in emergencies became a possibility.

This belief that telephone companies like Southwestern Bell can handle any problem, and do it immediately, has never left the public consciousness. Hurricanes, tornadoes, snow and ice storms? Well, surely the phones will be working tomorrow. . . .

Harold Miller, who came to engineering from plant in 1955 and retired as chief engineer of the Houston area, has seen his share of such emergencies. Some of them were caused by nature, and others were caused by man. He recalls two that must fit into the latter category. One was the establishment of Houston Mission Control for the country's space program.

The LBJ Ranch needed top-notch communications when Lyndon Johnson was president.

"We had some terrible deadlines," Miller says. "We were supposed to put all the equipment and circuits in NASA's building so they could monitor the space flights. We were all lined up to install our toll terminals, microwave, carrier and all that sort of thing.

"Then, at the last minute, the government decided that it couldn't be done that way. Instead we had to have a long-term lease on some of that land they owned. And when we finally got the red tape out of the way, then we had to rush and construct a new building for the equipment.

"And of course, there was a lot of competition involved in this. We wanted to provide all the terminal equipment, but we lost out to a private firm.

"Furthermore, NASA felt that it should have the same interconnection privileges that the government agencies had during the war—this was long before the FCC's Carterfone decision [allowing such interconnections], you realize. AT&T resisted the idea of interconnection, but eventually we worked out some kind of haywire arrangement that both sides could live with."

Another situation Miller recalls vividly was the communications emergency that burst upon them after President Kennedy was assassinated and Lyndon Johnson became president. Suddenly the Little White House was not at Hyannisport, Mass., but in the hill country west of Austin, which was in the Houston service area at the time.

"The LBJ Ranch was not in our territory; it was handled by the Southwestern States Telephone Company," Miller points out. "They agreed to let us come in and put in the long distance service. Southwestern States still took care of the local service.

"The ranch was about 65 miles west of Austin, out in the boondocks. Johnson had had some service out there as vice president, but nothing like what he needed when he became president."

How does one decide what communications facilities a president needs? The solution was a rough-and-ready one, but it worked. The company looked at what had been installed at Hyannisport for John Kennedy and doubled it.

"We were playing it safe," Miller says. "We wanted to be sure that if another tragedy occurred, no one could blame it on lack of communication.

"For a lot of the stuff, like all the mobile radio equipment, we just furnished the circuits; the equipment belonged to the government. Johnson had to have a telephone at his fingertips all the time. When we knew that he was going to come out there for his Christmas holidays, the service had to be there. And the supply of equipment kept growing and growing as he stayed there.

"It was touch and go, too, every time LBJ flew into Texas. We might know he was coming, but we were never told where the plane was going to land. So we had to be prepared with communications facilities at all possible landing sites.

"Another part of the problem was providing circuits for all the media people who were scattered all over. A lot of motels were built near the ranch, but some of the news people stayed at other places, like Fredericksburg and Austin. They wanted to have circuits going all the way in to the ranch.

"And throughout, we were constantly trying to meet deadlines—self-imposed deadlines. This all started the day Kennedy was killed. We had to move fast, without any service orders. The White House people came down a few days later and told us what they wanted; but it was just guesswork on our part as to what we put in there before we even heard from them. That was a hectic month of finding locations, putting up buildings, installing and testing equipment and doing whatever needed to be done."

Miller stresses that the LBJ and NASA situations weren't just Southwestern Bell projects. AT&T Long Lines and Western Electric were deeply involved, too. And of course, engineering couldn't have handled all these projects on its own. In every case he cites, the Southwestern Bell Plant Department handled most of the physical effort, and engineering's role was largely one of coordination. This always has been the relationship between the two departments. ∎

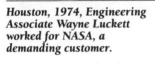

Houston, 1974, Engineering Associate Wayne Luckett worked for NASA, a demanding customer.

FROM COMPANY STEPCHILD TO "YELLOW PERIL"

CHAPTER EIGHT

THE ACCOUNTING DEPARTMENT (recently renamed Comptrollers Department) developed as a formal organization quite a bit later than the warhorses—plant, traffic, commercial and engineering. But the function was there from the start; no business could exist for more than a few days if nobody kept records on money spent and money received.

Until the year 1911, however, the operating departments just kept their own books and ran their own shops to a degree hard to imagine today. They had their individual operating funds from which they paid bills and met payrolls. They were answerable only to their department heads in St. Louis. Commercial's duties included billing customers and receiving payments from them; these payments were to be passed on to the company treasury, but the arrangement was a loose one and in danger of abuse.

When Theodore N. Vail returned in 1907 to head AT&T (he had held such a post once before but left the business), he instituted sweeping changes in the way the Bell System was organized.* The eventual creation of Southwestern Bell Telephone Company from four separate telephone firms was only one of a num-

---

*Much of the material in this chapter is based on the reminiscences of Harlan Gould, who was an Accounting Department employee from 1924 until he retired in 1968 as general accounting methods supervisor.

ber of such mergers around the nation. And the changes were far more extensive than just revision of corporate boundaries.

One of the first internal reforms instituted under Vail's new-broom policy was a uniform system of accounts for all the Bell companies. This system was set forth in detail in Accounting Circular No. 6. Thenceforward each company kept its records and made its reports under "Accounting 6" rules until the Interstate Commerce Commission stepped in.

The ICC, which then had jurisdiction over all interstate communications as well as transportation, put out its own system of accounts for all telephone companies (not just the Bell System). The Bell companies now followed Accounting Circular No. 8, which replaced No. 6 and made it necessary to convert most of the records to the new categories.

This change did not happen overnight; the ICC began work on it before World War I, but it didn't become fully effective until 1920. Besides the added work of keeping company books under a new, more carefully structured system, the Accounting Department acquired another function—billing customers (a responsibility removed from the Commercial Department). The extensive billing operation was handled by an organization known as "Revenue Accounting." The Commercial Department retained the collection function, but under a new set of guidelines ... guidelines which have remained essentially unchanged to the present day.

In 1926, Southwestern Bell General Auditor Edward W. Meyer, after a series of meetings with AT&T officials, instituted a wholesale expansion of the Accounting Department. A separate organization was set up in each area (four at the time) in addition to the general books department at headquarters. Each area accounting office did all the accounting work for the Plant, Traffic, Commercial and Engineering departments in that area, as well as billing the customers.

Kansas City, Mo., circa 1915.
The accounting office.

Haute Couture, Dogpatch Style

THERE SEEMS to be an impression abroad that telephone people fall into a predictable pattern, and indeed great numbers of them have many characteristics in common. But in an organization as vast as Southwestern Bell (about 75,000 employees as of January 1, 1984) there is an occasional person who doesn't quite fit the mold.

E. S. (Sandy) Bridges, retired from Arkansas revenue accounting, recalls one such individual, a supervisor who must have qualified with many people as "the most unforgettable character I ever met."

The man was not the easiest person to get along with, because of his fanatic attention to detail and his impatience with anyone whom he suspected of not sharing his passion for figures. But a zeal for accuracy is not all that unusual in his department. No, Mr. X stood out for other reasons.

He resolutely refused the standard office desk chair provided by the company. Instead, he insisted on a bentwood chair with cane-bottom seat, probably left over from very early days. On this he perched, leaning forward so the chair's back legs were off the floor and with his feet curled around the chair's front legs as he pored over the company records. He sat at the front of the office, with his back to the entrance.

Another memorable trait of Mr. X's was his extreme parsimony. He was hardly impoverished—he received what was then considered an adequate salary for a man at that management level, and he had outside business interests—but it galled him to spend a penny if it wasn't absolutely necessary.

One fine day in the forties, Mr. X arose and dressed, and when he belted up his trousers, the belt snapped in the middle. It must have been the only one he owned. At any rate, when he appeared at the office that morning and took off his jacket to hunker down over the books, the belt was held together at the back by a large blanket pin.

Although there was a bit of tittering in remote corners of the office, no one said anything to Mr. X directly. He was not the sort of person who invited personal comments. And he would undoubtedly have got through the day with no untoward developments if fate had not intervened.

That very morning, the general auditor from St. Louis headquarters, making an inspection tour of the area offices, paid a visit to Little Rock. He strode into the office, trailed by Mr. X's boss, who had gone to the railroad station to meet him. The first non-standard item which caught the visitor's notice was the belt with the blanket pin.

The two men retired to private quarters, and then Mr. X was summoned for a conference behind closed doors. The accepted version of the boss' message was, "If you're too poor to buy a new belt, by darn, I'll buy one for you."

At any rate, that noon Mr. X left his brown paper sack lunch on his desk and walked across the street to the Kress Five and Ten Cent Store. He returned wearing a new 50-cent belt, sans blanket pin. Everyone in the office noticed; nobody said a word . . . until he had left for the day. ∎

When You Goof, Admit It Quickly

SENSITIVITY to customers' feelings is an important quality for people who get ahead in the telephone business. If an error is committed, it's important to fix it as quickly as possible.

Those had to be the thoughts of a young accounting supervisor in the Kansas City office when he discovered that a batch of bills had been sent out with insufficient postage. This was back in the mid-1960s, and the current first-class rate was 5 cents. Many customers got their bills marked "postage due 2 cents," and they weren't happy about paying the charge.

Here's what happened next, according to a source who asks to remain anonymous:

"He saw the department had created a public relations problem, and the sooner something was done to fix the situation, the better. So he had a letter prepared to go to every customer in this billing group, apologizing for the error and assuring them that there would be a 2-cent credit on their next bill.

"The letters of apology went out promptly . . . with 3 cents' postage on each envelope."

Did this ruin the young man's career?

Obviously not; he now occupies a fairly high position in his department. He must have been given special credit for good intentions. ∎

Circa 1940. Women did their work with machines called comptometers.

"Accounting thus became an operating department," Harlan Gould says ruefully, "except we weren't paid as much. We were still looked on as a sort of stepchild in the company."

In 1930, the ICC put out still another revision in its rules for telephone company record keeping, forcing another overhaul of the books. But the ICC's days as a telephone regulator were numbered.

The election of President Franklin Roosevelt brought many changes. Among them was the institution of a new agency to oversee activities of telephone, telegraph and radio communication—the Federal Communications Commission. The FCC started off its job with a philosophical viewpoint which telephone companies found hard to accept—that capital investment, on which they based their earnings requirements, should reflect the original cost of plant "when first dedicated to public use," rather than what it cost the telephone company which now owned it.

For example, if the XYZ Company put up its poles and wires and installed its telephones in 1915 at a cost of $15,000, and Bell bought out the company (with regulatory approval) in 1925 for $50,000 because it was worth that much as a going business, the FCC wanted Bell to carry the plant for $15,000 (less depreciation, of course, since 1915). Bell felt it should start at $50,000 and depreciate only since 1925.

The matter went to the courts, naturally; the FCC won, and the only concession granted to the telephone companies was that they could amortize their losses over a 10-year period instead of taking their lumps in one year.

Another result of the Roosevelt accession to power was the creation of the Securities and Exchange Commission (SEC). While the telephone companies didn't see the SEC as hostile to them, nevertheless SEC regulations created much more work for all companies and specifically for telephone company accounting departments.

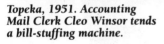

Topeka, 1951. Accounting Mail Clerk Cleo Winsor tends a bill-stuffing machine.

Clothes Make the Man...Look Unusual

PEOPLE WHO never worked in accounting may have the impression that it's a humdrum existence, that the most exciting event is when someone drops a tray of Addressograph plates or something of the sort. Not so, at least not so in Arkansas, says Bob Fleming, who spent most of his 48 years' service in that state.

"For a period in the fifties we had a midsummer department picnic every year," Fleming recalls. "That was when J. A. McCollum was state auditor, before he went to St. Louis and became the company comptroller.

"Each year, every unit in the department was expected to put

on a skit, and it got hard to think up anything new. But one year our group decided to really make an impression—and we did. We put on a style show. Women's styles. And the men in our unit were the models.

"I suppose the idea has been done to death since then, but it was a brand-new idea for us. We played it absolutely straight, just like the real thing. Warren Bock, who later became head of accounting in Houston, was the announcer and described all the costumes as the models appeared. We had background music, too. And the crowd was still laughing when they went home that evening.

"You know who was the star of the show? The man in this picture—the one in the white evening gown. That's Mr. McCollum himself." ■

Welcome To the Club

AL DUNSING started his Accounting Department career in the general books department at headquarters in August 1922. His first job was maintaining the records on "interest companies." These were independent, noncompeting telephone companies to which Southwestern Bell had lent money. Naturally Southwestern Bell insisted on knowing how these companies were doing

financially in order to protect its investment.

Al recalls that a man by the name of John Hughes was in a section which compiled "public returns"—those which were issued for the benefit of regulatory bodies and the like. Hughes had a somewhat forbidding exterior and a booming bass voice, well calculated to intimidate a newcomer fresh out of high

school as young Al Dunsing was.

"A good many years later, when I had lost my awe of the old-timers, I happened to stop and chat with Hughes," he recalls. "I said to him, 'John, when I first started with this company, I thought you were an old so-and-so.' John didn't change his expression as he retorted, 'Yeah, and now you're one of them.' " ■

These developments were especially important, coming at the time they did, because any company with long-term debt was busily engaged in refinancing that debt. The Great Depression was hard on many people, but it did have the effect of lowering interest rates. A firm which had issued securities with a yield of 5 or 7 percent was eager to recall these and replace them with other securities paying as little as 3 percent. Executing this maneuver under SEC regulations, however, was more difficult than it sounds. The new rules provided for severe penalties if data were presented in any way the SEC could construe as inaccurate.

Private enterprise was just beginning to adjust to the realities of the New Deal when it found itself confronted with a whole new set of problems occasioned by World War II. Suddenly a docile, dependable labor force changed its attitude . . . and its availability.

"From 1930 to 1945, Southwestern Bell hired no one, practically speaking," Harlan Gould explains. "For the first 10 years this was because we didn't need anybody. Business was stagnant and all our people were grateful for their jobs, even when they had to go on part-time schedules.

"Then when the war came along, the labor pools were depleted and we couldn't find anyone to hire. Wages were frozen by national wartime decrees and we couldn't meet the competition from the war industries. We were paying clerks about half what they could get if they went out to McDonnell Aviation in St. Louis County, which was making war planes. You could hardly blame them if they quit.

"I had a secretary and we were paying her what we considered a proper salary— about $90 a month. She said she could get $150 if she went to McDonnell. We had to argue pretty hard to persuade her to stay."

The unpleasant situation led to a post-war wave of strikes against telephone companies, which couldn't get approval to raise their rates fast enough to pay the wages the unions demanded.

San Antonio, 1971. Senior Audit Clerk Mary Dolle was still working with a mechanical calculator.

Meanwhile, back at the SWB Accounting Department, a whole new series of problems was arising. Zealous company leaders—Edwin M. Clark, as president, and J.A. McCollum, as comptroller—were determined to make the company a Bell System standout in every field. For accounting, this meant topping the System-wide statistics for cost, quality and productivity. It wasn't easy, but they often succeeded.

McCollum expanded the department organization to 15 division offices (in addition to the area offices—which had grown to five—and general head-quarters). Woe betide the bosses of these 15 offices if their groups didn't shine! Gould recalls one unfortunate whose office ranked only 17th among the 120 such offices in the Bell System. The other 14 Southwestern Bell offices ranked first through 14th, but somehow two other operating companies sneaked in entries ahead of SWB's "black sheep." Gould says that fellow was passed over when his next raise was due.

"Our company record was so remarkable that AT&T sent down investigators to be sure our reports were accurate," Gould recalls with a chuckle. "They were. We had our own internal auditors checking the same thing."

At the same time all this pressure was being imposed from above, the nature of the accounting operation itself was creating headaches comparable only to those faced by traffic about 1920. Right after World War I, so many local calls were being attempted that it wasn't possible to hire enough operators to handle them.

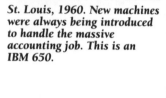

St. Louis, 1960. New machines were always being introduced to handle the massive accounting job. This is an IBM 650.

The Traveler's Tale

THE JOB of a traveling auditor is just what the words imply: He or she visits work locations throughout the company to check the records and make sure that everything is in order.

In the early days when the grapevine twitched with the news that a traveling auditor was in the territory, it was often cause for alarm: "I feel I did the right thing, but will the auditor agree?"

From time to time, the visitor did uncover some serious short-coming which would call for correction. Once in a great while, some outright dishonesty would be revealed, and the guilty party or parties would be discharged. As the years passed, however, employees began to realize that the traveling auditor was just doing his or her job and took no special pleasure in finding things out of line.

Robert L. (Corny) Cornielson, now retired and living in Ennis, Tex., was a traveling auditor for almost 14 years. In the beginning, he lived in Oklahoma City, reported to St. Louis and traveled through all six states (including a small portion of Illinois). Later he was assigned to a single area, first the western Missouri and

Kansas territory and then the state of Texas. He has many tales to tell, of which the following are just a few:

Once Corny found that a trusted employee was guilty of defalcation. Using the authority that goes with the job, he fired the employee. He then locked the office door and began poring over all the records—first, to make the case airtight, and second, to see if he had over-looked anything.

About 10 o'clock, there was a knock. Corny opened the door cautiously ("After a while, you learn to be careful at all times") and was greeted by the local marshal, who identified himself by his badge. The man came in and chatted a while. Finally Corny said he was just getting ready to leave and go over to his hotel.

"Fine," said the marshal. "I'll walk along with you." And when they reached the hotel, the lawman asked casually: "Are you about through here?" Corny replied that he would be finished in the morning.

"Well, I'm glad to hear that. You know, this person has been around here for a number of years and has a lot of friends.

If I were you, I wouldn't be out by myself any more at night."

That's when Corny realized that he had been in protective custody. He left town the next day slightly ahead of schedule.

At another time, he was audit-ing the records of the Harlingen, Tex., exchange. One of his audit duties was to verify outstanding bills, which could be done by letters, personal visits or a tele-phone call. In this particular case, he called a customer and the woman acknowledged that she had not gotten around to paying her bill yet. Then she went on:

"By the way, are you calling from the telephone business office?" Corny said he was, and the customer said: "Can I ask you to tell the girl in the office that I want my phone disconnected?"

This was during the Depres-sion, and the company was giving special credit to its employees for selling service or talking someone out of discon-tinuing it. So Corny began his carefully rehearsed Don't-Cancel-Think-Of-What-Could-Happen speech.

But the customer interrupted: "Oh, I'm not just giving up my telephone; I'm going to move. I've already got the house rented, and the lady that's going to be here will need a telephone, I'm sure."

"Fine," said Corny. "Give me her name, and I'll turn it in as a request for new service." When he finished the conversation, he turned over the slip to the service representative in the office, who looked at the name and burst out laughing. Then she explained:

"That woman is the town's most notorious character, and you just got in here yesterday. I'm wondering how you found her that quick!" ∎

"If I were you, I wouldn't be out by myself at night."

The answer, of course, was dial telephones, but the answer didn't take effect overnight.

After World War II, accounting had a similar headache, also related to traffic volumes. Pent-up demand for long distance service, occasioned in part by ever-decreasing rates and also by the mere fact that the number of telephones had mushroomed since war's end, produced a blizzard of paper toll tickets.

The practice called for traffic to sort the tickets when time permitted, before turning them over to accounting for billing. But human nature being what it is, "time didn't permit" a great deal of this work to be accomplished by traffic.

"We had so many toll tickets we couldn't hire enough clerks to handle them," says Gould. "So we grabbed any improvement suggested by AT&T. This usually helped our productivity and it *always* improved our indexes—because AT&T set its measurement standards to favor the innovators, and we were consistently first in trying anything new.

"We leased the latest IBM equipment for payrolls, for plant records, for everything possible, including general books. This equipment was still experimental in the 1950s; it used vacuum tubes instead of solid-state electronics. We changed our procedures every time IBM came out with improvements.

"And as for the specific problem of the toll tickets—we switched to mark sense cards, then punched paper tape, then magnetic tape. OCR (optical character recognition) cards came in there, too; these are cards on which the operator writes and a machine actually reads the handwriting. But the situation wasn't really brought under control until TSPS (modern operator stations) became universal, and all the billing information was compiled automatically."

Two other major changes in the accounting operation are matters of pride to Gould. One was the field-draft plan; in this case Southwestern Bell was only second in the System instead of the customary first to try an innovation.

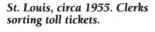

St. Louis, circa 1955. Clerks sorting toll tickets.

*Houston, 1972. As fast as IBM
turned out a new computer,
accounting found uses for it.*

Take a Break–Who's Got a Good Story?

EVER HEAR THE ONE about the accounting fellows who told off-color jokes as part of their work? Probably not. But it's true! To get the picture, you have to visualize how things were done before technology revolutionized the work of this department, just like the others . . . .

Today's record keeping is almost painless because of the help provided by modern computers. (Bell Laboratories gets much of the credit for this. The Laboratories developed specific applications of the computer art, responding to requests from operating companies like Southwestern Bell.)

But in the early days—say, in the 1920s—no such devices were available. What the accounting people had was this: paper and colored pens and pencils and typewriters and mechanical calculating devices, like comptometers.

Use of these items was a function of rank *and* sex in the department. Only a female clerk was supposed to touch a comptometer, for which she was sent to school and trained. A male clerk was supposed to use a non-electric adding machine to perform similar operations. Only typists—again, female—could operate typewriters. But paper, and colored pens and pencils, were available to both occupational *and* management forces.

Oh, yes: There were no photocopying devices. That's right; no "Miss Jones, will you make a picture of this for me before I send it back, please?" If the boss really needed a copy—or thought he did—Miss Jones would have to sit down and type it.

Naturally, there were a lot of times when the boss did without the copy. This saved typing drudgery, but the other side of the coin was that the boss might

hang onto the report when someone else needed it in his or her work. And a "minimum" number of copies still had to be made. Sometimes that "minimum" ran into the hundreds. Later on, commercial printing houses took over the task of reproducing original copies in bulk; but at first, a primitive technique was the only one available.

One of the most arduous parts of the reporting chore was the monthly summarization of all company activities. Items like the "16A" and the "16B" reports had to be assembled at St. Louis headquarters, then distributed around headquarters and down to the operating areas, at least as far as district level. Sets also went to AT&T in New York.

But without modern-day machinery, here's how this was done:

Individual reports would be carefully copied by hand onto large summary sheets and totals struck column by column. This work would be reviewed line by line and corrected where necessary. When a sheet was ready for typing, it was sent to a steno pool. The typist would make a top copy and five carbons, the absolute maximum that could provide any readability at all for the bottom sheet. (It took strong fingers on the manual typewriters to do this well.)

When the typist had made her six copies, she would pass the original on to someone else

(to break the monotony) and take up another original to resume the process. Conceivably, 20 typists might each make six copies so that 120 copies of an original could be completed. And this would be just one sheet of a thick report!

Proofreading? Aha! This was the *men's* responsibility. (They weren't called "lower management," but their salary treatment suggested that was their rank. When they had to work overtime, which was often, "the men" got no overtime pay; just 50 cents "supper money.")

To handle proofreading, a group of men would assemble around a table in a quiet room. The leader would have a batch of original reports in front of him; the others would each have a stack of typed copies, carbon paper and all. And for hours . . . and hours . . . the leader would read numbers off originals while the proofreaders eyeballed the typescripts.

The human body and mind can take just so much of this kind of drudgery without cracking up. Therefore, after each report was proofread, the leader would call for a break, and it was "blue story" time. To relieve the tension, the men would swap the jokes they had saved up during the previous 30 days.

There's no evidence that ability to tell the choicest story in these sessions led to career advancement. At any rate, as the old saying goes, "It didn't hoit." ∎

The field-draft plan restored some of the bill-paying authority which had been taken away from the operating departments back in 1920. Under the current arrangement, authorized persons can issue drafts (for limited amounts) to pay bills incurred in the field. The drafts, however, are liens on company (instead of departmental) funds, and their use is carefully supervised.

The other major change was the institution of what was nicknamed the "Yellow Peril." Its formal name is the "Schedule of Authorizations," and the nickname comes from the fact that this impressive loose-leaf tome was issued with a bright yellow plastic cover.

Until the time when accounting prepared and issued the authorization schedule (another change instituted by President Clark), there was no clear source of finding out who had authority to disburse company funds, to sign letters committing the company, and similar everyday problems. Some decisions rested with the board of directors, some were found in departmental practices or joint (interdepartmental) practices, some were in semiformal department letters . . . and some habits, like Topsy, jes' grew. Nor were the rules consistent from department to department.

Accounting set out to change all that, on instruction from Clark and General Solicitor Mark Garlinghouse. One individual, Tom Rostron, handled most of the task alone, since it wasn't the kind of assignment that could easily be split up. (Rostron, to be sure, had plenty of sideline coaching.)

When the "Yellow Peril" finally emerged from departmental eyeballing and board of directors approval, everyone knew exactly where he or she stood as far as responsibilities went.

And there was one special feature which might have been hardly noticed by the "Big Four" departments but was certainly appreciated by "stepchild" accounting.

Pay scales for accounting were equalized with those of the other departments. What this did for accounting's morale can well be imagined! ∎

Springfield, Mo. 1971. Employees Darlene McGlaughlin (left), Mary Herbst (center) and Linda Chitwood used an array of computers to track customer accounts.

These St. Louis telephone directories span 103 years

THE BOOK OF NUMBERS

CHAPTER NINE

ITEM IN the Dallas *Herald* for February 18, 1883:

"The telephone company requests subscribers to the telephone to secure a copy of yesterday's Herald, cut out the names and numbers of the new subscribers and paste it on their directories."

Editorial in the Kansas City *Star* for November 29, 1962:

"This month we have become a 2-phone-book town for the first time and, as might be expected, the change has been greeted with mixed emotions. . . . By any yardstick, the two volumes are big. They contain 415,000 listings on 1,702 pages and weigh 4⅛ pounds.

"Quite a change from 1880 when the first directory was printed. It consisted of a single sheet, listing 46 telephones in Kansas City and 12 in Kansas City, Kansas. And there were no two letters and five digits to worry about. Then the problem was to get Central, who presided over her switchboard at 12 West Fifth Street. If and when the connection was made, all you had to do was remember the Missouri number (1 through 46) or the Kansas letter (A through L)."

Today, of course, customers no longer have to "worry about" two letters and five digits; two-five numbering has made way for the seven-digit arrangement, and like everything else about the telephone business, the only constant in directories is . . . change.

It's hard to imagine using a telephone without a directory handy, although there are some members of the public who'd rather not be bothered. (It was this last group which was largely responsible for the fact that calls to "Information," long included in the basic service billing, have now become charge calls to "Directory Assistance"—a change that was instituted in the summer of 1968.)

Directory production, as a recent article in Southwestern Bell's *SCENE* magazine reminds us, is a big business. The company produces 466 different directories; more than 26.5 million individual copies roll off the presses each year. It takes 671,000 15-year-old loblolly pine logs to provide the paper for all these directories; 1.3 *billion* gallons of water, 607 tons of glue, 629 tons of black ink and 84 tons of red ink.

The directory story really involves two different entities: the "alpha" (alphabetical) or white pages and the "class" (classified), more familiarly known as Yellow Pages. This simple color scheme has now been augmented by the "blue pages"— the special listing of frequently called numbers and government agencies. Using the blue pages to separate residential white pages from business white pages was

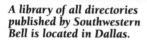

A library of all directories published by Southwestern Bell is located in Dallas.

Two early directories: at right, Little Rock, 1883; below, Dallas, 1902. The page below was on pink paper, a forerunner of Yellow Pages.

a Bell System first when Southwestern Bell did it in the Joplin, Mo., directory of 1977.* The rainbow effect has been further enhanced in recent years by providing red as a second color of ink for print advertising in the Yellow Pages.

And appropriately, the most colorful directory stories are related by the industrious folks who sell ads in those pages. Every business telephone is entitled to one listing there without added charge; the real revenue comes from the additional space sold as advertising. It's a lucrative medium for the telephone company, and obviously worth its while to the advertisers as well, for volume and revenue keep increasing with every directory issue. Since the Yellow Pages sales people

*"Blue pages" of frequently called numbers and government agency listings had been tried elsewhere earlier, but Southwestern Bell was the first to realize the advantage of splitting business from residential listings and using the color section to separate the two sets of pages on white paper.

work on commission, there's a very strong incentive to keep up that momentum.

But the alpha came first. It not only predated the Yellow Pages, it predated telephone numbers themselves. Early one-page directories show the names of subscribers, but not their numbers—because no numbers had been assigned.

No doubt there were quite a few persons who recognized that assigning numbers and placing calls by number would make service simpler and faster for everyone, as well as saving expense for the telephone companies. But it was feared that the public would resent such an innovation. It took a measles epidemic to bring about the change.

In the winter of 1879-80, measles broke out in Lowell, Mass. That was long before the days of gamma globulin and immunization, of course, and Dr. Moses Greeley Parker foresaw a serious problem. There were four telephone operators who knew how to connect the 200-plus subscribers by name; suppose all of those operators came down with the measles? How could untrained substitutes handle the calls, especially the calls to doctors and drugstores?

So Dr. Parker recommended the use of numbers to the Lowell telephone management, and even though they had their misgivings, these worthies decided to give the idea a trial. Perhaps to management's surprise, the telephone users immediately saw the practical value of telephone numbers and the system went into effect without any complaints. Within a few years, numbers were in use wherever there was telephone service.

To say that the Yellow Pages came after the alpha is not to suggest there was no advertising in those early directories. On the contrary; even the single-sheet listings usually carried a few special display ads, as the newspapers would call them. It was a logical place to put an ad. When Little Rock's first directory was issued in 1880, for example, it consisted of a single sheet of paper bordered with 18 advertisements.

Over the years the directories grew as the number of subscribers grew, but for a long while the books were a hodgepodge of listings and ads. In Southwestern Bell, it took until 1926 for someone to decide that this had to stop. The new-style directory was first tried out in Topeka and Houston, with advertising banished from alpha and concentrated in the Yellow Pages. In the latter section (which had been in existence since 1906, when it was introduced in Michigan Bell), a new method of indexing and grouping of listings was instituted.

Only three years later, Southwestern Bell, as well as the rest of the Bell System, made the Yellow Pages still more helpful to users by instituting National Trademark Service, in which dealers are listed under brand name as well as in alphabetical order in their appropriate section.

The Yellow Pages have remained essentially the same since that time. They have achieved a new, more complete style of indexing and in many larger cities they carry such user helps as locator maps and zip code directories. But the most significant change has to be their "divorce" from the white pages.

In all the large cities of Southwestern Bell and many of the medium-sized ones as well, the white and Yellow Pages now come out on different schedules and are separately bound and delivered. For Southwestern Bell, the split first took place in St. Louis (April 1955), followed by Houston (June 1956) and Dallas (November 1957); but now divided books are commonplace.

Directories have split and resplit, like amoebas, since that first division. For the convenience of the user, who prefers not to have to thumb through a 10-pound

Little Rock, 1880. This directory had no numbers. Operators knew how to reach everyone's phone.

The Marathon Yellow Pages Sale

A TOP-NOTCH salesman, in any line of business, is always willing to go the extra mile to "close." Harry Cradduck, who retired from the Dallas Yellow Pages sales office and now lives in Fort Worth, tells a classic story of a sale he made at Corpus Christi, Tex., December 19, 1957. Here's how it went:

"It was Thursday evening, and the book was going to close the next day. I had put in a full day's work—8 a.m. to 5 p.m.—but I still had a 6 p.m. appointment with Mr. Johnson,* who ran his appliance service business out of his home.

"I went back to my hotel room to shower and shave. I figured this last call would take only an hour or so and told my supervisor, 'Mac' MacBride, 'I'll be back around seven. Wait and we'll go to supper together.' We had connecting rooms at the hotel.

"I had no idea what I was in for. Mr. Johnson had just really gotten started with directory advertising; he knew he needed more space but wasn't sure about the details. Every time I thought we had an ad settled and started on something else, he'd have second thoughts.

"About 10 p.m., he asked if I didn't want to continue the following day since it was rather late and neither of us had eaten supper. I explained to him that the book was closing the next day, and if we didn't get this settled, he just wasn't going to be in the directory at all—why not wait to eat until we had finished?

"Around 12:30 a.m., Mrs. Johnson pointed out that we had talked for over six hours and urged us to take a coffee break. Well, we didn't take a break, but we did manage to drink several cups of the coffee she made. (She went to bed after fixing coffee.)

"At 3 a.m., we both ran out of cigarettes and Mr. Johnson suggested we continue later that day. Again, I said that since it shouldn't take us very long to finish, why not do so?

"About 4 a.m., no nearer completion of the sale than at 6 p.m. the evening before, I realized that I was about to lose a customer (physically) if I didn't close the account. His eyes were bloodshot; he was hoarse and talked with great difficulty; he was resting his head, eyes closed, on the kitchen table. He hadn't moved from that table since 6 p.m. the previous evening.

"About this time, I repeated the theme of the evening and brought Mr. Johnson back to the interview. I said, 'Mr. Johnson, this shouldn't take us very much longer.' He replied: 'I've heard that since 10 p.m. last night, but I won't give up if you won't.'

"At 4:45 a.m., Mr. Johnson (by now I was calling him 'Jim')

agreed on a program. I left him at 5 a.m., a very tired but convinced customer, with the understanding that we would meet at 9 o'clock that morning in the telephone company business office to sign the contract and copy sheets. He also needed some changes in his telephone service, and I would help him with this.

"I returned to my hotel room, wrote the contract, prepared the copy sheets and called MacBride, who by now was at our sales office. I told him I was going to be late getting to work because I had an early call.

"Mac had aleady checked my room before coming in, and he retorted: 'Late to work? Heck, you haven't even been home yet!' But when I told him what had happened, he laughed and said he'd meet me over at the business office.

"At 10 a.m., Mr. Johnson signed the contract for a $41 renewal and $87.15 increase—also the copy sheets. We shook hands rather weakly and Mr. Johnson echoed a familiar statement. He said, 'Let's get a cup of coffee. It shouldn't take very long.' Actually, the three of us had breakfast, and then Mac and I drove home to Houston."

Cradduck proudly closes his account with the observation:

"After working 16 continuous hours on one account plus working from 8 a.m. till 5 p.m. the previous day, I believe this sets some sort of a record in the state of Texas." For all anyone knows, this may be an all-time world record.

The aftermath? Mr. Johnson was so pleased with the results of his expanded advertising that he opened up a regular business establishment outside his home and increased his advertising even more in later years. ∎

*Not the customer's real name.

Today's Yellow Pages ads are composed on computers at the Graphics Center in Dallas.

directory to find a single listing, regional white pages and regional Yellow Pages books are issued now.

And the bulk of the standard books has forced a division even in them; Houston now has four basic telephone directories.

All this progress has naturally demanded that the latest advances in printing technology be employed. The old-style setting of subscribers' listings in slugs of metal type has given way to phototypesetting done by computers. As a result, the number of listing errors, which always was fantastically low, has been reduced even further.

Of course statistics are no consolation to the occasional customer whose listing isn't quite right. So telephone companies maintain specialized directory production organizations whose people have a passion for accuracy. Traditionally these groups were part of the Commercial Department, but when the Marketing Department was created, directory was transferred there.

The time when errors are most likely to occur is when there are wholesale number changes—conversion to the "Metropolitan Number Plan" of two letters, four digits; or its successor, two-five numbering (first printed in the March 1953 Little Rock directory); or again, All-Number Calling, which eliminates letters altogether in favor of seven-digit numbers.

It's at times like these that the horror stories originate—people dropped out of the listings altogether, or shown with the wrong number, or perhaps shown with the right number in the alpha and the old, wrong number, in the classified . . . for with the telephone book, as with horse races, there's only one way to win but a hundred ways to lose.

For many years the directories of the Bell System, including those of Southwestern Bell, could be instantly distinguished from any other books of their size. It was the emblem on the brown cover, the "Spirit of Service" (sometimes called "Golden Boy" by the irreverent). This was patterned after a gilded statue which once stood atop the AT&T building at 195 Broadway in New York City.

But there's a fine line between consistency and monotony, and the directory people came to realize that their product was on the wrong side of that line. When St. Louis cut to two-five numbering in April 1954, the people in charge of this staggering conversion wanted to be sure that everyone would know the difference between the old and the new directory. The solution: Use a different cover. A bright blue cover, to be exact. With red printing in it.

The ice had been broken. All sorts of variations on the directory cover were toyed with, and in 1957, Oklahoma City issued the company's first directory with a full-color photographic cover.

True, variations like this add to the expense, but the difference is not great compared to the total cost of producing a directory in hundreds of thousands of copies. And the public relations value of a carefully selected photograph, or a piece of representative artwork, has been immediately noticeable. People love the covers, say they're worth framing. More important, the individual covers underline the status of Southwestern Bell as a hometown enterprise with hometown people, regardless of where its corporate headquarters may be located.

And nobody misses "Golden Boy."

With divestiture, a big change has come to the directory organization. It is now Southwestern Bell Publications, Inc., a subsidiary of Southwestern Bell Corporation. The new subsidiary has been established to compete even more effectively in Yellow Pages and other markets. In fact, the subsidiary has established four subsidiaries of its own—Southwestern Bell Yellow Pages, AD/VENT Information Services, AD/VENT Grafx and Southwestern Bell Media.

Through these subsidiaries, Southwestern Bell Publications will handle traditional offerings and enter new fields, possibly including direct mail, graphics for outside firms and catalogs.

In directory, as in the telephone business in general, it's a brave new world. ■

SALES AND SERVICE

CHAPTER TEN

TELEPHONE PEOPLE are accustomed to hearing, "Why do you advertise? You already have all the business in town."

There are dozens of good replies to this, starting with the obvious one that, indeed, there is a lot of "business in town" that the company doesn't have; that there are competitors in the communications field, and their numbers constantly increase; that an operating telephone company's principal monopoly is of the unprofitable local exchange service. An operating company needs additional income from other products and services in order to remain viable.

Perhaps the most cogent response to the question "Why advertise?" is to point out that like any business, the telephone business had to be sold to the public when it started and, again as with any other business, selling can never stop.

In fact, selling has gone hand in hand with service ever since the earliest days. Managers went door to door seeking new customers. Before there were service representatives in business offices, operators took orders for service installation.

In 1917, when the Bell Telephone Securities Company was organized to secure new telephone capital and expand ownership of the Bell System, the first activity undertaken was a sale of preferred stock of the Southwestern Bell System.

In a two-week period in the fall of 1926, the Oklahoma area of Southwestern Bell put on a statewide sales campaign, with the slogan "Every employee a salesman." (Sales totaled 4,216 "stations"—main telephones—a good sales performance for those days.)

Later, when the Depression struck and people began removing telephone service as a desperate economy measure, operators who might have been laid off (because there were no calls for them to handle) were urged to find new customers and bring the old ones back. Contrary to what is generally accepted as a fact of life today, it is possible to survive without a telephone in the house. Very inconvenient, but possible.

It must have been in those Depression years that the leaders of the telephone business recognized an economic truth to which they had paid little attention when business was booming: Sales of extras, such as extension telephones, meant more than added revenue; they were insurance against losing the customer altogether.

When times are really tough, those executives realized, people might choose to keep main service and cut off their 50-cent-a-month extensions. But if they had no extensions to start with, there was only one place to cut as far as telephone service was concerned. And that was the basic service itself—POTS (plain old telephone service).

Of course, the rules have since been changed—many times, in fact. When the FCC ruled that customers could connect non-Bell equipment to telephone company lines, the "sale" (really, *lease*) of extensions was no longer an operating company monopoly. Furthermore, it forced the telephone industry to devise a different method of establishing tariffs for local service.

Until that FCC ruling, such tariffs had traditionally been based on the number of company-owned telephones that could be reached for the basic charge. But this statistic became unrepresentative when customer-owned extensions were numerous, so the companies had to institute a new measurement—"exchange access arrangements."

They're
Worried!
Call home and tell them you're safe and happy.

Rates are reduced after 7 P.M. on station-to-station calls. Just give the distant telephone number.

SOUTHWESTERN BELL TELEPHONE COMPANY

No. 14 X

GIVE YOURSELF a THRILL

Call her to-night by "Long Distance." The sound of her voice is next best thing to the look in her eyes. Worth a great deal more than it costs, and it costs very little.

SOUTHWESTERN BELL TELEPHONE COMPANY

Various appeals to emotion were made in these telephone ads promoting long distance and local service.

The girl without a telephone stays at home

MARY had hoped Jack would take her to the dance.

He had seemed interested the night she met him at Sara's party ˙ ˙ ˙ ˙

But when Jack tried to call her he couldn't find her name in the directory.

A telephone in the home may not be a sure aid to popularity, yet very often ˙ ˙ ˙ ˙

The girl without a telephone stays at home.

IT ISN'T A HOME
WITHOUT A TELEPHONE

AND YOU CAN HAVE ONE
FOR TEN CENTS A DAY

SOUTHWESTERN BELL TELEPHONE COMPANY

Sure Put my name in this book

Name

Address

Everybody's a Salesman

THE SELLING TECHNIQUES of early-day telephone people were a little different from the methods used today. In fact, an anecdote contributed by John W. Ripley of the Shawnee County Historical Society implies that free service for advertising purposes was part of the technique. Today this would be strictly forbidden by tariffs.

Nor would it be likely today that a telephone company president would be engaged in such activities—but times were different in 1905, when Charles Sumner Gleed became president of the Missouri & Kansas Telephone Company. Gleed was a Topeka attorney, prominent in organizing the Santa Fe Railroad, and, according to Charles McDaniel's memoirs, a former newspaperman. To quote John Ripley:

". . .Our neighbor Charles S. Gleed, about 1905, persuaded my mother, against her better judgment, to accept free installation and service of a Bell phone. At first Mother had refused the offer, telling Mr. Gleed that we had no use for a Bell phone; all of our friends had independents.

"But Gleed persisted and finally Mother agreed that she would allow a Bell phone to be placed on the wall (of course) in our front vestibule. No sooner had it been placed in service than Gleed spread the word through Potwin Place, recently annexed to Topeka, that the Ripleys had a long distance phone.

"After a month or so of getting up in the night to allow neighbors to place emergency messages, or worse, delivering messages to neighbors, my father (whose firm, the Topeka Laundry Company, had both phones) had the Bell phone removed from our house.

"Incidentally, the family-owned laundry was the first local firm to publish its phone number. An advertisement from the Topeka *Journal* of April 15, 1884, shows the business number, 153. This appeared nearly a year before the first Topeka telephone directory was issued to phone subscribers."

Gleed served as president of the M&K from 1905 to 1912 and as chairman of the board of directors from 1912 to his resignation in 1919. His name is perpetuated in the title of the Gleed Chapter of the Pioneers. ∎

What is an "EAA"? It's what most people think of as a "main line"—a connection from a customer's telephone or switchboard to a telephone company central office. Counting all of these in an exchange gives an approximate answer to the question, "How many different numbers can you call without using the long distance network?"

But aside from such changes compelled by government rulings, sales activity in the telephone business took on increasing importance as the years went past. Between about 1920 and the present day, what had originally been pretty much a sideline became a vital part of the operation.

Elementary economics caused the change. Providing local telephone service became increasingly expensive with each rise in wages and material costs. To keep the business solvent, there were three options:

(1) Rates might be raised (after negotiations with state utility commissions), but not by so much as to turn away from the System goal of "universal service," i.e., at least one telephone in every household and business.

(2) Service standards could be lowered, a possibility that was never seriously considered.

(3) Or a drive could be launched to develop and sell additional services—premium features. This would produce revenues which could maintain earnings and still hold down basic rates as much as possible.

Where absolutely necessary, operating companies like Southwestern Bell resorted to option No. 1, but the real revenue-raising impetus went to option No. 3.

This was not just a post-World War II development, although that's when the big rush got under way. As far back as 1937, Southwestern Bell distributed its first complete sales catalog of all products it had to offer. The catalog was nothing like the glossy full-color productions of later years, but at least the principle of selling, rather than order-taking, was recognized.

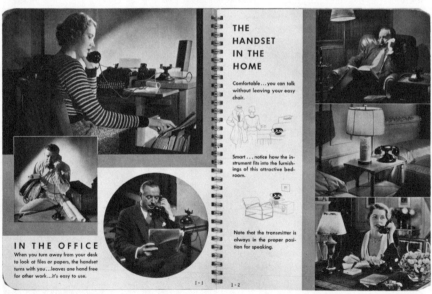

A two-page spread from the 1937 Southwestern Bell sales catalog.

The sales effort, for items like extensions and "advanced" instruments such as the 202 sets ("French handsets"), was at first principally a function of the business office—the Commercial Department. But the plant people who called on customers in their homes were in an ideal position to show and demonstrate desirable service items. So they were brought into the selling effort, too.

The outbreak of World War II brought this sales effort to a screeching halt. Southwestern Bell and other operating companies found themselves hard-pressed just to meet government and military demands for service, and there was no extra supply of telephones or central office equipment to serve civilians. In fact, Southwestern Bell did not begin selling residence extension telephones again until October 1949. From then on, however, selling became second only to service improvement as a goal.

It might be noted that service improvement itself has always been a selling tool in the telephone business. The better the service, the more the customer is inclined to buy. (Is a feature like Call Forwarding a service improvement or a sales item? Obviously, it's both.)

In the 1950s and 1960s, new products and services poured forth in a torrent from Bell Laboratories and Western Electric. In Southwestern Bell and the other operating companies there was a corresponding volume of sales campaigns, complete with newspaper, radio and television advertising, business office posters, bill inserts and all the other media.

Data-processing equipment from the mid-1960s.

Among the items presented to the public during this double-decade were color telephones;* hands-free speakerphones; Dataphone® service; the Princess® telephone; telpak and WATS, to be followed not long afterward by INWATS;** home interphone, farm interphone, Bell Chime, panel phone; the Trimline® phone, with dial or keypad included in the handset; Call Director® and a host of other equipment items to improve business service; the Touch-Tone® (push-button) phone; ECS (Emergency Call System); Centrex and, of course, Centrex II; the Dimension® PBX; electronic central offices and Custom Calling Services; the Horizon® communications system, and the electronic blackboard, to name just a few innovative products and services.

With all this increased emphasis on selling new products and services, Southwestern Bell could no longer confine its sales activities to what service representatives and installers could handle along with their regular duties. In the early 1950s "sales and service manager" was a title found in the Commercial Department; this individual had a small staff of specialists who kept in close touch with business customers. But by 1970, at the conclusion of a number of steps reminiscent of a caterpillar's metamorphosis into a butterfly, this activity had been concentrated in a Marketing Department, standing tall and looking the old Plant, Traffic and Commercial departments in the eye.

The first Marketing Department in Southwestern Bell was created September 1, 1967, in the North Texas area, but within a couple of years there was a full-fledged marketing operation in effect in all areas. This, however, was really just a preliminary to the complete reorganization of Southwestern Bell. Again, the change took place in stages, but by the mid-1970s most of the old depart-

---

*The idea of color telephones was not all that new. Western Electric had produced some model 202 ("French handset") telephones in 1927, and in 1937, at the depth of the Depression, a few color 302 sets were offered. Most of the latter were still in operating companies' stocks, waiting for a buyer, when the Bell System began its massive promotion of the new 502 sets in eight shades. These shades, incidentally, were considerably revised within a year of their appearance; contrary to market research findings, the public wasn't impressed with the "executive mahogany" telephone but craved sets in baby-blue and baby-pink. Ma Bell obliged.

**WATS (Wide Area Telephone Service) permits a customer to make as many long distance calls as desired at a fixed monthly rate. Inward WATS, or INWATS, is the familiar toll-free 800 Service which has been a remarkable sales tool for American business.

"Never Send a Girl..."?

THE SELLING PART of the telephone job wasn't always restricted to marketing people or commercial and plant forces before them. There was a period when it was thought that operators could make an effective sales force, too . . . not for selling equipment or special services but securities. J. R. Peterson's reminiscences of his early days in the Traffic Department include this anecdote:

"While I was in Houston as toll district traffic chief in 1922, Southwestern Bell put out an issue of preferred stock, a distinctive feature being that this issue was to be sold largely by employees. Russ Fields, the district man in charge of local service, and I went into this stock sale campaign in a big way. As many of my toll operators were acquainted (over the telephone) with many of Houston's leading businessmen, they did exceptionally well with the sales effort.

"In one case, however, this rather amateurish financing scheme backfired a bit. One of my toll operators called on Jesse Jones (Jones had not yet achieved national fame,* but he definitely was *Mr. Big* in Houston). He was annoyed at such an unorthodox manner of selling securities and asked the girl who had sent her. She gave him my name. Jesse telephoned me and asked that I come over to his office.

"Jones' tone of voice betrayed the fact that something was bothering him.

"He proceeded to chew me out for sending a young girl out on the town to sell telephone company securities but, apparently realizing that I was not to blame, ended up by telling the girl that he would buy 300 shares. When we sent in the order, it was returned by Dallas because it exceeded the maximum—250 shares per customer, as I recall it. However, when my boss explained the trouble we

had already had, someone wisely decided that the limit per customer had best be waived.

"Incidentally, I've often wondered what great financial brain concocted the financing plan, as I have always thought that Jesse Jones' criticisms were pretty sound."

Peterson was "promoted" (with no raise in pay!) within 10 months to the corresponding job in the St. Louis toll district. One might speculate whether his successful involvement in this "amateurish" stock-sale plan had something to do with the promotion, which may have gotten him started on his rise to a company vice presidency. ∎

*Peterson's reference may require clarification for those unacquainted with Franklin Roosevelt's presidency. Jones, who was chairman of the Reconstruction Finance Corporation and later secretary of commerce, gained national and international stature. As a cabinet conservative, he did much to hold business support for the New Deal administration.

ments had been swept away. There was no Traffic Department, no Plant Department, no Commercial Department, no Engineering Department . . . and no Marketing Department, either. Instead, the duties and responsibilities of these five were reassigned, on a sales and service basis, to the Network Department, the Business Department and the Residence Department.

Sales, later retitled "Marketing," had triumphed; but in its triumph, it had lost a little of its own identity. Now *all* of Southwestern Bell was a sales organization, and employees' titles depended not so much on what they did as on the "segment" of the customers for whom they were doing it. Telephone people shook their heads to clear them and settled down to learn a new way of doing business, and a new way of thinking about the business, as well.

There was still more upheaval to come. The FCC decided that companies like Southwestern Bell might have an unfair advantage over their competitors, who were seeking to sell equipment and hook it onto the Bell communications lines. As the upshot of its Computer Inquiry II decision, the FCC ordered that equipment sales must be separated from operations.

The government agency ruled that AT&T could sell or lease the equipment made by Western Electric only if it created a wholly new subsidiary to do so. This would avoid any suspicion that revenues from long distance, for example, were being diverted to hold down the cost of equipment and gain an unfair competitive advantage. Operating companies like Southwestern Bell, for the year 1983 only, were restricted to selling or leasing only the equipment they had in stock as of December 31, 1982.

And so, American Bell (since renamed AT&T Information Systems) came into existence January 1, 1983. Southwestern Bell bade farewell to some 2,800 of its employees—about 3 percent of the total—who took jobs with the new organization. The terms of the FCC order spell out that Southwestern Bell people must deal at arm's length with their former fellow employees. By word or act they can do nothing which would help the AT&T people sell equipment to Southwestern Bell customers.

Above: A 1966 ad urges customers to use communications consultants. Right: Austin, Tex., 1976. A youngster visits a PhoneCenter Store.

Cold Calling in Tough Times

IF A BUSINESS customer today expects the sales force to use the telephone in "qualifying" prospects, the telephone company will gladly put on training classes to show them how it's done most effectively. But back in the 1930s, Southwestern Bell employees were sent out to sell door to door and face to face. And no nonsense about "qualifying," either; *everybody* was a prospect.

Bill Wimsatt, customer service representative in Wichita, has two training manuals that were used in those days by commission salesmen, employees of the Commercial Department in Kansas City. One titled *Outline of Sales Procedures* is obviously intended to prepare a salesman to make a "cold" call on a single-owner small business. The other is labeled *Salesman's Aid—Residence Non-Users*. This latter carries a pathetic overtone of what people were facing during the Depression.

After the hearty introduction (one can almost see the carefully-rehearsed smile)—"Good Morning, Mrs. Blank (pause); I am Mr. Blank of the Telephone Company (slight pause)"—the salesman gets down to brass tacks: "I would like to talk to you about your telephone service." Then comes the first prospect objection: "We don't have a telephone."

Whoever wrote the manual had foreseen this response because the salesman is then instructed to say: "But you do have occasion to use a telephone sometimes, do you not? I am thinking of those times when you have occasion to use telephone service, and I wonder if I may come in and discuss it with you. There may be some way we can be of help to you."

And so forth. Anyone who has sold insurance or has been visited by insurance salesmen—and this must include practically all the population over the age of 12—can anticipate how it goes.

The situations which the manual suggests the telephone salesman may encounter are disturbingly familiar, too. . . .
□ "Since you are not employed regularly, I am wondering if you are trying to obtain part-time employment or odd jobs until you do get regular work again?"
□ "Yes, you can use your neighbor's telephone, in most cases, and it is nice to have such obliging neighbors, but I am thinking of those times when your neighbors are away."
□ "Yes, it is nice to be located so you can use the telephone at the store but, of course, you are not in a position to receive your incoming calls."

After a while....

they were doing so well they would take afternoons off.

□ "Yes, I can appreciate your position. Many of us are having to think about economy just now. But let us think also of the importance of telephone service to you at this time—(follow with sales appeal)."

The typical sales appeals seem just as compelling now as they were then: employment; protection; contacts; saves time and money; privacy and convenience.

How effective were these techniques? Despite the rather quaint wording of the coaching, it must have worked exceedingly well. Wimsatt obtained the manuals from an employee who worked with these salesmen, hired directly "off the street" with no telephone background, and this was the procedure followed:

The sales force would be assembled each Monday morning; the sales manager would distribute a stack of cards covering two or three blocks of the city. The cards carried names and addresses of people who were listed in the (non-telephone) city directory and who company records showed were non-users.

Each salesman was paid a straight commission. Every residence customer whom he persuaded to take telephone service and who kept service in for three months meant a dollar in the salesman's pocket.

If that doesn't sound like much, consider this fact: The manager's biggest problem was to keep the salesman knocking on doors all day. After a while, they were doing so well they would take afternoons off and hide out; they were making all the money they wanted and preferred to stretch the job out rather than to strip the vineyard completely by putting in an eight-hour day.

Even in hard times, a competent salesman can always make a buck! ■

Does this, then, mean that Southwestern Bell Telephone Company is no longer a sales organization? By no means. The selling structure is still in force. Account executives and their account teams continue to be responsible for assigned customers. And the company will continue to offer items such as these:

- Local exchange service
- Custom Calling Services
- Private lines
- Touch-Tone Service
- Dataphone Digital Service

A new Southwestern Bell business sales organization was announced just before the change took effect. This group comprised employees who did not transfer to American Bell at the beginning of 1983. For that year only, marketing personnel in the telephone company took care of network sales (like WATS and private line services), premises system offerings (like leased Dimension and Horizon systems) and Centrex service (the switching service that houses switching equipment in a central office, not on a customer's premises).

Ed Andrews, right, has been a popular spokesman for Southwestern Bell business services.

Of course, the biggest changes of all have taken place because of divestiture. Southwestern Bell Telephone Company has become one of four subsidiaries of Southwestern Bell Corporation. The other subsidiaries are:

☐ Southwestern Bell Publications, Inc., which competes in Yellow Pages and related directory advertising fields.

☐ Southwestern Bell Mobile Systems, Inc., which provides cellular mobile phone service.

☐ Southwestern Bell Telecommunications, Inc., which offers telecommunications equipment in direct competition with AT&T Information Systems and other companies. The network and Centrex sales force has remained with Southwestern Bell Telephone Company.

There can be no doubt about one point: This company, having become thoroughly geared to selling in a competitive market, never again will assume the role of a mere order-taker. George Durant sold telephone service in St. Louis when there wasn't a working telephone west of the Mississippi River. The heirs of George Durant's enterprise will carry on that tradition of overcoming any obstacle. ∎

GENERAL INSTRUCTIONS

FOR OPERATING

THE NEW SYSTEM.

Each station is connected with the Central Office by two wires—the "Private Wire" and the "Signal Wire."

But one subscriber is connected on each private wire, while the signal wire may be used by a large number.

The "signal wire" is used *exclusively* for signaling the Central Office to connect and disconnect the "private wires."

The Telephones are connected to the private wire, and are switched to the "signal wire" by shoving in and holding the push button.

(It should be understood that the above explanation *does not apply* to the change now being made in the system at the annex.)

After shoving in the button, if any other subscriber is using the wire do not interrupt him; wait until the operator has repeated his order correctly.

After giving your order to connect, hold the button until your bell strikes. If the wire you want is engaged, the central office will strike your bell four times slowly, or the operator on the signal wire will notify you.

When ordering your wire disconnected, hold the button until the operator repeats it correctly.

After ordering a connection, if the party does not respond promptly, shove in the push button, and ask the Central Office to ring them up again. For example: "Ring up 283 for 279 again;" or, "Ring up Simmons Hardware for 195 again."

Operators are stationed at the signal wires constantly from 7 A. M. to 9 P. M. At other hours they will respond within a few seconds from the time the push button is used.

No communication with Central Offices is allowed on the signal wire, except for connection or disconnection. Each office has a "private wire." No. 417 Olive street is number 100 and the Leffingwell avenue office is number 900.

Signal-wire operators are instructed to pay no attention to "Hello!" "Hello, Central," or any such useless exclamations.

WHEN YOU HAVE FINISHED USING YOUR LINE DON'T FAIL TO DISCONNECT, WHETHER OR NOT YOU CALLED FOR THE CONNECTION, OR IF THE CONNECTION IS MADE AND THE PARTY DOESN'T ANSWER.

If your line is connected, it is presumed at the Central Office that it is in use, and is so reported when called for.

When a station of the *new system* connects with a station of the *old system*, the latter is absolutely cut out of the Central Office, and cannot signal the office, and is dependent upon the strict observance of the rules at the new system station.

It is very important that subscribers should add the numbers of new system stations to the list as they are received.

After a subscriber has been changed from the old to the new system, the new number is necessarily substituted for the name at the Central Office.

These numbers will be supplied as fast as possible, and new lists will be issued about every week until the change is completed.

When subscribers call for connection with old system stations, and can hear the "rumbling" of the answer on the bell, but cannot engage in conversation, the trouble is in the transmitter or the cords connecting the Telephone. Please report such occurrences on the signal wire, in order that they may be speedily remedied.

TO SUBSCRIBERS.

Complaints of imperfect working of your line or instruments should be reported to No. 100 at once from the most convenient Station in your vicinity.

THE CUSTOMERS, GOD BLESS 'EM

CHAPTER ELEVEN

THEY SAT on a porch of a West Texas ranch house—the earnest young (36) Southwestern Bell executive and the courtly cattleman—and "dickered."

The telephone man, whose name was Drexyle Turner, had a serious problem. His responsibilities in the Pennsylvania-sized Midland district included maintenance of all plant facilities, local and long distance. This included the "Class A Lead" that ran from Midland to Seminole and then to Hobbs, N.M. By the miracle of "C" carrier, the 10 pairs of wires on those poles' two crossarms provided 25 precious circuits, over which government messages hummed between Washington and Hobbs. For it was wartime—1942—and the United States war effort included building airfields around Hobbs in southeast New Mexico and training airmen there.

Turner's problem? The toll line went across the ranch of B. B. Curry, the gentleman he was interviewing. Curry had a customer-owned service line running into Seminole—a single strand of wire with a magneto telephone at the ranch end but tied into the Southwestern Bell switchboard. It was a typical arrangement at the time, making it possible for ranchers to keep in touch with their markets even though they weren't on the regular telephone network.

The wire was strung on short poles which ran alongside the Bell poles; the wire had to be low so when repairs were needed, Curry's cowhands could fix the line by standing in or on their pickup trucks. This worked fine until the area became the scene of an oil boom. The big oil trucks, entering and leaving the Seminole-Hobbs highway, would snap the service line and sometimes drag down the poles.

So the cowboys were making their repairs by fastening the service line on the Bell poles . . . still low enough that they could reach the wire. The next time an oil truck came through it again would snap the wire, which would flip over the Bell wires and short out the Washington-to-Hobbs circuits. The Air Force didn't like this, and neither did Southwestern Bell. So Turner drove over to explain to Curry that this must stop.

Tall, courteous, graying ("a regular Gary Cooper type," Turner recalls), Curry listened to the visitor state his case. Then it was the rancher's turn to talk.

"Son," he said, "my service line is important to me. When something happens to it, I have to drive about 20 miles into Seminole to conduct my livestock business.

"I understand your problem. But let me explain some things that may not be in your records.

"When that line of yours was built, it ran along an old wagon trail across my property and no one ever obtained a right-of-way easement. Now I don't mind having your pole line there, but if you had to move it you'd have to build around the north end of my ranch to the place where they're building the new highway. That would require 25 or 30 miles of new construction for your company.

"Now don't you think you could help me a little by letting me use your poles through the oil fields?"

Turner's jaw dropped. "Maybe I had better think about this a little more," he said slowly.

"Good, son. You do that," Curry responded with a warm smile. "Meanwhile, won't you stay for supper?"

("He was a widower and lived alone except for his house boy," Turner recalls. "But that houseboy really knew how to fix a big steak. It was a delicious meal.")

After supper Turner drove back to Midland. The next day he called his Fort Worth division office, which advised him to discuss the problem directly with state headquarters in Dallas. Would they make a special exception in Mr. Curry's case—let him run his wire on the Bell pole line—in view of the fact that he could make it very tough for Southwestern Bell? "No way," said Dallas. "We have to stick to the practice."

Stalemate. Dallas said Mr. Curry would have to back down. And Turner knew very well that Mr. Curry was not about to back down.

In desperation he called a friend high up in the organization. Could they work out some arrangement that would keep everybody happy—say, establish a special toll station at the Curry ranch house, which could be linked to the Bell toll line so there would be no need for the service line?

The man he talked to grasped the situation immediately. Men and materials were in short supply; it made no sense to spend thousands of dollars to reroute a toll lead if Curry could be accommodated some other way and the present toll lead preserved, even though it might mean winking at the practice.

The upshot was that Southwestern Bell constructed a pole line from the highway to the ranch house, half a mile away, strung two copper wires on those poles and installed a toll station at the house. Curry paid the charge, roughly $1,500, for the work. As he handed over his check to Turner, Turner handed him a check for the identical amount as payment for a right of way for the toll line. Honor

St. Louis, 1899. The PBX at Union Station, one of the nation's busiest railroad terminals at that time.

was saved on both sides. And Southwestern Bell's cost to put in the special toll station was neatly balanced off by Curry's long distance billing the next month, which by coincidence was also $1,500!

Turner and the rancher became good friends as a result of what started out to be a problem. In fact, when Turner confided in Curry how difficult it was to patrol 1,000 miles of toll lines by driving a car through the West Texas sand hills, Curry suggested a horse would be a better way to do the job . . . and gave him Brown Jug, a long-legged animal the cowhands used when roping steers. Curry also presented Turner with a silver-mounted saddle, a bridle, blanket and "everything that a drugstore cowboy would need." Turner already had his boots.

Not every customer turns out to be so generous; in truth, few can afford to be. But on a lesser scale, the stories are manifold of customers who show their appreciation for considerate service. Flowers and candy are often sent to operators; sometimes service representatives are the recipients of similar gifts; craftspeople who go to customers' homes to install or repair service are often asked to stay for lunch (not permitted).

Yes, customers complain about their bills; service representatives know that every Monday, especially, will bring an outpouring of such complaints which built up over the weekend. But at the same time there are customers who have an abiding faith that any billing error must be unintentional and will be promptly corrected (as a matter of fact, that faith is fully justified).

Faye Williams, who was a service representative in Kennett, Mo., for 31 years before she retired in 1981, remembers the customer who came into the office, threw his bill on her desk and said:

"Mrs. Williams, will you look this bill over and tell me if there are any calls on it that I didn't make?" When she examined the bill and said it looked all right to her, he paid it without further question.

The relationship of the telephone company to its customers always has been a close one, closer than with most businesses.

Only the other utility services and the mails are so thoroughly involved in the day-to-day activities of the people they serve. When an emergency arises, the telephone company ranks right behind police and fire departments as the organization the public depends on. In fact, without the telephone there would be some difficulty summoning the services of the other two.

And if the public depends upon the telephone company, one can also observe the company is unusually dependent on the public, not just for financial patronage, but for cooperation in making the service *work*.

To drive the point home, one need only look at the Customer Guide section of a modern telephone directory. It carries dozens of pages explaining how to use the phone effectively. No such instructions are necessary to use the services of the gas, electric or water utilities.

From the very beginning, telephone service represented the interaction of an electrical system with two human beings, one at each end of the circuit. Customers had to learn to speak into the gadget, how to listen to it, how to crank up Central, how to give the number desired (the "Millie, let me talk to Dr. Jones" period lasted only a few years) . . . and then how to place a long distance call with the operator, how to use a dial telephone, how to master the area codes, how to dial a long distance number, how to use a Touch-Tone telephone.

Available today are the Custom Calling Services which, although convenient, require an informed user to give the machinery the right signals in order to benefit from Call Waiting, Speed Calling, Call Forwarding and similar special services.

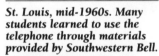

St. Louis, mid-1960s. Many students learned to use the telephone through materials provided by Southwestern Bell.

He Saw His Duty and He Did It

Service to customers can take unusual forms, and tearing down communications lines must be one of the strangest ways to provide that service. But K. G. (Red) Shell remembers a time when it was necessary. Shell retired in 1981 as a test center technician with over 40 years' service. Here's his story.

IN JANUARY 1949, I was directed to lead 20 repair and installation trucks to Durant, Okla., where residents were experiencing a terrible freezing sleet storm. When we arrived, we didn't have to strain our eyes to realize that the service we had been providing this community was flat in a pile of ice. In some cases, the cable and open wire were jumping up and down with a noise that we knew meant certain disaster for the plant.

We arrived late in the evening, with darkness just a few minutes away. Our supervisor, George Evans, said: "Let's have a big meal, get to bed and get some rest. There's no use going out in this. It surely will all be flat on the ground tomorrow." And indeed it was.

Early the next morning, Evans got word that a rancher one mile south of town couldn't get out of his driveway to water his cattle because five arms of No. 109 steel toll lead were down over the driveway. Evans told me to go out to survey the situation and to do whatever I thought was necessary to help the customer.

As I drove out, I could see that all the wires between the city of Durant and the ranch were flat on the ground. As it was still sleeting and freezing on the toll lead, I knew it was just a matter of time before all the poles would be down, too.

Meanwhile, a rancher's cattle would go without attention, maybe for days, until something was done about the wires blocking his driveway. I'd just have to speed up what was going to happen anyhow.

I stopped my repair truck across from the ranch house. The rancher was standing on the front porch, and when we greeted each other, he grumbled something about "this damned weather." I told him we were

going to help him but would he please go inside for his safety.

After he went inside, I took my side cutters and knocked the ice off the strands—that ice was three inches thick!—and then began to cut them. I had finished cutting about two arms (20 wires) when there was a roar like a tornado, and I could see the whole works was going. I got into my truck and watched as one mile of five-arm toll lead went down like dominoes.

I had a sort of sick feeling when it was over. I had spent about 10 years providing service for our customers in my small way, and now I had just torn down service to lots of people.

I'll never, as long as I live, forget that rancher's expression and what he said when he came back out on his front porch and saw the devastation: "My gosh, man, did you have to do that?"

After I explained why it was necessary and assured him that we had a lot of men from all over and would have service restored in a few days, he said, "Well, thank God for Ma Bell!" And so do I. ∎

Telephone Curfew, Courtesy of Grandma

THERE ARE still plenty of folks around who can remember when the telephone—that is, the sending and receiving unit—and the ringer box were separate. The box would be fastened to a wall at the most convenient access point, and a line cord ran from there to the telephone itself.

This arrangement usually worked well enough but caused intermittent trouble for the Anderson family, who lived 12 miles north of Odessa, Tex. Every few days, the Odessa *American* reports, Mr. Anderson would come to town and complain to A. Quincy Cooper (who owned and operated the local telephone company from 1921 to 1927) that he couldn't

make any calls at night. Service was all right in the daytime.

Cooper went out late one afternoon on one of these fruitless trouble calls. The phone was working fine. But because it was late in the day, the family invited him to stay for supper. After supper, he decided to try the

phone just one more time and, lo and behold, it didn't work.

Anderson's elderly mother had excused herself a bit earlier from the dinner table and gone to bed. It was in her bedroom that the ringer box was located, with a long cord leading from there to the telephone in the living room. Anderson knocked on the door and obtained permission to bring Cooper in to trace the circuit.

It took only a few moments' investigation to find the trouble.

On the bell box, which had exposed binding posts on top, rested Granny's glasses with their metal frames. That's where she had been putting them every night when she retired. And that's what shorted out the circuit so calls couldn't be made. ∎

The Customer's Always Right–Usually

THE TELEPHONE reminiscences of Henry Altepeter, who worked in Southwestern Bell's Plant and Engineering Departments from 1926 to 1964, cover far more than his personal job experiences. Watching the world with an amused and tolerant eye, he has stories to tell about customers, too. Like these:

The owner of a large and successful business had a number of peculiarities. He used to summon his secretary by blowing a whistle (startling, but effective!) and kept a stuffed horse in the board of directors' meeting room. This, of course, was of no concern to Southwestern Bell. What *was* disturbing was the fact that he suddenly stopped paying his firm's monthly telephone bills.

All the usual calls and letters got nowhere, but before suspending service, the routine final step, the local manager paid a call on the gentleman. There was a long discussion, but the prob-

lem finally came out: He said he would pay his past and future bills only if the company agreed to bill him the nearest dollar amount. He explained that he was tired of seeing bills and authorizing payments for amounts that weren't stated in whole dollars.

Fortunately, the telephone company was flexible enough to issue him special bills from then on, rounded to the nearest dollar, and there was no further problem with non-payment. Nor did it bother the company that he had the payment checks made out to "The Great American Octopus." Just as long as the dollar amount was right and the proper signature was penned in.

Another out-of-the-ordinary customer was the woman who claimed to be a clairvoyant and advertised as such in the newspapers. Although she conducted this operation at her home, she felt she should change her class of telephone service from residence to business.

No problem. But she wanted her listing in the Yellow Pages to be under the classification "Clairvoyants." There was no such classification (and still isn't), so the company refused this request. She filed suit to force the company to accommodate her.

When the case came to trial, the judge asked for stipulations from the attorneys. The Southwestern Bell lawyer asked that the plaintiff be required to establish that there was such a business as "clairvoyant" and that the plaintiff conducted such a business. He stipulated that the plaintiff must be able to prove she could foresee the future.

There was the usual preliminary legal skirmishing and then the judge dismissed the suit with prejudice. On the way out of the courtroom the plaintiff was overheard telling her attorney: "I told you I wouldn't win this case, so don't send me a bill."

Altepeter reflects that maybe the lady just might have been clairvoyant after all. ∎

And just ahead, the telephone scientists cheerfully assure us, are features the public will use to call home and turn on the heat, turn off the cooking roast and perform dozens of other handy helps. All these features, too, will require cooperation from the public to make them work.

In a nation of some 220 million, there's hardly anyone over the age of 8 who doesn't use the telephone; most people use it every day. They take it for granted, and cheerfully (for the most part) undertake to master each new advance as it comes along. "If the phone company says this will make service better, all right, let's give it a try."

How did this high regard develop? In a few words, it was earned. After all, the world went about its business for millenia before the telephone came along. As Corah Mooney Bullock reminisces in the Butler (Kan.) *Free-lance:*

"It was not easy to convince anyone in El Dorado that anyone in El Dorado needed a telephone. We seemed to be getting along pretty well. At our house we tied a white towel around a porch post to summon a neighbor across a vacant half block. It never failed.

"Each morning, as Father arose from the table, he would say, 'Want anything sent up today?' At noon he usually carried home a small package in brown paper.

"Nothing wrong with the system."

Yet it was Mrs. Bullock's father who was a prime mover in bringing the telephone to El Dorado, Kan., in 1896, and Corah's world was never the same. For the telephone was going to prove indispensable. No more white towels around porch posts.

In the earliest days, we find telephone companies, eager for more customers, offering services that—alas!—can no longer be provided. Thus the first (January 1901) directory of the J. S. Haley Telephone Company of Hays, Kan.—one of Southwestern Bell's hundreds of ancestors—includes these "SUGGESTIONS":

" . . . 3. Always ask Central for information regarding trains; railroad employees object to the annoyance of these repeated questions. . . .

" . . . 9. In case of fire or other occurrence of public interest, call Central and give the facts. . . . "

Yes, Hays had a newspaper then, the *Free Press,* but early on, people came to rely on "Central" for the latest newsbreaks. And Central didn't let them down. She knew where the fire was. She knew where the church picnic was being held this afternoon. More than the typical newspaper of the time, she was the eyes and ears of the community. She relayed messages or hunted down people who weren't at their regular place of business.

But as the telephone grew more and more useful, it could no longer be used for purposes other than straight people-to-people communication. Millie no longer knew Dr. Jones' number, or whether the 12:30 train was in the station; to speed up service, she was ordered not to answer questions like "What time is it?"

And with the advent of dial service, the public got its calls through faster, but it also lost the daily contact with the operator for local calling . . . and eventually, for long distance calling, too. As equipment grew more and more dependable, the average time between residence service calls lengthened to two years, and that means many people went far longer than that without a repair visit. Thus, another contact with folks at the telephone company became a sometime thing.

Small wonder that people gradually came to feel that their telephone service was impersonal, at least compared with the old days. And a byproduct of this

This operator of 1879 answered questions about everything from train schedules to the time.

changing attitude was an increased feeling of proprietorship on the part of the customer. That instrument was no longer "the telephone"; it was "my telephone." Who was this utility to say I couldn't do with it as I pleased—even hook other phones on the line if I wanted to? If I wanted to add another floor lamp, I didn't ask the electric company's permission.

An even stronger possessiveness developed on the subject of telephone numbers. The longer a number was used, the more it became part of the customer's personality—like a fisherman's old hat festooned with fishing lures. Sure, maybe the tariff (what's a tariff, the customer wondered) might say the numbers are assigned at the option of the telephone company. But after all these years—!*

Unfortunately, numbers *had* to be changed as the service grew. They had to be changed from single and double digits to three, four and five digits as dial service became available to more phones. Then came "metropolitan" numbering, two letters and four digits, which was supposed to be the ultimate. But that ultimate was soon succeeded by another ultimate, two-five numbering, and two-five's life span was far shorter than the telephone people expected.

With two letters and a digit to identify the telephone number's "prefix" (the part which picks out a specific switching unit), it had been confidently predicted that such a system would last at least until the year 2000. After all, there are 540 possible prefixes, even allowing for the fact that a good many combinations weren't available.**

Two-five made it possible to have, theoretically, 540,000 different telephone numbers within a single area code, and there would be enough area codes in the United States and Canada so that every telephone in both countries would have a unique number: Three-figure area code plus two letters plus five digits nearly equals infinity—or so it was thought.

But no one had foreseen the incredible demand for more telephones and more telephone numbers. A workhorse Centrex, for example, gobbles up an entire prefix because every extension with this PBX (private branch exchange) gets a unique number of its own, so that it can be dialed directly from outside. And Centrexes constitute only a small part of the total demand.

And so came ANC: All-Number Calling (called by its opponents "Digit Dialing," although digit dialing had actually been instituted with the first dial system). The letters had to go. All telephone numbers would consist of seven digits, with a dash between the third and fourth.

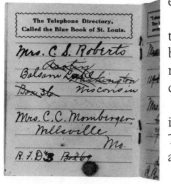

Southwestern Bell for many years has provided customers with personal directories.

Patiently, the telephone people explained why it was not possible to use all 26 letters of the alphabet. (That would make it necessary to junk the entire multi-million-dollar communications system, which is based on decimals, regardless of the letters on the dial.) Nor was it a very useful suggestion that all the old word-prefixes be retained and another digit added behind them, creating "two-six" numbers. That would have been horribly expensive, too . . . although telephone people—once bitten, twice shy—aren't about to say we'll *never* have eight-digit numbers.

*What's the record? We don't really know, but perhaps it was set by "No. 1" of Tahlequah, Okla., which was in service at the same location from August 18, 1896, to August 26, 1929, serving Mr. and Mrs. J. W. McSpadden.

**Regardless of the alphabet, there are only 10 openings in the dial wheel, and two of them have no letters associated with them. Thus only 64 (8 × 8) letter combinations were available, and some of these couldn't be made words—although digraphs like "KL" were used as a stopgap at one time. Without digraphs, the number falls to 54; multiplying this by 10 possibilities for the digit in the third position gives us 540.

Another suggestion came from the anti-digit dialers. This would be to increase the number of area codes; and this would have been possible—but at what cost! In a large city, it would often be necessary to dial an area code, using the long distance network, just to call across town. And the supply of area codes was not inexhaustible, either.*

What it came down to was the simple fact that many people weren't going to be swayed by logic. They *liked* their old numbers, and that's all there was to it. Many prefixes carried an aura. If your lived in Beverly Hills, Calif., and had a "Crestview" number, you felt it brought prestige that might help you get your next movie job. How many people would identify you with Beverly Hills if your number started with "27"?

The turmoil was incredible, and it's only in the past few years that some of the older cities, such as New York, have finally eliminated two-five numbers from their directories. Southwestern Bell, serving a newer and perhaps more adventurous part of the nation, did not have to suffer the same quantity of flak. After all, as far as the Bell System is concerned, here is where ANC started—in Wichita Falls, Tex., and some surrounding communities. (Independent telephone companies began making the change a few years earlier than Wichita Falls.)

The ANC affair could remind telephone people, if any of them needed reminding, that customers are not to be pushed around. They can be marvelously

Dallas science demonstrator Glenn Scott traveled 1.5 million miles and talked to more than 8,500 groups before he retired.

*For example, a new area code—409—was assigned in 1983 to about 450,000 Bell and 200,000 independent main telephones surrounding metropolitan Houston, and the north of Texas 214 code is expected to need a similar split in 1985. By the year 2000, a completely new system may be needed in the United States.

cooperative when they can see that a change benefits them. And they can dig in their heels if they feel someone is playing games with them.

Like a housewife in Gainesville, Tex., for example. Central office repairman R. B. Head, in his reminiscences, referred to a "Don't Answer" study conducted by the Traffic Department in the mid-1930s. One phone wasn't answered on two call attempts within a 30-minute period, so the matter was turned over to the Plant Department to check possible equipment trouble. The test desk reached the customer, who answered in obvious exasperation:

"Yes, my telephone rings all right, and when it rang this morning I was giving the baby her bath, and then when it rang the second time I was taking my bath, and anyway I don't think it's any business of the telephone company what I am doing when I don't answer my telephone!"

(And the truth is, it isn't. But sometimes it's necessary to disturb people just to be sure service is up to standard; it was possible that people could call her number, hear a ringing signal and assume her telephone was ringing when it really wasn't. This was not unheard-of with some older equipment.)

Well, if what the customer does is none of the company's business, what the *company* does is certainly part of the public's business. And early on, Southwestern Bell began to spend a lot of time to let the customer know what was going on. This activity comes under the umbrella of "public relations."

The phrase "public relations" has acquired unpleasant connotations in some places because it has been used to mean its direct opposite—the cover-up. But in the telephone business, there's a wistful desire to have people know *everything* about the enterprise. Even if they don't particularly care!

The number of different media employed in this effort is impressive. There is paid advertising in newspapers, on radio and television, and occasionally on billboards. Other efforts include open houses, lecture demonstrations and the like. People in all five states are responsible for turning out news releases when these are called for.

Direct mail is employed extensively—after all, the company has a ready-made mailing list that can be screened to select exactly those customers who would be able to use a service. And perhaps the most cost-effective item of all is the monthly bill insert, which has been issued for decades and seems to be one of the best-read media of all.

Communication with employees to keep them aware of what's going on includes area newspapers, a company magazine—and other internal publications, call-in daily telephone reports and even closed-circuit television. The philosophy behind all this activity is that the well-informed employee is necessary in a high-technology enterprise and that he or she is the company's best ambassador to the public.

Does all this effort to communicate pay off in better customer attitude? Southwestern Bell is always trying to find out. In the fifties there were the customer attitude surveys, in which trained interviewers visited selected homes on a random-sample basis. These surveys were replaced in 1966 by the Service Attitude Measurement plan, and this in turn yielded in the seventies to TELSAM—Telephone Service Attitude Measurement—which employs a bank of telephones in a central location to canvass customers at random. Mail questionnaires are still used as a supplement to TELSAM, especially in canvassing employees (and also retirees—another important group of company ambassadors). Recently, a new

Southwestern Bell has always felt an obligation to communicate to customers and employees.

One Moment, Please, While the Operator Changes Reels...

TELEPHONE CUSTOMERS today, who fret if dial tone is delayed a few seconds when they start to make a call, may find it hard to believe the patience of customers 90 years ago.

G. W. Foster's reminiscences (compiled in 1908) of early Texas telephone history provide this example of the public's tolerance:

"J. C. Maben recalls that when he went to work in 1888 we had about 275 subscribers (in Dallas). The rates were: business connection, $5; residence, $4 flat. There were five or six long distance circuits. . . .

"The employees consisted of the local manager, an inspector who also strung the lines and put in telephones, three 'day' local operators, one 'night' local operator, one toll operator and a general roustabout, which Mr. Maben says was himself. . . .

"When B. H. Johnson, a fore-man, built a new toll line from Dallas to Fort Worth along about 1893, bringing in about three copper circuits, there was much rejoicing, and it was thought the long distance business had reached its zenith. But it was not very long before Johnson was back again stringing additional toll circuits, and also many new local lines, some of them 'large wires' (50 and 100 pair cables). This necessitated building a distributing frame. . . .

"After it was used about 12 months, it was the hardest proposition on earth to find a wire or get one to it.

"The central office was moved to Sixth and Houston streets along about '95 or '96. Then it was thought ample room had been provided for many years to come, this being one large room about 40 by 20 feet plus two more small rooms.

"It was an easy proposition to move in those days. First we notified all subscribers that on a certain day and hour we would move and that all telephones would be out of service for 24 hours. Then we would cut the switchboards loose, haul them into the new location, set them up and proceed to get busy connecting the lines to the various numbers, and in 24 hours, things would be running again, barring misconnections, cross-connections and lost wires.

"Our subscribers thought that this was very fast time and waited patiently.

"In Mr. Maben's opinion, if we were now (1908) to tell all our subscribers that they would be out of service 24 hours there would not be room enough in the different undertaking estab-lishments in Fort Worth to hold the suicides."

Well, good storytellers know when to draw the long bow. ■

It was an easy proposition to move in those days.

Cheaper Than Calling a Plumber?

ANYONE WHO DEALS with the public learns that at times the hardest part of the work is putting up with occasional injustice and getting on with the job. Witness the story told by Forrest Gilliland of Fort Worth, who retired in 1974 after 46 years' service.

When Gilliland was an exchange repairman at Amarillo, Tex., in the early forties, he was dispatched one day on a "telephone does not ring" report. The telephone involved was located in a garage apartment behind a house. Gilliland found that the trouble was a loose ground wire on the party line, and the faulty connection was in the apartment's bathroom.

Gilliland replaced the ground clamp to clear the trouble, and in reporting to the young woman who lived in the apartment, he pointed out to her that water had been leaking on the bathroom floor. Then he went on another trouble report.

When he called in at completion of this task, he was told to come back to the garage and pick up his supervisor. It turned out that the young woman in the garage apartment had called in again, this time to report that Gilliland had caused a water leak in the bathroom. Of course, he denied this, but he and his boss picked up some plumbing repair material and went back.

The young woman's mother-in-law, who lived in the main house, was present this time and carried on a constant conversation while the two telephone men repaired the water leak. When she was assured that the repair was complete, she left. As the door closed behind her, the young woman burst into tears.

She explained that her husband was in the Army and her mother-in-law had insisted she would have to move unless she reported that the telephone man had caused the water leak. She apologized profusely.

"I really felt elated as we left the premises," Gilliland recalls, "and my boss appeared to be pleased at how it turned out, too." ■

Step-by-Step? That's for the Birds

BACK IN 1951, we were busy converting the remaining Kansas manual central offices to step-by-step dial offices. We felt that was a great step forward for our customers," reflects Ralph Louis of Topeka, a retiree from the Kansas engineering department. "Now we're making bird houses out of the switch covers used in those dial offices. That's because these days, everything is going electronic."

Louis suggested the birdhouse idea when the Topeka Pioneer Life Member Club was thinking up community service projects. The now-useless covers were going to be taken to a dump because they weren't worth salvaging for their metal content, so the chief engineer gave the project the go-ahead.

Louis drove down to Wichita, where the Amherst office was being converted to ESS, and brought home about 400 of these cylindrical switch covers in the back of his station wagon. Then the Pioneers cut holes in

them for birds to enter, put a Pioneer emblem on them and gave them to the city parks system.

"At first, we made wren houses out of them—putting the covers in a horizontal position," Louis explains. "We built 50 of them and hung them in trees in the city parks, using telephone cable ties made of plastic. The people running the parks didn't want us to attach any kind of metal hangers to the trees because some day a chain saw might hit

that piece of metal when the tree was being taken down.

"Next, we got the idea of making birdhouses as a fundraiser. We sold several hundred dollars' worth of them in the next couple of years at $5 apiece, mostly to telephone people who thought they were cute. We sold them about as fast as we could make them. People bought them for nostalgia, I guess.

"Later on, we conceived the idea of hanging the covers in a vertical position and making the opening larger so bluebirds could use them. We've given the state 50 or 60 of these, and they've been placed in various parks around Kansas. The Fish and Game Commission told us in 1981 that these had been used almost 100 percent, and they asked us for more, which we were happy to supply."

One of the nation's big meat-packing firms used to brag in its advertising, "We use every part of the pig except the squeal." Topeka Pioneers are equally resourceful. ■

customer attitude survey was begun to take quarterly measurements of attitudes in five areas—pricing, rates, openness, management and service.

To make sure that all departments get into the communicating act, and not just some public relations specialists, Southwestern Bell has developed and is extremely proud of its community relations teams. These are interdepartmental units which deal on the local level with local problems, showing the company's desire and ability to be a good citizen and a good neighbor.

There is a concerted effort to see that, so far as possible, no citizen is excluded from the use of the telephone because of physical disabilities. Special telephones are available for the hearing-disabled, and those who are completely deaf can use devices which display light signals transmitted over telephone circuits. Even the person who can neither see nor hear can use the telephone. This is accomplished by hooking up a fan to alert that person to an incoming ring. A vibrating disk is used to receive Morse or other code signals, while another device allows the disabled person to reply in similar fashion.

Public telephones, which used to be too high for the average wheelchair user to reach, have been lowered, especially in areas like airports and bus stations. And in some company locations, teletypewriter service for the deaf has been installed so that such customers can communicate directly with the business office. This was first put into effect in the Little Rock–North Little Rock metropolitan area. Braille PBX switchboards, which enable blind attendants to receive incoming calls and transfer them to the desired party, are becoming increasingly common.

A complete report on all the things being done to serve the disabled today would make a book in itself, so this is only a hasty summary. The point is that Southwestern Bell is concerned about its public image but knows the first requirement for being well-thought-of is to *deserve* such a rating.

In becoming involved with such activity, the company is following the pattern set by Alexander Graham Bell himself, who considered his proudest claim to fame not the invention of the telephone, but the fact that he was a "teacher of the deaf." The Telephone Pioneers for years have emphasized service to the disabled, especially children.

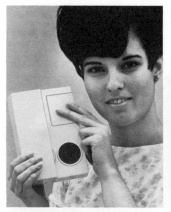

Above: This device helps customers who are deaf and blind use the phone by stimulating touch. Right: Alexander Graham Bell, top of the stairs at right, was a teacher of the deaf. The year was 1871.

In 1892, Southwestern Bell started its "Let's Talk" program as a concerted effort to get the public involved in an ongoing dialogue. Many changes were in the air; parts of the company were being split off to create a new marketing operation, and the remaining organization was being realigned. It was hoped that by creating a centralized question-answer group, the public's apprehensions (and misapprehensions) about what was happening could be addressed. The answering group was established in Little Rock, and customers were encouraged to call there (without charge) any time they had questions about the business.

"Let's Talk" assumed a new role, and new importance, when the decision was made in 1982 to break up the Bell System. All the public, not just the curious, now had a vested interest in finding out what was going on.

To meet the public need, Southwestern Bell undertook what Gerald D. Blatherwick, vice president-public relations, described as "the biggest explanation job any corporation has ever had to conduct." The information blitz involved a multipronged approach: public talks, meetings with key community leaders, advertising and news releases.

Oklahoma managers literally "walked the streets" visiting businesses and residential areas to discuss the implications of divestiture.

In Dallas, Houston and San Antonio, business and civic leaders, educators, city officials and representatives of minority and consumer groups were invited to meetings called " '83 Key Issues Seminars."

In Kansas, trained employee speakers made more than 600 public talks in 1983. Missouri prepared and distributed a booklet entitled *The Effect of Change.* A new Missouri Consumer Advisory Panel includes 12 consumer representatives to provide feedback on the company's information efforts.

In Arkansas, which has the nation's second highest percentage of residents 65 and older, special talks have been prepared addressing the interests of senior citizens.

If trying counts for anything, Southwestern Bell's customers should be some of the best-informed citizens in the nation — when it comes to telephone industry matters, anyway. ∎

West Memphis, Ark., 1977. Dr. Dexter Johnston of Bell Labs talks with high school students.

No "Mañana" for This General!

MOST CUSTOMERS are reasonable enough about necessary inconveniences in their telephone service, if the situation is explained to them.

Some customers won't accept explanations. They write letters or call up phone company and public officials. They report the problem to the local newspaper and get themselves feature stories complete with photos . . . and generally raise all kinds of sand.

And then there are customers who have some very persuasive counter arguments. Like the Mexican general at Piedras Negras back in 1921.

At that time, the border town's telephone service was provided by the Southwestern Bell exchange at Eagle Pass, Tex., across the Rio Grande. The two cities were connected by a cable which had absolutely no conductor pairs which were not in use.

Until someone's service was disconnected, no customers could be added in Piedras Negras; even service transfers would involve complicated re-arrangements of the circuits.

So a problem was created when the military office was moved from one location to another. Southwestern Bell was notified to move the telephone service also—"inmediatamente."

The Eagle Pass manager went across the river to explain that it would take several days, at least, to make such a change. But the explanation didn't convince the Army.

Two days later, the Southwestern Bell repairman went across the Rio Grande to clear a case of trouble. He was arrested by Mexican soldiers and taken to their barracks. The general had ordered that all Southwestern Bell people be held under guard

until the telephone was connected at the new office. The general had gone out of town. No soldier was about to disobey his order, and there was no one to appeal to.

Since the repairman longed to see Texas again, he did the only thing he could think of, rules or no rules. Escorted by four soldiers, he went to the old military office location, removed the telephone, brought it to the new location and connected it to a line already in use.

Then he rang the Piedras Negras customer whose line he had appropriated and explained the situation. This customer, fortunately, was understanding. He agreed to do without telephone service for a few days. Anything the general wanted was all right. The repairman heaved a sigh of relief as he was allowed to cross the river again. ■

PIONEER TELEPHONE COOPERATIVE

CITIZENS TELEPHONE CO.

ALLIED TELEPHONE COMPANY
ONE ALLIED DRIVE

Sunflower Telephone Co., Inc.

STEELVILLE TELEPHONE EXCH.

CHEROKEE

W.A.M.E.C.O. TELEPHONE COMPANY Inc

HINTON TELEPHONE COMPANY

OUR BUSINESS BROTHERS

CHAPTER TWELVE

ASK THE PROVERBIAL man-on-the-street: "Who supplies the country's telephone service?" He'll probably say "Bell Telephone," or something like that. But even after the transformation of the Bell System into AT&T and seven separate operating entities, these regional companies still are only seven of the 1,466 telephone companies operating in the United States.

Southwestern Bell people sometimes use the expression "the territory we serve" in speaking of five states—Arkansas, Kansas, Missouri, Oklahoma and Texas. However, the company would be strained to the breaking point if it suddenly had to provide the plant, manpower and financial resources represented by the 241 independent companies which operate 2,449 exchanges in those states— "the territory we serve."

Some of these independent companies are quite large. General Telephone, for example, has $21 billion in assets (about a sixth as much as AT&T before divestiture). Other large companies which operate in the five-state territory include United Telecommunications, Continental Telephone and Allied Telephone. At the other extreme, some are tiny—only a few dozen telephones.

But whether these companies are large or small, the people who own and run them are much the same breed as Southwestern Bell people. They're proud of the work they're doing, and they're determined to keep doing it better.

A Friend in Need Is a Friend Indeed

COOPERATION between Southwestern Bell and independent companies isn't confined to friendly discussions or even the coordination of operating techniques. There are times when material assistance is required in an emergency. And when this happens, it's given without reluctance.

In 1936, the owner of the independent exchange at Redfield, Ark., was relocating his central office. The move was from the second floor of one building to a new location in larger quarters. The owner was going to shut down service on a Saturday midnight, move his equipment to the new location, and hook it up. He expected service to be back to normal by early Sunday morning. Obviously such a maneuver required careful planning and timing.

He planned to reuse the main distributing frame. This steel frame consists of an array of vertical and horizontal strips fastened together. All the wires that enter the office from outside are terminated on this frame, and conductors run from the frame to the switching equipment. Also mounted on the mainframe are the protective fuses, or "heat coils," which keep unwanted stray electric current from damaging equipment.

The operation might have come off without a hitch if the telephone man hadn't hired some local help for the non-technical part of the move—local help that hadn't been briefed too carefully.

To move the mainframe, the owner had arranged for a boom to be installed on the roof of the old building. A block and tackle was suspended from this boom to lower the various items to the ground. After the cabling had been disconnected, the mainframe was pushed through a

window and the block-and-tackle attached to it.

With all in readiness, the owner shouted to his temporary helpers: "Let her go!" And they did.

The mainframe crashed to the ground and was bent out of shape. To add insult to injury, the small fuses were now scattered all through the grass.

Fortunately, the owner knew he could turn to Ma Bell. In response to his frantic call for help, a Southwestern Bell crew rushed over with a spare mainframe of the type he was using. Working throughout the night, they had his service back in shape by 10:30 a.m. that Sunday.

The neighborliness works both ways. When a small Bell town in Arkansas was extensively damaged by a tornado, the community dial office (unattended) was put out of service. Independent people from neighboring towns came in with materials, tools and know-how and restored emergency service to their neighbors. ∎

Today's independents are not competitors of Southwestern Bell in local exchange service. They have their exchanges, and Southwestern Bell has its exchanges. Lines of the two entities interconnect. When a customer calls from one company's territory to another's, he or she isn't aware of the differences because the facilities have been engineered to be "compatible."

It hasn't always been like this. In the early days of telephony, Bell and non-Bell companies often were bitter enemies, fighting to drive each other out of the more lucrative territory.* The public's sympathies were often with the independent because it was seen as the "underdog" compared to the gigantic Bell System. This attitude was especially prevalent in the Midwest, where the anti business philosophy of the Populists was well accepted.

One of the leaders in the establishment of the Missouri & Kansas Telephone Company, which became a Bell subsidiary, was Charles McDaniel. McDaniel has some stirring tales to tell of those days. Unfortunately, he is inclined to see every issue as black hats and white hats, good guys and bad guys; his recollections require some salting before they are swallowed whole. Taking this into account, however, there still seems little doubt that the Bell enterprises were more sinned against than sinning, and it required a good deal of determination and ingenuity to keep their franchises in effect.

Consider one sample of McDaniel's narrative, which might bear the title, "How the M&K Was Won." He talks about starting up the Hannibal, Mo., exchange in 1879. After he put together the required financial backing, the next step was to get a city franchise. Unexpected opposition arose from the Western Union company, represented by J. R. Woodward, Burlington Railroad's general superintendent, and W. B. Jones, superintendent of telegraph.

Western Union knew its way around. For the attorney to represent them before the city council they hired George M. Harrison—who was a member of the city council! Niceties like "conflict of interest" apparently didn't bother anyone in those days.

But McDaniel was not without political resources: "Col J. T. K. Hayward, formerly general superintendent of the Burlington, and an intimate friend, was a member of the council and worked in my interest. He and Mr. Harrison were about as far apart politically and socially as men can be, and were bitter enemies.

"There were oratory and fireworks for a while and it looked as though the police would be needed. It was the old Hannibal boy versus a great and overbearing corporation—I finally won out."

If the point isn't clear, McDaniel himself was the "old Hannibal boy," since he was born in that city. This would have been one of the few such encounters when he could enlist local sympathies in his behalf—most of the time a local citizen would be fronting for the competition and McDaniel would be cast in the role of the interloper.

"This was the first of my 35 years of fights," McDaniel observes, "and my present associates can understand how it is that I can now enter into a fight and take a licking so gracefully; the years of practice account for it."

McDaniel also tells how he was riding in a buggy with Hannibal's Mayor W. A. Munger when the latter observed:

Independent company telephone poles were sometimes makeshift in the early days.

*This was chiefly when the two companies were trying to serve the same territory. As far back as October 10, 1882, the St. Louis *Globe-Democrat* reported that telephone communications had been established between St. Louis and Alton, Ill., across the Mississippi River; the two companies involved agreed to split the cost of the line connecting their exchanges.

"Mack, a man could make big money by infringing the patents of the Bell Company and getting into a fight with them."*

The relation between the Bell companies and the non-Bell enterprises went through several phases. In the beginning, Western Union, which inadvisedly had rejected an offer to buy the Bell patent rights, decided instead to drive Bell to the wall by establishing the rival Gold & Stock Company. For a while it appeared that WU might succeed, but Bell brought a successful suit for patent infringement. Thereafter, for the 17-year life of the patents, Bell had things pretty much its way, but other entrepreneurs were only biding their time.

G. W. Foster's reminiscences of early telephone days in Texas and Arkansas include this passage:

"At the end of 1891, the Southwestern Telegraph & Telephone Company was the only company operating telephone exchanges in Texas. There was one opposition exchange at Fort Smith, Ark., which had been built by what was then known as the Pan Electric Telephone Company, prior to the settlement of the Drawbaugh litigation, which was decided in favor of the Bell patents. This opposition exchange was considered of too little importance at that time to warrant an expensive infringement suit, and it was then the only opposition telephone exchange in operation *in the United States*."

One wonders how Foster could make such a sweeping statement about the situation in all 44 states and several territories, including what would become Oklahoma. At any rate, the tolerated competitor in Fort Smith managed to hang on until 1911, when Southwestern Tel & Tel bought the property of the Southern Telephone Company of Fordyce, Ark. The deal involved 68 exchanges and 9,000 subscribers in Arkansas and Louisiana. Picking up Pan Tel at this time, SWT&T combined its operations with the Bell lines. The next year the Little Rock Telephone Company, "only remaining competition in the city," sold out to SWT&T.

The Pan Electric Company was a thorn in the SWT&T flesh in several locations. The Little Rock-based corporation had the Fort Worth territory to itself for only a short period after it opened for business in 1881. Pan Electric came in

G. W. Foster

*McDaniel tells both these anecdotes twice, a few pages apart, in his memoirs, and the accounts differ in small details. This helps prove the adage that memory is a treacherous servant.

Arkadelphia, Ark., 1913. The Southwestern Bell Telegraph & Telephone Company building.

You Win; I'll Buy the Beer

RIVALRY between local telephone companies didn't always involve a Bell entity. In fact, in the early days many a struggle for survival matched up two or more small independents.

For example, at the turn of the century, A. A. Sharp and H. T. Taylor owned the Larned (Kan.) Telephone Company, which had an exclusive franchise in the town. C. E. Clutter, also of Larned, and E. S. Lindas owned the Rock Telephone Company, operating out of Pawnee Rock, which was extending toll lines to Great Bend and Larned.

But Sharp wasn't about to allow Clutter-Lindas to connect its lines to his system, or even to construct lines into Larned. He said he'd have the law on the interlopers if they tried.

Clutter-Lindas, however, did just that on a Sunday, a day when the courthouse was closed and Sharp couldn't get a restraining order to stop them.

Sharp took his defeat with good grace. "All right," he said, "I'm licked. You can connect with my lines; all I ask is that

I get to make the first toll call from Larned."

And he did. On March 2, 1902, Sharp called the M. K. Wolf Brewery in Ellinwood and ordered a keg of beer. It was shipped out on the afternoon train.

Incidentally, the Rock Telephone Company later bought out the Larned exchange, extended its lines to other points, and changed its name to Arkansas Valley Telephone Company. In 1917 the firm was sold to the Bell interests. ■

Wandering Switchboard

INFRINGEMENT of the Bell patents on telephone equipment was not taken lightly. To protect their interests, the patent owners didn't hesitate to use the law.

And so it came to pass that a switchboard in use at Peabody, Kan., was determined to be in violation of the patent and an order was issued to seize it.

But when agents appeared on

the scene, telephone service in Peabody had been discontinued and no one knew what had happened to the switchboard. The agents spent quite a while trying to run down various leads and finally gave up their search.

This was in 1883. Several years later—after the original Bell patents had expired—the Butler County Telephone and Electric Company established a small

telephone exchange at El Dorado, Kan. And lo and behold, the switchboard being used was unmistakable: It was the one long missing from Peabody.

Someone must have known where the switchboard was all that time, and how it traveled the 30 miles from Peabody to El Dorado. But whoever knew wasn't telling, and the mystery was never solved. ■

1884 and signed up about 300 subscribers—probably as many as or more than the Southwestern Company had. A patent suit put them out of business in 1886.

Pan Electric also operated in Dallas from 1885 to 1886, barely getting under way before it had to cease operations.

New competition arose for the Southwestern Company in Dallas in 1907. A group of citizens was granted a franchise by the city commission to establish and operate the Dallas Automatic Telephone Company.

The Southwestern Company was infuriated and demanded a citywide referendum on the issue. Full-page advertisements appeared in the local papers to dramatize the evils of having two telephone companies operating in the same city. Their catchy slogan was "One Flag, One Wife, One Phone."

SWT&T sold its Dallas exchange October 1, 1918, to its rival, and the combined operation was renamed the Dallas Telephone Company—an independent. Southwestern Bell started up again in Dallas a few years later, however. The competition was not finally eliminated until 1925, when Southwestern Bell bought the Dallas Telephone Company.

Dallas, circa 1920. The logo of the Dallas Telephone Co., seen here on vehicles, displayed an automatic dial.

But the typical independent telephone company was not a competitor of the Bell interests; rather it tended to make its presence felt in smaller cities and in rural areas. Bell people didn't see the situation quite the same way. To many Bell people, their campaign for "universal service" necessarily implied that one company must own and operate all the country's telephones, and a policy of wholesale acquisition got under way.

To protect their interests, the independents organized the United States Independent Telephone Association at a June 22, 1897, meeting in Detroit. The 400 people who attended hardly constituted a group of Johnny-come-latelies. There are records of independent telephone companies dating as far back as 1889, and some of these companies had been operating for several years previously. There were manufacturers, shut out of the Bell company market, who were eager to supply instruments to the independents.

The situation is well expressed in an article which appeared in the *Public Utilities Fortnightly* for September 25, 1947:

"...The telephone was not simply a gadget which made life a bit easier. It was a thing which changed ways of life. ... New customs were made possible and new methods of doing this came into being.

"The telephone was, in short, too important in the lives of many people to be left to the control of any one set of people. The whole country was unwilling to wait until Mr. Bell and his associates got around to supplying it with telephones. It wanted, and needed, its telephones now. It got them in very many cases from locally organized and locally owned companies—the independents."

The stage was set for a donnybrook, and Bell and non-Bell set to with a will. The independents had two major grievances: Bell was building up a large long distance network and would not allow independents to connect with it; Bell was gobbling up every independent in sight. When the situation is viewed dispassionately, it's hard not to sympathize with the independents.

But the situation changed in 1910. That was the year AT&T acquired a controlling (30 percent) interest in Western Union, the same outfit that had once haughtily refused to buy the Bell patents when they were offered for a mere $100,000. There may have been some poetic justice in AT&T's triumph over its adversary, but the virtual merger of the two firms raised the specter of a communications monopoly. The postmaster general, the attorney general and prominent congressmen discussed the possibility that the government might take over Bell.

AT&T President Theodore Vail tried to stave off the assault by issuing a statement of Bell System policy: Under certain conditions (non-competing exchanges, for instance) Bell would permit interconnection by independents with its long distance network.

This sounded good, but the independents found that even Vail couldn't turn AT&T around that quickly. Individual Bell System operating companies often dragged their feet. Furthermore, on examination, Vail's offer turned out not to be as lucrative an arrangement for the independents as they had anticipated.

E. C. Blomeyer, writing in the *Public Utilities Fortnightly,* sums up how it looked to the independents:

INDEPENDENT COMPANY
STATISTICS
1982
Annual Report

Industry Relations   Southwestern Bell

"This expression of policy turned out to be more shadow than substance ... Little progress was made under it in bringing about actual Bell toll line connections with independent companies. Some of the Bell System operating companies were not disposed to go along with policy; the contractual terms offered independents were in many cases unsatisfactory, and the whole proposition sort of bogged down as time went on."

Then came a truly profound change—a watershed in Bell-independent relations. No doubt influenced by the dire threats of a government takeover, Nathan C. Kingsbury, a vice president of AT&T, made a startling proposal to the attorney general of the United States.

Here was Kingsbury's offer, dated December 13, 1913:
☐ Bell promised to dispose of all its Western Union holdings;
☐ Bell promised to provide connection of Bell System long distance lines to independent telephone systems, where there was no local competition; and
☐ Bell agreed not to purchase any more independent telephone companies except as approved by the Interstate Commerce Commission.

This proposal (known ever since as the "Kingsbury Commitment") was to a representative of the federal government, it should be noted. Vail's earlier proposal was to the independents themselves and, however well intentioned, hardly had legal standing.

The attorney general accepted Kingsbury's proposal. AT&T did dispose of its Western Union holdings in due course; interconnection with non-competing telephone companies became a fact; and perhaps equally significant, a clear line had been drawn for the first time between "mine" and "thine." From that December day forward, no Bell company has acquired an independent exchange without getting federal approval—first the ICC, then the FCC—and also that of the state regulatory commissions involved.

The rule has sometimes worked minor hardships. State commissions, bowing to public demand, have sometimes ordered Southwestern Bell to take over exchanges it didn't really want because they were unprofitable. In trade for these white elephants, the Bell company would be compelled to dispose of something it wanted to keep.

It is true that even this self-restraint, and bowing the corporate neck under the government yoke, did not stave off a successful government antitrust suit in the 1970s. But an important point should not be overlooked: For 70 years, under the terms of the Kingsbury Commitment, this country's telephone service grew to become the envy of the civilized world. Everyone benefited—Bell, independent companies and, most of all, the customers.

Two final items illustrate the harmony which has developed between the erstwhile competitors:

Fifty years after the United States Independent Telephone Association was founded, the Bell System's Telephone Hour presented a special broadcast October 13, 1947, from the stage of Chicago's Medina Temple as a feature of USITA's annual convention there.

And on March 2 and 3, 1953, when nationwide dialing began to take form, groups from AT&T and USITA met to discuss plans for integrating Bell and independent plant. Thus, any customer would eventually be able to dial any other customer, whether the two telephones were both Bell, both independent or one of each.

Peace. It's wonderful. ■

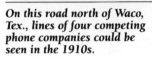

On this road north of Waco, Tex., lines of four competing phone companies could be seen in the 1910s.

THE PUBLIC BE...SERVED!

CHAPTER THIRTEEN

IT IS CONTENDED that if there is to be no competition, there should be public control.
— *Theodore N. Vail, 1907*

People sometimes say that Bell invented the telephone, but Vail invented the Bell System. Twice president of the parent company, he spent the years from 1907 to 1919 shaping the nationwide organization according to his vision of the future. He recognized the wastefulness of duplicative telephone service, but he recognized, at the same time, that if there was to be a telephone monopoly it should be a *regulated* monopoly. Regulation would take the place of competition in serving the public interest—in keeping service standards up and rates as low as was consistent with the financial health of the supplier.

The ideas he expressed were not original with Vail. What made them unusual at the time he first expressed them was that he was a businessman. Many people who were not in business—at least, not in a position to prosper from a business monopoly—saw the situation the same way. Political leaders, especially in the Midwest and South, made political hay (votes) out of expressed hostility to Big Business, regardless of what their private convictions may have been.

Telephone service was not especially singled out for this antagonism. There were the railroads and the gasworks and the grain elevators and the emergent electric utilities to go after. If the telephone business seemed unusually subject to government scrutiny, it could have been because it was perceived as an interloper come out of the East, like the railroads, and yet too young and puny to put up any serious resistance. At first the long distance portion of the business (which fell under the supervision of the Interstate Commerce Commission) was too small to worry the city fathers. But the local operation, with its overhead wires fastened over rooftops or along poles on the public streets, was a sitting duck for ordinances and rules which could be aimed merely to control . . . or to eliminate.

In this atmosphere of suspicion, often inflamed by editorials in the Populist-leaning newspapers of the time, those firms which were apparently locally owned were looked upon with favor; Bell companies, even if they got there first, were considered intruders. And when the local firms went broke because of inadequate rates and incompetent management, and the Bell company bought them out, the political hue and cry was something fearful to behold.

Municipal franchising was an obvious outgrowth of the situation, but even so the city fathers often suspected that the city slickers were charging all the traffic could bear—and then some. Rates were written into franchises in some cases, and then would come the discovery that the rates at Siwash down the road a few miles were 25 cents a month lower.

An example of this attitude comes in a 1900 news item from Wichita, Kan. The city council put the Missouri & Kansas Telephone Company on notice that its franchise would expire April 1, 1901. By that time, said the council, the company would be required to have removed all its poles and wires from the city streets. Police were instructed to arrest any company employees doing any work in the streets other than what was necessary to remove the offending equipment. Yes, the dispute was eventually settled, but it gives the flavor of relations with some city governments of the period.

Another news item reports that in 1907 a bill creating a St. Louis city public utilities commission, to regulate all public utility corporations, was introduced in the municipal assembly. The measure's proponents said some method must be found to control rates charged for gas, electricity and telephone service. (The city owned the water system.)

So the cities had their franchising power—and used it. But there still seemed to be a need for some type of authority to be sure that utility rates were uniform throughout the state for equivalent scope of service. This led to the establishment of state commissions, empowered to approve rate structures and set other rules to ensure that customers were treated even-handedly.

Apparently Wisconsin, in 1907, was the first state to establish a commission specifically to regulate public utilities, including telephone service. Other states soon followed Wisconsin's example.

In Southwestern Bell territory, the state of Arkansas may have been the first with such a commission, although the trail through a thicket of statutes is difficult to follow. The Board of Railroad Commissioners, established by an act of 1883, was followed by the Railroad Commission of Arkansas, which in turn gave way to the Arkansas Corporation Commission in 1919; this body had telephone service spelled out in its responsibilities. However, it appears that one of the earlier commissions had begun regulating telephone service some time between 1900 and 1910. The current telephone regulatory agency is the Arkansas Public Service Commission, established in 1945.

The history of regulation in the other four states is easier to follow. Oklahoma was certainly in the forefront of these and may actually have anticipated Arkansas with an effective mechanism. The Oklahoma Corporation Commission was created at the beginning of statehood, dated from adoption of the state constitution November 16, 1907. The ninth article of that constitution created the commission and spelled out that its jurisdiction covered "*transmission* and transportation companies doing business in this state." The clarity and cogency of this article is something to marvel at; it's still the law of the state and has not required any change to keep it current for more than 70 years.

The Kansas Public Utilities Commission came into existence next, in the year 1912; it was followed a year later by the Missouri Public Service Commission. Each body had jurisdiction over telephone service from its inception. The Missouri commission has retained its title throughout the years; the Kansas PUC later became the Public Service Commission (1925) and, in 1933, the Kansas Corporation Commission, its present name.

For decades thereafter, Texas and Iowa shared an unusual distinction: They were the only two states which left jurisdiction over telephones to the municipalities affected. On July 4, 1963, Iowa's new state Commerce Commission took over this power in the Hawkeye State, and Texas became the last holdout.

The Texas Public Utilities Commission finally went into operation September 1, 1976, following passage of enabling legislation by the state legislature 15 months previously.

Even before the first state commissions came into power, the federal government exercised some authority over the telephone business through the Interstate Commerce Commission, which, as the name implies, had jurisdiction over communications which crossed state lines. Since the Bell System was involved from the beginning in interstate enterprise, it naturally had to check out its actions with the ICC, which prescribed methods for keeping records under the Uniform System of Accounts.

Under the New Deal, the ICC was supplanted by the Federal Communications Commission, which had nothing to do with railroads and buses but everything to do with telegraphy, telephony, radio and eventually television. The FCC has been a stern taskmaster for telephone companies, and its ruling in the "CI II" case (Computer Inquiry II) led to the separation of equipment sales organizations from Southwestern Bell and other operating companies as of January 1, 1983.

Does regulation mean that government (federal, state or local) actually manages the business regulated? Of course not. But it does mean that every significant act is subject to commission scrutiny. Regulatory commissions have the power to approve or disapprove rates, but that is only the beginning of their authority.

In every dispute that comes before them, the commissions have the responsibility to determine where the public interest lies, always bearing in mind that a utility which is not earning an adequate return cannot, in the long run, give adequate service. The problem is to determine what is an adequate return. This is the subject of many scholarly dissertations and many heated commission hearings, not to mention court suits after the commission issues its decisions.

The Carterfone made by the now-defunct Carter Electronics Corporation of Dallas. The corporation's successful petition to hook its equipment to the Bell network eventually led to the breakup of the Bell System.

But this is hardly the same as actually running the business. The United States has had one experience of what this is like. On July 31, 1918, the federal government assumed control of the country's telephone system by a wartime act of Congress. This condition lasted one year to the day. When the companies were turned back to their owners on July 31, 1919, it was generally agreed that service standards had slipped. There was no question that long distance rates had increased 20 percent.

The mistake was not repeated. In World War II and all subsequent wars, this country's telephone system has remained in private hands and has done yeoman work supporting the country's needs. ■

"ONE BIG HAPPY FAMILY"??

CHAPTER FOURTEEN

So far this book might have given the impression that, among telephone people, everyone loves everyone else—the boss and the bossee always get along swimmingly. Not so. Telephone people are human beings, prone to disagreements and misunderstandings, possessed of tempers that can flare up. Injustices occur on both sides of an argument.

What is notable about the telephone business is that with the rise and maturing of unions there has been, not a mellowing, but a realization that both parties have a stake in getting along, and that they share an obligation to think of the public welfare as well as their own.

Yes, there have been strikes—many of them, over the course of years. It would be hazardous to predict that there will never be another. Still, the trend is clearly toward peaceful settlements.

Management has learned a salutary lesson, and not since the earliest days of the business has it tried to employ strikebreakers, local or imported, when a walkout occurs. The management force itself provides man- and woman-power for a skeleton crew which tries, albeit in a relatively inexperienced way, to keep service going. Both sides know this crew wishes heartily to get out of those jobs and back to their real jobs. By and large, the strikers accept the situation; in many Southwestern Bell towns the pickets and the management people can be observed engaged in guarded, but not uncordial, conversation. Just as long as the conversation doesn't touch on the reason they're both there. . . .

The Truth, the Whole Truth...

THELMA KREEGER, who retired in 1973 with almost 31 years' service, was a union representative for the last 22 of those years, which she spent with the Accounting Department in Arkansas. Of all her experiences as a union representative, this one stands out most in her memories.

"The company wanted to discipline this little girl because she had done several things wrong, and we decided to bring a formal grievance. So eventually we marched in to Jim Hughes' office—he was the auditor, the top man in Arkansas accounting. There were the girl involved, the regular steward—another woman, who happened to be wearing a tight-fitting raincoat— a plant man also representing the union, Mr. Hughes and I.

"We started to go over the list of things the girl was supposed to have done, and the girl interrupted. She said: 'That's not all I've done,' and she went on to tell about some other things none of us had heard about.

"Just about that time the buttons started popping off the steward's raincoat—I don't know what caused that, but I think she got excited over what the girl was saying—and Mr. Hughes grabbed his head and spun clear around in his chair.

"You see, what the little girl had told us was a pretty serious offense, and she didn't even know the difference. I asked the plant man to take her out in the hall while I gathered up my things and bowed out of Mr. Hughes' office.

"Well, that was one case the union didn't win, and small wonder. But I have to laugh every time I think about it."

Mrs. Kreeger went on to become more than just a local union spokesman. For 17 years, she was on the national bargaining committee for the CWA-CIO, as well as being a bargainer in Southwestern Bell contract negotiations. But the incident of the girl who wouldn't stop talking is her most vivid memory of her union career. ∎

When was the first telephone strike in Southwestern Bell territory? It may have been the one in the fall of 1900 against Southwestern Telegraph & Telephone Company. A majority of the operators went out at Houston, San Antonio, Temple and Waco. A colorful account of what happened appears in the memoirs of G. W. Foster, assistant to the general manager; unfortunately, it is decidedly one-sided and does not even hint at what caused the walkout. Nor does Foster tell how the strike was settled.

The end of the Texas strike didn't mean a long period of labor peace. There was a strike among the "outside men" at Kansas City which started September 1, 1906, and was not called off until two years later. The company report of the incident describes the strike as a "dismal failure."

And in 1907, according to the memoirs of Mima Blanchard, then an Oklahoma City operator, a union organizer came to town and would appear to have made headway for a time. In the summer of 1913 there was an operators' strike in St. Louis. In 1917 operators went on strike for three months in Fort Smith; it was the first operators' strike in Arkansas.

This period—during and immediately after World War I—was a time of labor unrest everywhere, not just in the telephone business. There was a streetcar strike in St. Louis, and the company hired "as many automobiles as it could find" to transport operators to their jobs. A month later a "general strike" in Kansas City caused the company to resort to the same expedient.

And with the war over, there was a "second strike of telephone operators," apparently confined to St. Louis, in the summer of 1919.

The advent of the Depression might have discouraged union activity except for a counterbalancing factor: It swept the New Deal of President Franklin Roosevelt into power. One of the early creations of this administration was the Wagner Act, which sheltered union organizers from management harassment. As a result, unions sprang up everywhere, including the telephone business. At first the organizations created in Southwestern Bell were comparatively docile, and then the outbreak of World War II made labor disruptions appear unpatriotic.

But once the war was over the wraps were off. The National Federation of Telephone Workers, as it was then called, staged the first nationwide strike in telephone history. It began April 7, 1947, and lasted 41 days. A 10-day strike occurred in 1950 (not involving Southwestern Bell to any extent), and for a while it seemed that a strike every three years was an established routine. By now the national union had changed its name to the Communications Workers of America, affiliated with the CIO.

A strike in 1953 led Missouri's governor, Phil Donnelly, to implement the King-Thompson Act, which prohibited utility strikes in the state. That worked only once; the union forces used their legislative muscle to get the act repealed.

After this, there was a period of relative calm, and then a 1968 strike began on April 15 and was not completely settled until September 21, setting a record up to that time. For Southwestern Bell, however, the walkout ended after 18 days.

Three years later there was again a nationwide walkout. It began July 14, 1971. Although it was over in six days for most telephone employees, including those of Southwestern Bell, the plant unit of New York Telephone smashed the old record by holding off ratifying a contract for seven months, until February 16, 1972.

What had to be the last nationwide strike in Bell System history ran for 21 days in the summer of 1983. All three major telephone unions (Communications

Workers of America, Telecommunications International Union and International Brotherhood of Electrical Workers) took part. Besides the customary disagreement over wages, there were special circumstances about this strike. For it was indeed the last time the Bell System would bargain collectively; in a few more months there would be no Bell System.

"What will happen to our jobs? And what will happen to us?" This was the primary concern of the workers. Management's previous reassurances were not enough; the unions wanted the terms spelled out in the contract, which would be binding not only on the new, greatly diminished AT&T but on the "divested" operating companies as well.

In the settlement, the unions got a package of victories. In addition to improvements in the pension plan, these concessions were included in the package:
□ The companies are to provide two types of training programs—career development training for employees with at least a year of net credited service, and job-displacement training to help employees whose jobs might be phased out because of technological progress.
□ The Supplemental Income Protection Program was improved to provide additional compensation to employees who might lose their jobs because of technological changes or other force-adjustment needs.
□ A new Voluntary Income Protection Program was set up for employees faced with layoffs or permanent reassignments. Payments under VIPP can include reimbursement of some expenses, including relocation and retraining.
□ Medical insurance coverage was extended for six months for any employee who leaves the company under provisions of a force-adjustment plan.
□ A new mortgage money plan was established to provide funds at fixed rates for as much as 95 percent of the value of the property.
□ All active and retired employees already receiving concession services received the terminal equipment they had in place in their homes as of July 1, 1983.

In all bargaining sessions, the latest as well as those that went before, the negotiators for both sides face a difficult task. For the union, the goal is to get the best deal possible without resorting to the unpleasantness of a strike; for management the objective is to achieve a settlement that will not only keep the business sound and be fair to employees but be acceptable to regulatory bodies and the public they represent.

Contrary to a statement frequently made by the uninformed, a regulated telephone company cannot automatically pass on its increased costs—for materials or labor—in the form of higher rates; it must get permission to do so. Regulators are always on the alert for any suggestion that negotiators are not bargaining in good faith—and in this case "good faith" must include the interest of the public.

In recent years a new spirit of cooperation has developed between management and non-management people in the telephone business, exemplified by the "Quality of Work Life" program. QWL, as it is commonly referred to, involves getting representatives of both sides together on a regular and frequent schedule to discuss problems and to seek together to solve those problems. A byproduct of the meetings is that the participants find there is more agreement than disagreement among them on a number of issues. QWL can help maintain labor peace. ■

Thankee for the Small Apples...

THE DEMANDS—"requests" might be a better word—of union negotiators in early days were modest indeed, but they did mark the opening of a dialogue between management and non-management. And the discussions marked a turning point from the patriarchal attitude of earlier days—"We know what's best for you, but if you don't like it, you always have the right to quit."

Lillie Richards, who died in January 1982 at Nacogdoches, Tex., got her first job as a Jacksonville, Tex., telephone operator in 1911. She quit several times for various personal reasons, then settled down at Nacogdoches in 1927 for a career as an operator. Twenty-one years after her retirement in 1960, Lillie could still name many of the traffic and plant people with whom she had worked, and she summed up:

"We all cooperated in our work and felt as if we were one big family. A number of times when I would look over our clean, neatly dressed people, I would think the company should be proud of their employees.

"Later, we were union organized. I was chairperson for a while, and we needed a few changes made. I called Mr. Jackson (district traffic superintendent) and asked him to come out and have a meeting with us. He wanted an idea of what was to be discussed so he could be prepared when he came to our meeting.

"When the meeting was called to order, the first item mentioned was some improvement to help cool the office. We had three ceiling fans, which were not very effective. In those days, we had a metal plate to which our transmitters were connected. The piece sat on our chest with a strap around our neck to hold it in place. I would have heat (rash) over my face and neck so badly I could hardly stand myself.

"Our improved cooling was three large washtubs placed on the floor at our backs with a tall stand placed by the side of each tub. A large electric fan was placed on the top of each stand. The ice company would deliver large blocks of ice and place them in the tubs. The fans were then turned on, and the cool damp air blew on us—mostly on our heads.

"We asked to have our floors covered and our worn cane-bottom chairs refinished to keep them from tearing our clothes and scratching. We also asked for better lights so our shadows would not be over us while we were trying to write ticket details.

"We also needed a small fan placed in our two-foot by four-foot toilet room. We got a six-inch fan and not any light; when the door was closed, it was as dark as if you were blindfolded.

"We got a couch, one small table, two straight chairs and a stand made of three pieces of lumber placed together, which made a shelf for our needs. A rod was placed underneath the shelf for us to hang our coats or wraps on.

"I was sure Mr. Jackson came prepared, for what we received did help some." ∎

Manhattan,
Kansas 1951

READINESS TO SERVE

CHAPTER FIFTEEN

More than 1,000 Southwestern Bell men have saved South Texas from what could have been total paralysis. These wire-splicing, spurred heroes still are wading water and climbing poles throughout the vast flood-wrecked Rio Grande Valley area to restore vital lifelines more than a week after Hurricane Beulah wrote a new destruction chapter in Texas weather history. Before I left Harlingen . . . I turned to E. H. Sonntag, construction foreman over a San Antonio crew. "When will you get through with your job?" He quickly replied, "When the last phone in this valley is working."

—*Dallas Times Herald, October 1, 1967.*

Heroes? Heroines? (That's what the reporter called the operators who stuck to their posts and never stopped trying to get the calls through.) Yes, many telephone people qualify for such praise, and some have Vail Medals to prove it.*

But who's to define the terms? Surely no organization can claim to be made up 100 percent of heroes and heroines. Yet when disasters knock out or endanger service, Southwestern Bell employees always respond to the call. They work long hours, sometimes under grueling conditions and occasionally to the point of actual exhaustion.

It won't do to make too much of this—to imply that only Bell people, or only telephone people as a whole, are unselfishly devoted to the public well-being.

*Vail Medals, discussed at greater length in the appendix, are awarded to telephone people who display heroism in public service.

Eureka Springs, Ark., 1913. The aftermath of a telephone office fire.

Certainly employees of other public utilities share this attitude. With that acknowledged, however, the record of Southwestern Bell people in maintaining and restoring service has indeed been outstanding.

An instance, only one of thousands which might be cited, is the major fire in Fort Worth in the spring of 1908. The blaze raged out of control for four hours on a Saturday afternoon, making a clean sweep of a half-square-mile area on the edge of the business district. J. C. Maben, who later became Fort Worth district manager, reported:

"Everything the telephone company had in the burnt area . . . was destroyed. Our work of reconstruction started immediately after the fire department allowed us to enter the burning area. By Monday our north-south and east-west leads were up and subscribers were receiving service. It took all Saturday night, Sunday and Sunday night to do this, *but the Bell Company has always been equal to any emergency.*"

A proud boast, justified at the time it was made and since that time. But in the earliest days of the telephone, the claim might have been questioned. Consider the case of Junction City, Kan., where the exchange building was badly damaged by fire September 12, 1888, and the switchboard was rendered unusable. It took the Missouri & Kansas Telephone Company seven weeks to order, ship, install and hook up a new switchboard to service Junction City's 46 subscribers.

Such a delay would be both inexcusable and incredible today. Of course in 1888 the M&K was expanding so rapidly it had not had time (nor, probably, capital) to build up a stockpile of replacement equipment. What's more, at the time neither the company nor the employees nor the customers had yet recognized telephone service as indispensable to the community.

Maben's boast—"the Bell Company has *always* been equal to any emergency"—isn't literally true, then. It took many years, years he must have overlooked, before today's proud tradition was established . . . a tradition exemplified by what occurred in the St. Louis Jefferson dial building in 1939.

Besides the dial equipment, the Jefferson building also housed a substantial operating force, since it was the principal trunking unit which linked the city's numerous central offices.

When a high-voltage power transformer in a basement vault began to malfunction, the resultant heat caused vaporized oil to penetrate all the building's electrical conduits and ducts. Thus when the transformer finally burned out, the oil was ignited and an explosion rocked the entire building.

Plaster was blown off walls and ceilings. Damage was especially severe to the women's restroom; there, tile had been dislodged from the walls and floors, and the ceramic fixtures were reduced to fragments.*

A personnel check made immediately after the blast indicated that all operators were accounted for and all were working at the switchboard. To be sure there were no injuries, the chief operator asked the women who had been in the restroom whether they were hurt. Fortunately, no one was. But when one of the operators was asked: "What happened in there?" her reply was: "I don't really know, but it certainly was different!"

Repairing the damage to the Jefferson building cost more than a million dollars. But customer service was hardly affected. Not one operator left her post.

They were not, and are not, superhuman, these telephone men and women. Intelligent and courageous leadership—or its opposite—can play a role in the way people react to emergencies.

There is the tale of the male traffic supervisor, endowed with more zeal than common sense, who observed that the operators were not taking fire drills seriously. To create a dramatic lesson, he arranged to have some smudge pots set off behind the switchboard just as he sounded the alarm. He proved his point that the operators were not prepared to react to a real fire; they panicked, ran in all directions, and several of them were slightly injured. He also proved that he wasn't ready for the authority he had been granted, and he was quietly shipped out a week or so after the incident.

Contrast that with the case of the supervisor who assembled a crew of plant men and took them out in a large boat into Galveston Bay to repair an underwater cable break. It was a winter's day, and in winter even gulf water is dauntingly cold. The boss observed that the men were grumbling and suspected that if he sat in the boat while he ordered them to jump overboard, he might have a mutiny on his hands. So when they reached the trouble spot, he said calmly, "Okay, fellows, let's go," and went over the side himself. Not wanting to be shown up, all the work group followed the boss' example, and the cable was quickly repaired.

Galveston provides another example of leadership in times of stress; this time

Wellington, Kan., 1892. The remains of a switchboard after a "cyclone."

*As a result of this accident, all such transformers throughout the company were inspected to be sure there was no hazard, and most of them were relocated.

it was the 1900 hurricane in which an estimated 8,000 people lost their lives.

At the height of the storm and the flood that accompanied it, water stood four feet deep in the manager's office, the storeroom and the terminal equipment room, all of which were on the first floor of the telephone building. Windows were blown in on all sides of the building. Portions of the switchboards (on the second floor) were soaked with water. Telephone pole lines throughout the city were badly damaged or destroyed, and there was a tangled mass of wires and cables in all directions.

Manager Herbert Snelling forbade the day operators to leave the building, a wise decision for more reasons than one. In the first place, it was far too dangerous—a bookkeeper who attempted to reach her home never got there but was added to the long list of drowning victims. In the second place, it was impossible for the night operators to get to the building, so the day force had to be available to handle what few communications lines were still working.

To keep up the spirit of the operators, Snelling had them sit on a broad iron stairway in the north end of the building. Then he got them singing and telling stories. The strategy worked only in part; some of the young women fainted and others became hysterical as the storm raged outside. But without Snelling's outwardly calm demeanor, there probably would have been a complete panic. And the telephone building, damaged as it was, became the central point for citywide restoration efforts. The adjutant general made the building his headquarters.

The understanding (there was no formal order) that all telephone employees who could do so should report for emergency duty even carried over to those not directly involved in service restoration. Cashier Gordon Bell reached the building on Sunday morning after the storm—"bruised, battered and nearly naked," according to the report at the time.

Restoration of communications lines got under way as soon as possible, with all the resources of the Southwestern Telegraph & Telephone Company put at the disposal of emergency crews. It was weeks before service could be described as "normal," and of course some service was never restored, in cases where homes had been converted into vacant lots by the gale's fury. But there was service by telephone even while the citizens were still picking over the rubble of the once-proud Gulf resort.

Today telephone "outside plant"—the circuitry that runs from central offices to other central offices, to customers' premises, or between exchanges—is largely buried cable, aerial cable or microwave facilities. It requires a stretch back in memory to recall the days when virtually all such circuits were open wire. Many telephone people active today can't remember the years when copper strands ran along pole crossarms from city to city; yet for most of the telephone's first century, this was the only way long distance service could be provided.

Henry Altepeter (to quote again from his reminiscences) says: "I have seen instances where entire states, or even several states, were paralyzed by lack of communication after a natural catastrophe. Restoring service ... was usually accompanied by extraordinary difficulties—icy roads, cold weather, high water, fallen electric wires and, last but not least, pressure from the customer."

Competition among work crews made something of a game out of what would otherwise have been an unrelieved ordeal. Altepeter tells of a restoration job where supervisors had to report, at the end of each workday, how much their crews had accomplished. Naturally each man making out a report would ask his fellows

Cable repair technicians work long hours to rebuild what nature destroys.

Judgment Call

SPOKESMEN for the telephone company have it drilled into them that telling the unvarnished truth is the best policy in the long run. Aside from the ethics of the matter, it's a certainty that any deviation from the facts will be quickly uncovered. (A Southwestern Bell vice president-public relations was fond of saying, "We run our business in a goldfish bowl.")

Still, there are times . . . or to quote from Grover Cleveland's third annual message to the nation, "It is a condition which confronts us, not a theory." That was the spot in which J. R. Peterson, head of the St. Louis long distance operations, found himself when a tornado hit the city in September of 1927.

"The big blow hit shortly after noon," Peterson relates, "and within a few minutes a flood of outgoing and incoming long distance calls swamped the switchboard. Several times the increased power load, caused by thousands of burning unanswered signals, blew out fuses. Also, all local telephonic communication with the western part of the city and county was disrupted, as was all public and most private transportation. Quite a few operators not already on duty made their way to the office, many walking several miles through the debris."

Since the operators on duty would have a hard time getting home, and a maximum work force was needed in any case, it was obvious that some plan was needed for providing emergency housing near the toll building. Peterson found rooms for about 50 of the operators in a hotel a few blocks away, but quarters were needed for a couple of hundred more.

"It so happened," Peterson says, "that just across the street a three-story home for orphans was being completed. I went over there to inspect it. It was just what the doctor ordered, rooms furnished and ready."

But the caretaker knew his job; he wasn't about to let this telephone man move a couple of hundred operators into the building without proper authorization. And that meant an okay from the board of trustees, headed by a well-known society woman. When Peterson finally got her on the telephone, she said she would have to poll the other board members.

"Night had fallen," Peterson goes on. "We had a hundred or more operators almost exhausted, and with no way to get home. So I decided to take a chance. I went back to the orphans' home and told a white lie to the caretaker, that the board had granted permission for us to use the home in view of the emergency.

"The tired operators slept between clean sheets that night and were available bright and early the next morning. Of course, the board chairman was furious and threatened all sorts of things, but the substantial check I delivered to her in payment for our use of the home calmed her very nicely."

And one presumes that Someone up there at that Great Switchboard in the Sky smiled and passed up the chance to make still another notation in Peterson's book of missteps. ■

what their reports showed; and naturally he would come back to tell his men, "So-and-so's crew put back more poles and strung more wire than we did." No further pep talk would be needed!

Altepeter isn't exaggerating when he speaks of "entire states, or even several states" being paralyzed by storms. Southwestern Bell's territory seems unusually vulnerable to such natural disasters, and as the telephone plant became more widespread, naturally the damage increased in proportion.

The chronology of the telephone's first century in the Southwest includes reports on damage from flood, snow and ice as far back as June 1908, when "unprecedented floods throughout Texas and Arkansas" caused extensive damage to telephone property. But that was only the beginning. We find items like these:
□ December 18-19, 1924—Sleet storms level 34,000 poles in Missouri, Kansas, Oklahoma, Texas and adjoining states. Ten days required for emergency restoration; complete restoration takes many months.

Above: Kansas City, Mo., 1903. The "Hickory" office fell victim to flood waters. Right: San Antonio, 1921. The Travis Street office went under this time.

□ December 3-4, 1925—Sleet storm covers entire state of Oklahoma and portions of Kansas. Takes 60 days to replace 3,000 poles, 1,260 crossarms, 175 anchors and 380 miles of wire.

□ January 21, 1926—Sleet storms hit northeast Texas and part of Oklahoma. About 1,750 poles down in the two states; service temporarily restored by January 25.

□ Summer 1935—Great dust storms affect service in West and Midwest, chiefly Kansas, Nebraska and Oklahoma.

□ September 1936—Floods in west central Texas.

□ November 23, 1940—Freak ice storm in Texas Panhandle; ice two to five inches thick on telephone wires.

□ February 1945—Worst ice storm in years sweeps through Kansas, Oklahoma, Arkansas and Texas; 1,500 circuits out of service for varying periods.

□ January 1949—Ice storms in all areas of Southwestern Bell territory during

Travis St. looking West to St. Marys St. from Nava... Flood

three-week period cause $10 million damage; most expensive and costliest disaster in the company's history.

□ February 2-5, 1950—Severe ice storms in Texas, Oklahoma and Kansas cause $1.5 million damage to telephone property.

□ January 29-February 2, 1951—Ice storms in all five Southwestern Bell states cause about $2.5 million damage to telephone property.

□ July 1951—Disastrous floods in Missouri, Kansas and northeastern Oklahoma cause $3.69 million damage to telephone property.

Leavenworth, Kan., 1898. A sleet storm forced down aerial cable in the town.

Sleet, ice, high winds and floods continue to plague the Southwest right up to the present, but damage to telephone property from these causes has begun to lessen. In May 1983, two waves of tornadoes swept through southwest Texas within 24 hours. More than 200,000 electric customers lost power. But only about 21,000 telephone customers were knocked out of service.

"More of our cable [compared to electrical facilities'] is buried and was unaffected by the high winds," said Larry Laine, whose title is district staff manager-network distribution operations-Houston east. "In the areas where the twisters hit, more than 60 percent of telephone cable is underground. However, we had extensive damage in other parts of Houston, and in Port Arthur, where we still have a good deal of aerial cable."

In the districts where underground cable had not yet been installed, five miles of aerial cable had to be replaced, as well as 270 poles and 8,600 "drop wires" leading from poles to customer premises. Nevertheless, all repairs were completed within a week. It would be a fair guess that the same weather conditions a decade earlier would have caused far more trouble.

J. R. Peterson's memoirs provide an illuminating insight into how and why the change occurred. He recalls:

"One night, in 1924 I think, the night chief operator at the St. Louis toll office woke me to tell me that all her long distance circuits were out of order. I told her that there must be a power failure, but she insisted that the sleet storm that had descended that night was responsible. Grumbling at the chief's stupidity, I dressed and went to the office . . . to find that she was absolutely correct.

"In those days the long distance circuits were all open wires. The necessary loading and amplification for long distance cables had not yet been developed, and, besides, the cost of stormproofing facilities was then deemed prohibitive anyway."

But things were due to get worse—much worse. The 1927 sleet storm flattened the entire long distance plant thoughout Missouri and most surrounding states. It was more than a week before service was restored from St. Louis to Kansas City or Chicago, and almost two *months* before all facilities were back to normal.

The extremely prolonged breakdown of long distance service created a serious revenue loss at Southwestern Bell. When people became accustomed to being told, "I'm sorry, there's no service to ———," they got out of the habit of using long distance. It took almost a year for long distance calling volumes to achieve the levels attained before the storm. And as telephone economists like to say, you can't manufacture telephone calls, wrap them up and put them on the shelf until a customer comes in. Revenue lost today is lost for good.

Peterson goes on to pay a deep-felt tribute to E. M. Clark, Southwestern Bell's seventh president (1951-1965), for what Clark did to fix the situation permanently.

"Coming to the Southwest from Pennsylvania, where most plant had been stormproofed, Mr. Clark was astounded to find out how little had been done in this territory," Peterson says.

"There were, of course, many obstacles in the way, not the least of which was the sizable capital investment required. Nevertheless, Clark would not take 'no' for an answer, and the happy result has been that, by and large, Southwestern's long distance facilities are now as stormproof as any. Besides the revenue losses that will be avoided, millions of dollars in maintenance and storm repair costs will be saved."

But all of Clark's efforts couldn't do much to tame nature's deadliest onslaughts against the Southwest: hurricanes along the Gulf Coast and tornadoes, the hurricanes' land-based relatives.

Replacing open wire with pressurized cable has helped, true. But when a hurricane really makes up its mind to get nasty, there's not much human beings can do other than take cover, wait for the storm to blow over, and then come out to rebuild. Likewise, when a tornado decides to wipe out all or part of a town, including central office buildings, no one gets a chance to raise an objection.

It's in the rebuilding effort after the catastrophe has passed that Southwestern Bell's star shines brightly, and there is no need for the company to brag about this record; letters from appreciative customers, news reports in newspapers, radio and television broadcasts, and editorials all provide testimony enough.

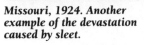

Missouri, 1924. Another example of the devastation caused by sleet.

What seldom appears in these tributes is a recognition of the staggering financial burden imposed, and the necessity to maintain sizable stocks of replacement equipment to meet such emergencies. Only a strong, well-financed enterprise can afford to put enough aside for the inevitable rainy days.

But enough; the public does recognize the efforts of the *people* who keep the service going as long as possible—and, if nature proves too hard to handle, their efforts to restore that service as soon as it can be done.

Resources of material and people—and the know-how that comes with years of experience—have stood Southwestern Bell, and the public it serves, in good stead . . . before and since that Galveston hurricane referred to earlier.

In 1900 weather forecasting was primitive and communications were skimpy; this accounts for the awesome loss of human life at Galveston that year. More recently newspapers, radio and television have given the public more warning; and weather forecasters, using radar and now satellites, enable disaster aid teams and utility repair crews to be ready when the blow hits.

Still, the Texas Gulf Coast has suffered many blows since 1900—blows, literally, that can keep telephone old-timers reminiscing for hours.

There was the September 1919 "cyclone" (in those days hurricanes and tornadoes went by the same name, although they are quite different) which hit Corpus Christi, Galveston, Port Aransas and surrounding towns. "Operators stayed at the switchboards relaying weather information until the lines went dead," we are told.

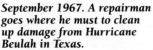

September 1967. A repairman goes where he must to clean up damage from Hurricane Beulah in Texas.

There was the September 1933 hurricane in the Rio Grande Valley, which caused (overall) property damage of $45 million. And the one that hit Matagorda in September 1941. And the one in July 1943 that struck Houston and Galveston.

And then there was Hurricane Carla, which lashed the Texas coast from Port

A Day To Remember

No ONE can predict when or where lightning will strike, but telephone lines today are amply protected against such mishaps. Not only are protectors routinely installed where the lines enter the customer's premises, but fuses and other types of grounding are used around the central office equipment as well. Today's plant investment is too substantial to permit unnecessary risks.

It hasn't always been that way, however, especially with outlying customer-owned rural lines. Sometimes lightning would strike such an unprotected line and then travel to the switching center itself, causing all sorts of damage within the center.

In one such incident at Ola, Ark., in 1935, the customer line was connected to a Southwestern Bell agency office in the agent's home. When the lightning hit, it knocked out the entire rural communications system.

When a Bell representative arrived to see what was being done to restore service, he found the living room of the agent's home in considerable disarray. The agent's elderly father was sitting in a rocking chair amidst all the bustle and activity. Near him was a cannonball stove which looked as though it had been blown apart with explosives. Wood, ashes and other debris were scattered on the floor.

The visitor asked the old gentleman: "Where were you when the lightning hit, and what happened?"

"Waal," he drawled, "I was settin' ratcheer when a ball of far came in the winder and bounced around on the floor and then jumped inter the stove and blew her up. Than all those farcrackers (fuses) started shootin' too."

The Bell representative asked him if he had been hurt or had felt anything while all this was going on. He replied: "No, but when it was all over, the chair seat was a mite wet." ∎

"Where were you when the lightning hit...?"

Arthur to Corpus Christi in September 1961 and put 166,000 telephones out of service. Remember Carla—and remember the 166,000 telephones. Because only two years later Hurricane Cindy struck Texas—a storm that was about as bad as Carla, but this time only 8,000 telephones were out. The difference? Cable had been pressurized in the meantime.

This was part of Ed Clark's stormproofing program—to keep the air pressure inside telephone cables higher than the atmosphere outside, so that water would not creep in through tiny holes developing in the cable sheath. In later years this technique was made obsolete by a new type of cable ("Icky Pic") which embedded the conductors in a type of jelly; but at the time it was instituted, cable pressurization brought a dramatic change in cable's vulnerability to adverse weather.

When disaster causes widespread damage to an area, caravans of workers come from all over Southwestern Bell territory to lend a hand.

Possibly the worst storm, at least in terms of overall property damage, ever to strike the Texas coast was Hurricane Beulah, which occurred in October 1967. It was so devastating that 10 Southwestern Bell exchanges were put out of service, but only 66,710 telephones were affected. It was followed by Hurricane Celia in August 1970. Celia concentrated its assault on one city—Corpus Christi.

There have been others, and there will be more. Nature is not about to take a Dale Carnegie course. But at least the people of Southwestern Bell know that they have done everything they can to be prepared when the next storm sweeps out of the south.

So far, little has been accomplished toward preparing for tornadoes (the other kind of "cyclone"). And Southwestern Bell territory includes the principal part

Dallas, 1957. A tornado poised to strike.

of "Tornado Alley"—a stretch of land about 300 miles wide running from southwest to northeast.

This vaguely defined territory starts in northern Texas and runs through Oklahoma, Arkansas, Kansas and Missouri before it crosses into Illinois and ends in Wisconsin, Indiana and Michigan. Within this strip occurs the majority of the nation's tornadoes, and the vast majority of the twisters that kill.

As far back as 1893 the telephone chronology notes that a "cyclone" (that word again) destroyed the Missouri & Kansas Telephone Company's facilities at Wellington, Kan. As the Southwest grew and telephone facilities spread to accommodate the population, tornadoes seemed to become more frequent; at any rate they became more newsworthy for the damage they caused.

Thus we find reports of cyclones at Ardmore, Okla. (1915), and Hot Springs, Ark. (1916); at Andale, Kan. (1917), and Iola, Kan. (1918), followed by another two months later at McNeil, Ark.; a July 1924 tornado at St. Louis, followed by the "granddaddy of them all" at St. Louis in September 1927; an April 1924 tornado at Pryor, Okla., and one in April 1947 at Woodward, Okla. (as far as tornadoes are concerned, April seems to be the cruelest month); a tornado at Warren, Ark., in January 1949, quite out of season. . . .

In the last three decades there have been noteworthy tornadoes at Waco, Tex. (1953), Dallas (1957), Wichita Falls, Tex. (1958), St. Louis (1959), Wilburton, Okla., and nearby areas of Oklahoma and Arkansas (1960), Conway, Ark. (1965), Topeka and Manhattan, Kan. (1966), Jonesboro, Ark. (1968), Lubbock, Tex. (1970), Joplin, Mo. (1971), Sedalia, Mo. (1977), and Camden and Hamburg, Ark. (1978). Small books could be written about many of these incidents and, indeed, several have been.

Another of the disasters that Southwestern Bell is heir to is fire: fire in telephone equipment and quarters or fire in the community which affects communications.

As far back as 1885, the "Law" switchboard in St. Louis at 417 Olive Street was destroyed by fire. It was replaced by a similar board in a building a block away. And at that time all the branch offices were discontinued, so the entire St. Louis area was served from this downtown location. Several other cases of fires in switchboards were reported in the early years, giving rise to the speculation that slipshod wiring might have caused electrical hazards.

But fires in central offices themselves, as distinguished from fires that started

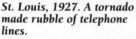

St. Louis, 1927. A tornado made rubble of telephone lines.

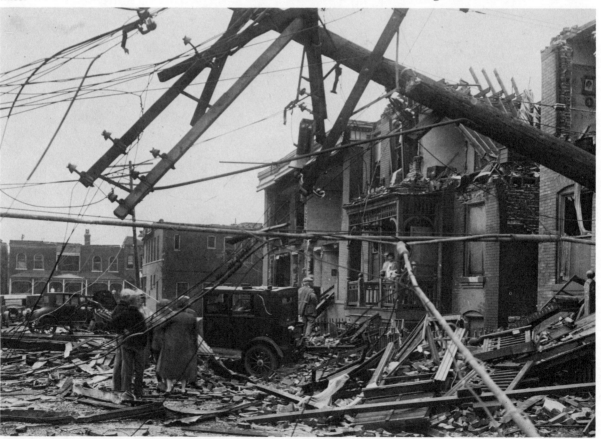

Topeka, Kan., 1966. A repair technician responds to tornado damage.

elsewhere and spread to central offices, seemed to have become a thing of the past by the early part of this century. Then came the shocker.

On May 1, 1963, the fire broke out on the main distributing frame of the "Whitehall" central office in Dallas, the hub of the interoffice truck network in the south and southwest part of Dallas. The blaze was discovered by a switchman who had been sent to clear a case of trouble.

Both the local people and the city fire department attempted to control the flames with carbon dioxide extinguishers, but when this didn't work, the firemen used water. This stopped the blaze but caused extensive additional damage. Technically oriented people will get some idea of its extent by two statistics: More than 7,000 jumpers and 18,000 protector blocks and heat coils had to be replaced.

Regular service was not restored until Monday, May 6. But as soon as the blaze was put out, a service restoration center was established to take care of the most urgent needs of the fire and police departments, hospitals, military services and other essential customers. Emergency radio units were rushed to the hospitals, and the largest one affected was served by a three-channel mobile microwave system. Private lines serving the military were rerouted from Dallas to Fort Worth.

Here was one of the unusual cases where the fire broke out on telephone prop-

Celia Was No Lady

From time to time someone makes an effort to capture in words and pictures the complex story of a Southwestern Bell restoration operation. Because this essay about Hurricane Celia sums up, in comparatively few words, a routine that applies to many other disasters, it is excerpted here.

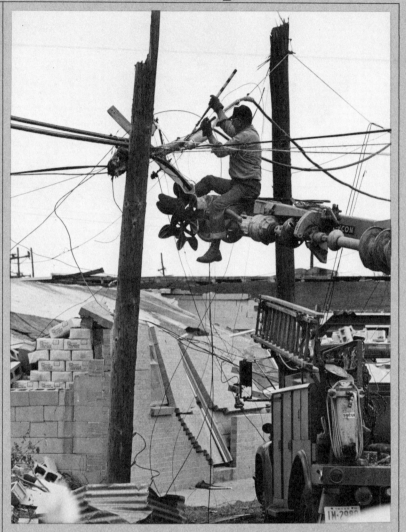

SHE STRUCK Corpus Christi at 3:45 p.m. August 3, 1970, with unexpected fury, leaving in her wake widespread devastation and more than $9 million damage to telephone facilities.

Before Hurricane Celia's winds touched the city, telephone men and women throughout the United States were hard at work preparing for her devastating blow.

Trucks and planes in Chicago, Omaha, Phoenix, Houston and Dallas were being loaded with equipment from Western Electric, the supply arm of the Bell System.

Telephone repair crews from Dallas, Houston and West Texas were moved into key locations on the fringe of the anticipated storm area. In addition, repair crews from Kansas, Arkansas, Missouri and Oklahoma were put on standby, waiting for the call that would send them to the Texas Gulf Coast.

Telephone operators from throughout Texas were already on their way to the storm area—racing Celia to the switchboards in anticipation of the surge in demand for long distance service that always follows a disaster.

Southwestern Bell's restoration efforts hit full stride during the night as Celia pushed westward toward Del Rio, leaving in her path $9.1 million damage to telephone facilities.

While people in Corpus Christi were still dazed by the fury of the storm, telephone restoration crews were fighting rain and debris to determine the damage to telephone facilities. It didn't take long.

Within a few hours, telephone men and equipment from throughout the Bell System were en route to the storm area to help those already working around the clock.

By early Wednesday, less than 48 hours after the storm struck Corpus Christi, more than 1,000 telephone people were either headed toward the city or already working in the storm area, in addition to the 400 local telephone people.

Weather experts agree Hurricane Celia was unique. With gusts of wind as high as 180 miles an hour and little rain, her performance was more characteristic of a tornado than a hurricane.

Although the storm was unique, Southwestern Bell's response was not. Whether it's a tornado in Lubbock or a hurricane on the Gulf Coast, the goal is the same: to restore telephone service as quickly as possible.

Restoration time varies with the nature and scope of each disaster. What doesn't vary is Southwestern Bell's commitment to fast restoration. ∎

erty. Most of the time, however, the telephone company is the hapless victim of someone else's fire; such incidents are numerous. In 1913, fire swept through the southern portion of Hot Springs, Ark. Included in the total damage of $5 million was a figure of $125,000 for telephone plant and equipment losses.

Two different fires in 1916, three months apart, destroyed the central offices at Paris and Jefferson, both in east Texas. Other community fires over the years wiped out service at Austin, Tex.; Marianna, Marshall, Benton and Forrest City, Ark.; Tishomingo, Okla.; Bells, Tex.; and as recently as October 1978, Hillsboro, Mo.

The fire god indulged in a bit of whimsy April 25, 1920, to shut off communications between Laredo, Tex., and Nuevo Laredo, Mexico. The outage occurred when the international foot bridge between the two cities burned.

But it was no jesting matter when a French freighter caught fire April 16, 1947, in the port at Texas City, Tex., just north of Galveston. The flames ignited a waterfront chemical plant, and the resultant blast turned the port area into an inferno, killing at least 461 people (some reported missing were never found). Four thousand people were injured, and damage was estimated at $67 million.

The disaster knocked out 400 phones in the waterfront area. Two cables serving the chemical plant were destroyed, and long distance lines were damaged between Texas City and LaMarque. Within minutes after the blast, Southwestern Bell repair crews mobilized to restore crippled circuits and maintain service.

Telephone calls for emergency assistance jammed the switchboards. Every available employee was pressed into service to handle the overload. And when off-duty operators in Galveston and Houston heard the news, many of them rushed back to their jobs to help route calls to and from the stricken city.

Two and a half millenia ago, the Greek historian Herodotus praised the king's couriers in these words:

"Neither snow, nor rain, nor heat, nor gloom of night stays these couriers from the swift completion of their appointed rounds."

If Herodotus were around today, he might adapt his words to apply to the Southwestern Bell people who maintain and restore the public's communications. ∎

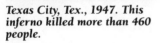

Texas City, Tex., 1947. This inferno killed more than 460 people.

WAR COMES TO ARKANSAS!

EXTRA — St. Louis Globe-Democrat. — SECOND EXTRA

VOL. 44—NO. 176   ST. LOUIS, MONDAY MORNING, NOVEMBER 11, 1918.   PRICE TWO CENTS

GERMANY HAS SURRENDERED
WAR ENDS OFFICIALLY AT 5 A. M. TODAY
KAISER AND HIS STAFF FLEE TO HOLLAND

WASHINGTON, N...
...ington tim...
...ntatives...
...50 o'clo...

WAR MATTERS GENER...

GENERAL REPORTS

CHIEF OPERATOR

RADIO BULL...

National Security Award Emblem

NATIONAL SECURITY AWARD

Here is your emblem of the National Security Award, which was given to the Southwestern Bell Telephone Company by the Office of Civilian Defense for superior standards of plant protection and security.

You and 6,500 other Southwestern men and women are entitled to wear this button for the part your OCD activities played in bringing this recognition of our company's plant protection program.

Maj. Gen. Clarence H. Danielson, commanding officer of the Seventh Service Command, Omaha, presented the award, and it was accepted by Mr. A. C. Stannard, president of Southwestern Bell, who praised the job being done by our "home-front workers." The presentation ceremonies were at company headquarters in St. Louis, but the award is for the whole company.

Col. Joseph W. Leedom, acting regional director of the Office of Civilian Defense, presented a lapel emblem to Mrs. Katherine Moore, chief operator, St. Louis, during the ceremonies. She represented all employees who participated in OCD activities for the telephone company.

SOUTHWESTERN BELL TELEPHONE CO.

"Going our Way?"

YOU can give them a lift in more ways than one if you will go easy on Long Distance between 7 and 10 each night.

That's the time many service men in the camps are calling home and they'll appreciate your help in leaving the lines for them.

BELL TELEPHONE SYSTEM

IN THE SERVICE OF THEIR COUNTRY

CHAPTER SIXTEEN

WHEN THE service was held at Heartbreak Ridge in Korea, Jim Brummett was there, and he described the scene in a letter home:

"Word got around that there would be church services held at 11 a.m. at the foot of the hill. It was raining, and the guys had had a pretty rough night, but all who possibly could go, went. I'd say there were approximately 40 men at the service. The chaplain, who is a wonderful guy, said that anyone who didn't want to sit in the rain could feel free to leave. I don't know why he said that, because we had been out in the rain all night. But no one left. It was a short sermon. As we were standing in closing prayer, tears rolled down the chaplain's face as he asked us to bow our heads. When he had finished, we all stood there for a moment and slowly turned to our duties. As we turned, he said, 'To conquer, have faith in God.' "

Ernie Pyle, the G.I.'s newsman, might have written the item in different words, but he couldn't have written any more sincerely. Brummett sent along a drawing he made dated "Korea 4 Oct. '51." Brummett, an installer-repairman from Lee's Summit, Mo., had been in Korea since July 1950. A long time to brave enemy fire, far away from home and family. But there had been thousands of Southwestern Bell men who served in the military overseas before him, and there would be still more in Vietnam. It is a proud tradition: service to the public, service to the country.

There seems to be no record of telephone people involved in the Spanish-American War. But when the country entered World War I on the side of the

Allies, Southwestern Bell employees (along with others from the Bell System and independent telephone companies), played a major role in its successful outcome.

Actually there were 1,268 Southwestern Bell people who served in the First World War, and 15 died in the course of that service. Most of these were assigned to units made up in their hometowns or states; however, the 206 enlisted men and nine officers who were the original core of the 412th Battalion, U.S. Signal Corps, constituted an elite group that gained special recognition.

Excerpts from the 1919 annual report of the chief signal officer of the United States Army paint the picture of how badly the 412th and its companions from other companies were needed:

"**The Signal Corps is a small, compact service . . . which in a peculiar sense serves all branches of the Army as perhaps no other service does . . . If at any time prior to the signing of the armistice we were to subtract from the American Army the Signal Corps in its entirety for a single hour, the whole military machine would utterly collapse. . . . On April 6, 1917, the Signal Corps of the regular Army consisted of 55 officers and 1,570 men, and the**

St. Louis, 1917. The 412th Battalion of the U.S. Signal Corps assembled at Jefferson Memorial.

problem confronting the corps was how to provide in the shortest possible time for an installation in Europe, as well as in the United States, which should extend from every factory door and training camp throughout the United States to the front-line trenches in France. . . . The importance of this was so evident that some time in January 1917, prior to the entrance of the United States into the war, the chief signal officer of the U.S. Army . . . had an informal conference with [leaders of the telephone and telegraph industries]."

One outcome of this advance planning was the action by Southwestern Bell, also before war was declared, to organize a Signal Reserve Corps battalion from its employees. The battalion would comprise two companies, one recruited from Texas employees and one from employees in Missouri and Kansas. Officers were selected by Southwestern Bell officials and cleared with AT&T officials who were working with the U.S. government.

A pamphlet dated April 4, 1917, was issued to company employees to announce the battalion. (Congress declared war April 6, an action foreshadowed by Presi-

Right: Two Southwestern Bell employees, "Baldy" Wright and Harry Brashear, on duty in Le Mans, France, during World War I. Below: H. J. Pettengill (left), the first president of Southwestern Bell, greets two members of the 412th Battalion at Camp Morse, Leon Springs, Tex., in 1917.

dent Wilson's second inaugural address in March.) Those who wished to volunteer were instructed to send their applications—through "lines of organization," of course—to the general managers in their states. The response was, as expected, gratifying; Texas alone sent in enough applications to make two battalions.

The organization was complete by May 15. Company E, which represented Texas, consisted of 97 enlisted men and three officers; Company D and the head-quarters unit were made up of 109 men and six officers from Kansas and Missouri. Five of the contingent from St. Louis and six from Texas, incidentally, were telegraph operators not employed by Southwestern Bell.

The making of soldiers out of this group of civilians is well detailed in a formal memoir of the battalion. They were given some preliminary training while still at their regular jobs, then assembled at Camp Morse, Leon Springs, Tex., for fur-ther training.* On December 1 they left Camp Morse, but it was January 26, 1918, before they finally arrived in France, and February 9 before they reached their first work base about 170 kilometers from the front-line trenches.

From then on, the story of the 412th is their part in construction of a tele-phone and telegraph line 400 miles across France, doing it according to American specifications where the American Expeditionary Forces were concerned, and according to English standards where the British were to use it. They took special pride in winning an unofficial race with the 52nd Signal Corps Battalion, a regu-lar Army outfit, to see which could string the most miles of wire per day.

Soon the work of the 412th put them right on the heels of the retreating Germans; sometimes they were able to use poles and wire left in place by the enemy. They were often under fire, but only one member of the battalion was wounded. Two members died in France of influenza. The battalion was mus-tered out March 31, 1919, although a few volunteers remained in France to help in reconstruction.

*Joseph M. Smith, an accounting clerk who rose from private to top sergeant with the battalion, interjects a human touch here in his history of the group: Besides sports like baseball and basketball, "another very novel way of entertaining the soldiers at camp . . . was the letters writ-ten to them by girl employees of the telephone company. Some of the men who probably lacked experience in writing letters to girls very often went begging for information as to what to say and how to say it. If some of the suggestions given to these fellows found their way into letters, it certainly would not have been the men's fault if many romances failed to develop."

Lineman, Spare That Wire

DURING WORLD WAR II, a new invention—radar—played an important role in detection of enemy aircraft. Although the United States itself (aside from bases in Hawaii and Alaska) was virtually immune from aerial invasion at the time, the military could hardly be faulted for taking every precaution; and so a network of radar stations was installed around the country's perimeter. Naturally this included the southern boundary of Southwestern Bell territory.

Many of the radar stations had to be installed in remote locations where it was difficult to bring circuits in to them. One such aerial copper line was constantly in trouble; about once a week the wire would be cut and service disrupted, and a repairman had to be rushed to the scene on an emergency basis. After a few such incidents, the military's G-2 section became quite concerned and launched a fruitless investigation to determine who or what was sabotaging the installation.

One day the local repairman was up on a pole, replacing a newly cut span of wire on the circuit, when he heard a voice below. Looking down, he saw a man pointing a shotgun at him. The man ordered: "You get down from there right now, because I don't want you-all to fix them 'wars' any more."

The repairman was prompt to obey the order to come down, and then asked why the shotgun-wielder didn't want the repairs to be made.

The reply: "Ever since they put that thing (the radar) in down thar, I've been gettin' headaches from the waves it puts out; and it's got to stop workin' or I'll go crazy."

It turned out that the poor fellow was already in that condi-tion. Eventually he had to be put into an institution.

The inflexibility of the military is legendary, and telephone people had their problems trying to get someone to listen to reason when things didn't work out the way the paperwork indicated they would. On one occasion a routine order was issued for service to be available to a particular post by a certain date. As this due date approached, there was very little activity in the area, and there was no building in which a telephone could be installed.

When this fact was called to the military's attention, the response was that under no circumstances could the service due date be changed. So on the appointed date an installer appeared on the scene. Lines had been brought in to the entrance point shown on the map, and the fact that the "post" was still open fields was not going to stop the telephone company from meeting its national defense commitment.

As he had been instructed, the installer fastened a small outdoor-type booth on a tree and installed a working telephone there. On the instrument he hung the regulation tag: "Your telephone man was here. Please call telephone number _____ when you are ready to have the rest of your telephones installed." Months later, they were. ∎

Australia, World War II. Soldiers had field communications through message centers like this.

No such specialized organization of Bell Signal Corps units under government aegis was created for World War II. The idea did not completely disappear, however. K. D. Hammond, who retired in 1972, reported 10 years later:

"About 40 years ago several Southwestern Bell executives, administrators, supervisors, wire chiefs, linemen and cable splicers joined with others to form a nucleus which developed into the U.S. Army's 436th Signal Construction Battalion.

"After months of training in building telephone communication lines (using Bell System Practices) at Camp Bowie, Brownwood, Tex., and at Fresno and Bakersfield, Calif., this battalion was sent to Australia, New Guinea, Netherlands East Indies, the Philippines and Japan. Mission—to build telephone lines that would link MacArthur's headquarters to the Air Corps."

After the war ended, the group kept in touch and came together for a 40th reunion June 2-3, 1982, in Branson, Mo.

In World War II, more than 3,000 Southwestern Bell people, male and female, took part, and the company was well represented in the Korean and Vietnam wars as well.

Female? Yes, of course. Southwestern Bell women have served their country as WACs, WAVEs, WAFs, SPARs and in all the other branches open to them. Not a few have risen to officer rank. Telephone women have always shown a desire to be involved, even in the days of World War I.

In those days there weren't as many opportunities for women who wanted to see actual military service. But we do see a May 1917 *Southwestern News* picture of Myrtle Brazena, stenographer in the Kansas City Plant Department, who has become a "yeowoman" (shades of today's "chairperson"!) in the U.S. Navy. Phoebe Neidenberger, health supervisor at Kansas City, enrolled as a Red Cross nurse. Leota Capps, chief operator at Taylor, Tex., joined the Salvation Army canteen service, and so did Jessie Winter, matron, and Cecil Burdick, chief operator of Houston's "Preston" office.

But the special military job for a woman in World War I was that of telephone operator in the regular Army in France—"in the uniform of a girl soldier of the United States." In truth, many were called but few chosen. In November 1917, when General Pershing announced creation of a Women's Telephone Operating

Unit in the Signal Corps, there was a deluge of 7,600 applications, but only 100 were accepted initially.

The major stumbling block was that the applicant had to be fluent in French as well as English. Eventually 233 American women got overseas, and some of them worked under combat conditions, close to the front lines.

First to be accepted from Southwestern T&T (as the Texas unit of the Southwestern System was still known in February 1918) was Pearl Virgie Baker of Dallas, who was of French descent; and one of the the first to be *rejected* was Elizabeth Browne, toll school instructress at San Antonio, because she spoke no French. The reason for singling out Miss Browne for recognition is that, undaunted, she

France, 1918. American operators serve near the front.

spent all her spare time studying and practicing the necessary second language until she could qualify and did indeed enlist in August 1918.

"For heroism in risking his life to save a fellow soldier during training in Louisiana, SFC J. T. Jones, installer, of Southwestern Bell at Stillwater, Okla., and now serving in Korea, has been awarded the soldier's medal . . . Sgt. Jones pushed a live hand grenade, badly thrown by a recruit, from the top of a sandbag shelter where it had landed, and as the recruit ran from the grenade, pulled him down with a flying tackle and lay on top of him to protect him from the blast." —*Bell Telephone Magazine, Summer 1951.*

The stories of heroism by Southwestern Bell people in military service could provide several books, and the pages of company publications during wartime are filled with such stories, as well as their letters home. Yet it should be borne in mind that they wore their country's uniform not as telephone people, but simply as loyal Americans. Some acknowledgment needs to be made of the service rendered by those who stayed behind, on telephone jobs essential to the country's war efforts.

In 1918 the federal government formally took over the telephone and telegraph industries in this country, just as it took over the railroads. During World War II the takeover was far more subtle and yet more effective; the companies were left nominally in the control of their managements, but a constant stream of directives and regulations meant that in reality those companies were "working for the government." Of course, it could not have been any other way.

A "Record of War Activities (1941-45)" compiled in 1947 gives some idea of Southwestern Bell's involvement in World War II. The report, never quite completed and described as "not exhaustive" in its foreword, still comprises 261 typewritten pages plus numerous charts and tables. Skimming through its pages, one gleans some interesting insights.

In July 1941, five months before the United States formally declared war, engineering, plant and commercial forces held a series of conferences to discuss priority use of scarce materials like copper and rubber. It was set out that the order of importance was: maintenance of present plant; provision of facilities for defense purposes; and civilian requirements.

Actually, it appears that the number-two priority quickly became number one. But number three, civilian requirements, lagged far behind from the beginning to the end of the war.

The conservation program decided on was not a matter of high-flown philosophy. It went into great detail—"drop wires were painted in place to extend their life," for example. One of the most significant items was a slight downgrade in service by filling central offices beyond their rated capacity. This still left thousands of civilian held (unfilled) orders until the war was over, of course, but it did help meet the essential communications needs of war industries.

Houston, World War I. Operators on duty at Camp Logan.

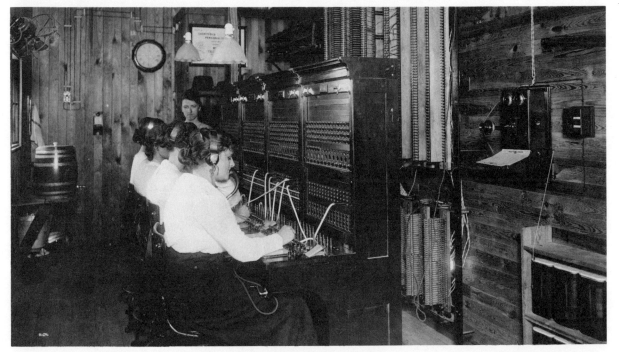

Southwestern Bell's five-state territory was important to the war effort in several ways. It was naturally and traditionally a training area for military forces; it contained the country's largest known resources of petroleum, and it became a war materiel production center which combined manufacturing facilities already in place in such older cities as St. Louis and Kansas City with brand-new industries springing up in what is now called the "Sun Belt." It was for such reasons that scarce supplies of equipment items like telephone sets were transferred from other operating companies to Southwestern Bell's inventory.

Of course the Traffic Department was involved in all these readjustments, too. Soon after the war started, long distance conversations became noticeably longer, as well as much greater in number. There were long delays on many calls and congestion at military camp pay stations as well as those in hotels and other public places.

What to do? The company could have simply clapped a limit on the length of calls. Instead, it was decided that operators should ask customers to restrict their calls, and the company supported this operating practice with advertising campaigns. (It's interesting to read, in these days of ample facilities and strenuous promotion of long distance calling, how 40 years ago telephone companies were trying to discourage its casual use.)

"Will you limit your conversation to five minutes, please? Others are waiting," and "You have talked over five minutes. Can you limit your conversation now?" became familiar phrases which helped reduce conversation time a little less than

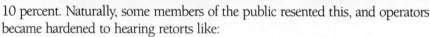

Above: A World War II long-distance operator's identification badge. Right: San Antonio, World War II. Operators were on duty at the Aviation Cadet Center to place long distance calls.

10 percent. Naturally, some members of the public resented this, and operators became hardened to hearing retorts like:

"Yes, I will, Operator. You tell me that every time I talk."

"We'd get through quicker, Operator, if you wouldn't butt in."

Or even, "Operator, will you *please* get off the line?"

But the vast majority of telephone users took the reminders in good spirit, and it probably helped the company's "image" as an organization trying to help in the war effort, especially to expedite servicemen's calls.

The Accounting Department, too, got into the act, when it was decided that operating companies like Southwestern Bell should take over operation and maintenance of Army telephone systems. At the end of World War II, the company was operating 71 separate government telephone systems. Special Accounts—Account 770, Operation of Army Telephone Systems, and Account 771, Maintenance of Army Telephone Systems—were established. Special billing procedures had to be set up

All these changes, plus the fact that company rates were frozen and profits cut, cannot be construed as hardships, certainly not in the light of what most other peacetime enterprises were going through at the same time. The hardships, after all, were endured by people, not companies, and the Southwestern Bell employee publications tell inspiring stories of how the home front rallied to the cause.

Over the years the events and the style of the writing change, but the essence remains the same. In August 1917, the editor waxes almost poetic:

" 'The war has brought tears to the eyes of one of our girls,' writes the correspondent from Hartshorne, Okla. 'Yes, and the war will cause rivers of tears to flow before it is ended. This girl at Hartshorne sits at her board and the tears blind her eyes so she can scarcely see the multiple jack into which she thrusts her plug for a connection. Someone she loves has gone to war. And she must stay behind. But she, too, has a part to play. And it is just as important as that of her soldier-

Is Nothing Sacred?

THERE ARE STILL plenty of old-time plant men around who remember when Southwestern Bell supplied spittoons—all right, cuspidors—for the use of its male employees. (Female employees weren't expected to smoke cigars or chew tobacco, so they weren't given the devices.)

A wire chief would take it for granted, as one of the perks of his position, that there would be a shiny brass target-bowl on a rubber mat beside his desk. Cleaning these objects every evening was one of the more distasteful duties of the house service people.

Then came the war—World War II, that is—and the government cast a greedy eye on all this brass, which might well be re-employed as shell castings and the like. So the word went out: no more cuspidors!

People who have grown to maturity since that war can hardly imagine the uproar this edict caused. Grown men who had felt their first sign of man-hood was spitting, a practice they had indulged in since the age of eight or nine, now faced a dilemma. Certainly they weren't about to give up cigars; and for that matter, even men who didn't smoke cigars were accustomed to using a cuspidor.

This seems incredible, but it was told to the writer by "Scotty" Kelso as the truth, and Scotty was an honorable man: He and some other members of the Plant Department were detached from their regular assignments to go around to each 1010 Pine (St. Louis headquarters) office where a spittoon was due to be removed.

Their mission: to visit the affronted dignitaries, explaining where to expectorate in the future.

Fortunately the headquarters offices in those days were amply supplied with washstands—another executive perk, now restricted to upper management levels—and so Scotty would walk over to the washstand, spit in it, and turn on the water to wash the basin clean. "See how easy it is?" he would say, or something to that effect.

Somehow the management men survived this indignity. Whether they followed his example for a few days, Scotty didn't know. Certainly by 1951, when he told this story, if this washstand spitting custom was still in vogue, it was practiced in private. Maybe the decline in cigar smoking among manage-ment men was related in some way to the absence of the familiar brass cuspidor and its rubber mat. ∎

sweetheart . . ." [and on and on went the prose for several more paragraphs. . . .]

" 'Men must work and women must weep,' sang the poet in the olden days, but now the women do both the work and the weeping while the men are at war. And this girl at Hartshorne who sits at the board with tears in her eyes is one of the countless sisters who must work and wait and watch and weep till the war is won."

Half a century later, in March 1968, the story of Service Representative Donna Hillmer, whose husband went to Pleiku as an artilleryman, is told this way:

"She was restless. Looking out into the early morning darkness at Lambert Airport, she squinted, trying to see if a plane was moving toward Gate 28.

"It had been a year—369 days exactly—since she had seen Darrell. Now, this morning, he was somewhere on a plane nearing St. Louis. 'Could he *really* be coming home?' she thought . . . She tapped the window and stared restlessly into the early morning darkness waiting for a year of waiting to end."

The reader turns the page, expecting the article to go on, but instead is faced with two unposed photographs filling the entire spread with the ecstatic "head-line" at the bottom:

"HOME, HOME, HOME . . . HE'S HOME!"

There is nothing more to say.

home, home, home . . . he's home!

But there is more to service on the home front than waiting for loved ones to return . . . or the heartbreak of learning they will not return. There are also the multitudinous fund-raising, material-conserving, pep-rallying activities that go on, not only to support the war effort but to keep back-home morale high.

We get some of the flavor of this in the lengthy memoirs of Mima Blanchard, Oklahoma City operator, recalling the 1917-1918 period:

"As if by magic our trained force [of 500 operators] disappears. We struggle to give service, employing almost anybody. We are all overworked and overwrought.

"The first draft of able-bodied men is called and on May 31 we go down to see them leave, some of them not to return. . . .

"By now we press any and everybody into service. Girls faint at the switch-board and have to be carried out. They have epileptic fits and everything from the itch to the smallpox. Dr. Rolster, the company doctor, vaccinates us all. Mary Cheatham, relief operator in toll, doesn't want a scar on her arm and is vaccinated on the leg. It takes and she comes limping to work.

"Our wages leap high and higher, and prices leap too. We go clothes crazy— we are the best-dressed working girls in town. Our wages are spent months in advance.

"Along comes the 'flu' epidemic and everyone is in a panic. We cannot answer half the calls. The company places a notice in the newspaper asking the public to restrict their calls, but we notice no decrease in traffic.

"Mother Cook, the matron, has more than she can do looking after the sick— a good many of them are more frightened than sick. . . . Eleanor Fulton, relief toll operator, dies suddenly at home of heart failure after having the 'flu.' All that can be spared go to the funeral, and some of the girls act as pallbearers.

"Time passes and the service gets no better. We have pep meetings and gather in the restroom every day for a 'sing.' We sing whether or not we can carry a tune—all the latest songs, 'Tipperary' and 'Over There'— anything to keep up our courage.

"It is nearly fall, and Mrs. Allen tells us we are to sell Thrift stamps on the streets for one day. Ruth Thagard says her feet hurt and begs to be excused. I suspect it is timidity rather than her feet. Fern Mitchell has charge of the toll squad of 10 girls and I have charge of the local. We go to a booth near the Huckins Hotel and they issue us, if I remember rightly, $10 worth of stamps for each girl. We stop people on the street and ask them to buy a stamp for 25 cents. Sometimes the buyer tells us to keep the stamp and gives us money and again some of the men paste them on their hats. It is a huge joke to the public. . . . By night we are dead on our feet.

"On a hot fall day we are told to march in a Liberty Bond parade. Everyone who can be spared marches and Ethel Mayo buys a new pair of patent leather shoes to march in, and she comes back to the office crippled in both feet. . . . When it is over we are all exhausted and we decide to ask to ride if we have to do it over. . . .

"The winter of 1918 is extremely cold and on many evenings at home we hover around the small gas stove in the bathroom as the gas pressure is too low to light any other stove in the house. We are almost frozen and Aunt Jennie remarks she knows now what makes the Russians so mean. . . .

Below left: Tulsa, 1918.
Women celebrate the arrival of
peace as World War I is over.
Below right: Chanute, Kan.,
Nov. 11, 1918. More
celebrating outside the
telephone company office.

What Stopped the Telephone Clock?

ONCE UPON A TIME, telephone customers took it for granted that they could ring up the operator, ask what time it was and get the answer. Then this service was cut off. What happened? World War I happened, that's what.

Southwestern Telephone News tells the story, laying the blame—or credit—for the change on patriotism, the war effort and all that. In today's cynical atmosphere one might suspect that the war was as much a pretext as a reason; remember "Lucky Strike Green has gone to war"?—using another war as an explanation of why a tobacco company had changed its package.

At any rate, here's how the August 1918 *News* told the story:

"From the beginning of Bell telephone service, it has been the custom of our company to answer requests for the time. It was a service not included in the contract, merely a courtesy in which the Bell was delighted to indulge. But war times brought the need of curtailment. Rigid economy and conservation became imperative, and steps were taken to learn just where and what could be eliminated to help keep up the standard of service.

"During October and November 1917, a study was made in St. Louis to determine how many requests were received daily for the time, and it was found that these calls amounted to 4 percent of all originating calls, or about 24,000 a day. With the equipment in use—which was practically all the available equipment—working under a maximum load, it was seen that by eliminating these 24,000 non-essential calls daily, considerable relief would be afforded."

At first the company met the issue head-on: It ran some newspaper ads asking people to please stop asking for the time because of war conditions. "There's a war on" appeals were persuasive with the public of that time; the calls dropped one half. But as advertising people could have predicted, the effect of the appeal wore off after a few days and the number of calls began climbing back to the old level. What to do? Keep up the ad barrage, or just abolish time-of-day calling? The decision was easy, and the last ads in the campaign told the public that the service was going to be discontinued.

All telephone people know how such a change is handled. First the chief operators and central desk supervisors were briefed and provided with the rote response: "I am sorry, but the heavy demand for necessary service, due to war conditions, has compelled us to discontinue the time service." Then, the day before the change was to become effective, the "A" operators (the ones who handled incoming local calls) were instructed that from the appointed day onward, they were to refuse to give the time; if the customer persisted, the operator was to connect him or her with the chief operator.

Then at 12:01 a.m. Monday, June 17, 1918, these printed instructions were placed before each "A" position in the St. Louis central offices:

On all requests for "the time" say, "The time service has been discontinued."

If the subscriber insists upon receiving the time, connect him with the chief operator.

There was a phrase appointed for step B, too, of course: "Will you speak to the chief operator, please?" Traffic in those days, and for decades thereafter, lived and died by the appointed phrase. However, a little flexibility was provided. Desk supervisors were instructed to use their own discretion—for one week only—as to whether the customer would be given the information after all.

This discretion period also provided data on why the customer was flouting the company edict by asking for the time. Most common excuses were that the clock was out of order; that the subscriber used the telephone for time service only (!); that the subscriber had not requested the time for two months and felt he was entitled to it; that all the clocks had stopped; that he had no clock.

The bottom-line payoff was that the change brought fewer than 10 official complaints (i.e., those directed to the company president)—and that "we have been enabled to take from four to seven operators from our early morning rush hours for use to greater advantage elsewhere."

The article doesn't say so, but one presumes the success of the St. Louis experiment impelled the company to institute the change throughout the Southwestern System. And for about four decades customers had to wind their own clocks, or get electric clocks, or listen to the radio, or look out the window at the city hall clock if they wanted to know what time it was. Finally, telephone time-of-day service, with on-line advertising to pay the costs, came into general use. Advanced technology, once again, had turned back the clock . . . to the customers. ∎

"We hear rumors of the armistice being signed. Finally, one of the papers announces it has been signed, and what a disappointment—-the report is false. Again we read it has been signed and this proves to be true. There is much rejoicing, and most of the operators stay away from work without reporting. Here I am trying to run a 53-position switchboard without any operators. I am disgusted and I tell Mr. Allen so. He thinks it is all right for the girls to celebrate and I disagree with him. I tell him, 'You would think they had won the war instead of the boys in the trenches.' Perhaps they have played a greater part than I imagine."

Mima's attitude about the role of the operator was not a common one. In all the wars, it has been generally recognized that the people who kept telephone service going deserved some share of the credit in the final outcome.

Such credit goes not only to the operators, but to all the people who buckled down to the task of getting the traffic through; the linemen, the installers, the repairmen, the forces in the central offices, the engineers who figured out still more ways to make do with less than adequate supplies and facilities; the accounting people who struggled with new regulations; the service representatives who spent most of their time on the telephone explaining why people couldn't have the service they wanted, when it would have been much more pleasant to say, "Will tomorrow be all right?"

After every war, Southwestern Bell has had to regroup and find its way back to normal operating conditions. Fortunately, it has been able to welcome back a sizable group of employees who have lost few if any of their skills but who have gained added maturity. What's more, they can really appreciate a peacetime job after what they've been through. ■

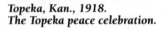

Topeka, Kan., 1918.
The Topeka peace celebration.

FROM TIN CANS TO TRANSISTORS

CHAPTER SEVENTEEN

TODAY, when the newspaper comic strip shows Nancy talking to Sluggo by means of two tin cans connected with a length of string, the average reader probably chuckles and dismisses the idea as a cartoonist's fantasy.

But it works.

In fact, the principle was already well established before Bell invented the telephone; and in Topeka, citizens actually paid money to buy wireless, electricity-less "telephones." This was back in February 1877, and the promoters were described as "city slickers" when disillusion set in.

The scam went like this: One of the out-of-towners stood atop the old Bank of Topeka building while the other collected a crowd on the street below. Each held a tin-can "telephone" with a parchment diaphragm across one end, and the instruments were connected by a taut cord, 300 feet long. The man on the building talked into his "telephone" and the local folk listened in at the other end of the line. The "telephones" sold like hotcakes, says the report; and at 50 cents a pair, one might think the customers got their money's worth for a misnamed toy for children. After all, 300 feet of cord. . . .

The Topeka incident illustrates how eager the public was to experience the wonders of the telephone. It also shows that they were often less skeptical of the medium's possibilities than those who were actually involved with it.

Walter Clower, son of the man who brought the telephone to Dallas, felt he had somehow inherited expertise on the subject. The youngster was fascinated by the magneto telephones of the day. He often stopped just to watch someone turn the crank, ask the operator for a number and then talk. One time a man standing nearby observed that this wasn't very efficient, and some day calls would be put through mechanically without the help of an operator. Clower, the young expert, turned to the man and said flatly: "You're crazy."

That would have been about 1881. Clower was wrong, of course, and the man's prediction did come true, perhaps even sooner than he expected. In fact, a machine-switching telephone system had been patented two years previously! David Connoly, T. A. Connoly and J. T. McTighe were granted their patent December 9, 1879. And although the system was not successful, that patent was the first of some 2,500 issued for "dial" telephones.

In the beginning, however, dials weren't used. Connections were set up by pushing buttons or turning rotary switches. The first successful system used push buttons (but not Touch-Tone buttons!). This was the Strowger system, the ancestor of the step-by-step equipment still in use today in many countries, including the United States. And it all started because Almon B. Strowger suspected the telephone operators of conducting a vendetta against him.

A wall model telephone used in the 1890s.

Strowger is one of the many colorful characters of early telephone history. A native of Penfield, N.Y., he served as a cavalry lieutenant during the Civil War, then took up farming and school teaching in Ohio. He also taught school in Anna, Ill., and at three locations in Kansas before changing careers again to become a Topeka undertaker in 1882.

The story of Strowger's feud with the operators and his inventive response has been told many times. Here's how it goes:

According to unverifiable tradition, Strowger's interest in telephones began when a close friend died. He expected the bereaved family to hire his professional services, but he never heard from them. He convinced himself that the operator who handled the call intended for him was in cahoots with his competition; that she reported his line was busy, although it wasn't, and then connected the call to the rival establishment.

Strowger may have believed this; it's hard to imagine that it could have happened—that someone would talk to Party A when Party B had been asked for. More likely, the family was not as friendly to the irascible undertaker as he assumed.

In 1886 Strowger bought a Kansas City undertaking firm and moved to that city. Again he had telephone problems, and again he displayed his persecution complex, as it might be diagnosed by a modern psychiatrist. He often had trouble raising the operator, or got no response at all, and sometimes days went by when no one called his place of business.

It's interesting to reflect that Strowger's paranoia might have been cured if anyone had invited him to visit the central office, which was only three blocks away from his place of business. But telephone companies didn't think of central office visits as a public relations device until decades later. If Strowger had seen the volume of calls the operators had to handle, he'd have realized they had no time to indulge personal grudges. And then someone else would have had to invent the first successful dial telephone system.

But if Strowger never saw the central office, he certainly was in the company building a lot—to complain. His story was the old one familiar to telephone plant men since the earliest days—"Trouble not found" (NF). Strowger would discover his phone wasn't working and walk over to report the trouble. The telephone company would make all the standard tests and visit Strowger's place of business, but find nothing wrong. . . . The telephone was functioning normally. And the next day Strowger would come in again.

One day Strowger appeared, furious, to report that his phone had been dead for two days. Herman W. Ritterhoff, the telephone company's assistant general manager, decided to go along with the repair crew to see for himself what was going on and perhaps placate this difficult customer.

Yes, the phone was working when they got there. But while Ritterhoff was talking to Strowger, someone opened the front door. A gust of wind whipped through the office and blew a hanging metal sign against the exposed contact posts of the telephone. Result: a short circuit and no telephone service.

Strowger took away the sign, eliminating that problem. Now the undertaker was in a better mood, and he invited Ritterhoff to sit down; he had something to show him. It was a small round collar box with a pencil standing upright in the center. Pins were arranged in a spiral around the pencil. As Strowger rotated the pencil, these pins made contact with other pins he had stuck to the inside of the collar box.

What Strowger was displaying was the first model of the step-by-step switch. He asked Ritterhoff if he thought it would work; Ritterhoff was favorably impressed. Then would Ritterhoff be willing to help get the device into production, in return for 10,000 shares in the company Strowger planned to found? Again Ritterhoff's reaction was cautiously favorable.

Encouraged by this reception of his idea, Strowger talked things over with his nephew Walter, who was farming near El Dorado, Kan. Walter fancied himself something of a scientist—he had taken a course in science at a Fulton, Ill., college—and suggested that a precision model be built by a Wichita, Kan., jeweler.

But this was not to be as easy as Almon and Walter Strowger expected. Before a prototype could be constructed, Walter had sold everything he owned to raise working funds and enlisted the help of a wealthy El Doradan, N. E. Frazier, who was willing to take a flyer on the new invention.

Strowger also got financial backing from a commercial traveler, Joseph Harris. This encouraged him to apply for a patent, which was granted March 10, 1891.

When the model was complete, Ritterhoff apparently—the story is not clear on this point—arranged for Strowger to meet some possible backers in Chicago, and he went there for a demonstration. Up to this time Ritterhoff had not set eyes on Strowger's "working model." When he did see it, it appeared so ama-

Left: The first phone used in St. Louis, 1877. Right: The Strowger automatic telephone, 1905.

teurish to him that he burst out laughing. Strowger's hair-trigger temper flared again. He ordered Ritterhoff out of the room, slammed the door behind him and never saw him again.

So Ritterhoff never got his 10,000 shares. He later said that one spasm of injudicious laughter cost him a million dollars.

In 1891 Harris and Strowger, bolstered with their patent, formed the Strowger Automatic Telephone Exchange. And the Automatic Electric Company used Strowger patents to install the world's first commercial step-by-step switching system at La Porte, Ind. It went into operation November 3, 1892, with 75 subscribers.

Taking a leaf from P. T. Barnum's book, no doubt, Automatic Electric arranged a special train from Chicago, complete with brass band, to herald the event. Chicago newspapers praised Strowger's invention as the "girl-less, cuss-less and wait-less telephone."

The new system wasn't very user-friendly. To place a call it was necessary to punch buttons the correct number of times. For example, to call number 87, the telephone user had to punch the "tens" button eight times, and then punch the "units" button seven times. This procedure set up the connection to number 87, and then the caller had to turn the crank to ring the distant telephone. And at the end of the call, another button had to be punched to break the connection and clear the line.

Each telephone had not one, not two, but five wires connected to it. It also required much more powerful batteries at each phone in order to make the system work, because these batteries had to supply power to move magnet switches at the central office. And this initial installation, with its "tens" and "units" buttons, was capable of making connections to only 98 telephones other than the one that was doing the calling.

Still, it worked, and now that a layman had come up with the basic idea, engineers took over and improved it. The multitude of wire connections was quickly reduced, and four years later, at the Milwaukee, Wis., city hall, Automatic Electric installed a system which actually used dials.*

Strowger's system didn't win acceptance everywhere it was installed, however. In Southwestern Bell territory, it was tried out at Hannibal, Mo., in 1894, but was found unsatisfactory. Two years later the automatic switching system at Clinton, Mo., was changed to a manual system—that is, one that used operators to complete the calls.

In 1896 the first telephone system was installed at Concordia, Kan.; it was a "Swedish-make dial system and served 75 telephones." Corcordians were pleased with their dial telephones, but there was one drawback; they didn't work successfully. So they were replaced the following year with manual equipment. Likewise, the Larabee family, which ran the telephone business in Stafford, Kan., decided to switch from magneto service to dial. But it didn't work out, and the old magneto crank instruments were put back in use.

This early phone required the customer to maintain the LeClanche battery at right. The phone was made by Western Electric.

*Even the dial had come before the telephone, curiously enough. The late-model switching telegraph exchange—like the one run by the American District Telegraph Company in St. Louis—used dials. Pull "1" and let it come back, and the telegraph exchange office got a message: "Tell the livery stable to send around a horse and carriage," for example. Dialing "2" might tell them you needed a doctor at your house or place of business.

For that matter, dials had been used in telephony itself starting in September 1885. They were employed to set up connections on interoffice trunks between Worcester and Gloucester, Mass. This could be called "Operator Toll Dialing," a term that acquired a completely different meaning in the late 1940s.

The Peculiar Case of the Bull in the Pasture

Outsiders are likely to think that technological expertise is the domain of scientists, engineers and technicians at Bell Laboratories or Western Electric. But since the things they develop eventually find their way to the operating companies, it's necessary for the field people to work out problems from time to time, too. All of which leads to this entertaining anecdote contributed by Jess Villareal, manager-network management in Oklahoma City.

IN THE SPRING of 1958, while I was wire chief in Elk City, Okla., a rural subscriber reported that her telephone would ring, but when she answered, no one was on the line. A repairman was dispatched, but he was unable to find any trouble. Repeated reports by the customer and repeated visits by the repairman resolved nothing.

One morning the customer called repair service and gleefully announced that she had figured out what was causing the trouble. There was a bull in the pasture across the road from her house; she had noticed that each time the bull scratched his back on the guy wire coming down from the pole, her telephone would ring. She said that all we had to do to fix her telephone was to get rid of the bull.

I wondered how much a bull would cost and what I would do with it after I got it. However, I knew there must be a better solution to this problem. This would mean another visit to the customer's location to see if we could re-create the trouble. This time the repairman and I drove out together, enjoying many belly laughs about the absurd story on the way.

When we arrived, we saw the bull in question grazing in the pasture. He also saw us and came toward us to investigate, snorting and pawing the earth. He was an enormous creature and proved to be very uncooperative. He wouldn't scratch for us—he was itching, but it wasn't the type of itch that makes a bull want to scratch; he was itching for a fight.

Somehow, we had to find a way to get to the guy wire and try to duplicate the action that a bull would cause while scratching. While I distracted the bull with my talents as a *torero* (I'm Mexican, you know), the repairman crawled over the fence and proceeded to scratch his back on the guy wire. The customer yelled from her front door, "My bells are ringing, my bells are ringing." Her story had really been true!

Up to this point, we had proved just one thing: We could make bells ring as well as a bull could; but why? It took a while to figure it out.

In the 1950s, a new type of radio-telephone was being used to serve rural customers without having to build expensive pole lines to remote areas. This type of service, designated M-1 Carrier, was provided via Rural Electrification Administration (REA) power lines. A coupler between the REA line and the telephone company drop wire and equipment was placed on the pole. This coupler protected our subscribers and employees from electrical hazards, and all connections to the electric lines were made by REA personnel.

We found we could re-create the trouble by shaking the guy wire. When we did this, the pole moved jerkily and created a make-and-break connection in the lead from the coupler to the electric line. This made the customer's phone bells tap or jingle (it wasn't a true solid ring).

Once we knew what the trouble was, the solution was simple. We called REA, their repairman was dispatched, he tightened the connection and the trouble was cleared; no bull. ∎

And an intriguing item from 1912 tells us that "Cleburne, the first automatic telephone exchange in Texas, was declared a failure; the plant was disassembled and the poles chopped down"—which seems more like a fit of pique than a considered judgment. The trouble was blamed on climatic conditions and the wearing effect of dust on the delicate machinery.

Machine switching, however, was an idea that would not disappear. Engineers for Bell, and for many other firms engaged in manufacture of telephone equipment, concentrated on getting out the "bugs." By the 1920s dial service was becoming common. Actually, Bell companies, including Southwestern Bell, lagged behind the independents. Even though the sender, a device that came to be the heart of mechanical switching, was patented by the Bell System in 1906, it was many years later that dial service became standard in the larger Bell cities.

Ironically, it appears that the first dial service in a large Southwestern Bell city was not a Bell installation. It was instituted in 1921 at the Dallas "Woodlawn" office; but at this time the city was served by two competing companies, and the Woodlawn office was operated by the independent Dallas Telephone Company. A few months later, however, two Southwestern Bell Dallas exchanges—"2" and "X"—were cut over to dial, and the "2" office became the first in the country to use equipment manufactured by Western Electric and installed by Bell employees.

In 1922 dial became more widespread, with Oklahoma City, Little Rock, Topeka and Kansas City following the trend. Kansas City, incidentally, was the first to use the Bell System's new "panel" system, which at the time was hailed as a major advance over step-by-step. But panel never lived up to its promise; it was used in Kansas City and St. Louis, but Southwestern Bell found that step-by-step, with the latest improvements, was more reliable and trouble-free.

Oklahoma City. A step-by-step switching system.

"A Shocking Occurrence"

IN THE DAYS before the development of modern ringing machines, several methods were tried out to eliminate the need for operators to "ring up" subscribers by hand, using a crank on the magneto switchboard.

One such experiment at San Antonio, according to T. W. Milburn, an early executive of Southwestern Tel & Tel, "included a big wheel and a boy to turn it, when he wasn't doing

something else. He was usually doing something else."

Next tried was a water-driven motor connected to the city water supply. The waste water ran into a well, which showed no sign of increase after a month's operation. But the meter attached to the line "registered about a million gallons," and the first month's bill was $50. Another experiment discarded.

Finally a generator was hooked up to a nearby machine shop's belts and pulleys. This plan worked pretty well, but the power which was produced was hazardous.

Nevertheless, the system was installed in many locations besides San Antonio. At Galveston such a generator was placed in a printing office. The wire carrying the current to the telephone central office was placed on a pin and insulator at the very top of the entrance pole. Both pin and insulator were painted

red, so that linemen would be sure to give good clearance.

From that point the line continued into the cupola on top of the office building. It was carefully separated from the other wires; but, for testing purposes, a branch from it hung down inside the cupola.

This led to an incident reported by the Galveston *News* under the headline, "A Shocking Occurrence." The item said that a "bright young inspector and a handsome operator" visited this cupola. He was explaining how the incoming telephone wires were distributed to switchboard positions; she was smiling and looking wise, or so the report alleges, and the *News* goes on:

"The retirement of their position, added to the close proximity of an enticing pair of red lips, tempted him to the theft of a kiss. It so happened that she was toying unconsciously with a wire leading to a source of electrical energy pretty nearly equal to a small bolt of lightning, while he leaned carelessly against the cupola 'ground.'

"Their lips met; there was lurid flash between two pairs of startled eyes, a smothered scream and a suppressed yell, and a double backward jump that would have shamed professional acrobats.

"Thereafter, until the day of their wedding, each made sure of the complete insulation of the other before any osculatory exercises were allowed to take place."

Just another tall tale? Apparently not. Telephone historian G. W. Foster reported that the young man in the incident served several years as manager of important exchanges, "but has long since dropped to sleep for the last time." His widow remarried and was still living in Galveston in 1908. ∎

In the early days of telephony, however, telephone companies and their customers were finding a far more serious problem to contend with than the manual-vs.-dial controversy. The problem was caused by a Johnny-come-lately public utility: electric power, first for lighting, and then for streetcar operation. Both uses played havoc with the telephone.

The earliest type of telephone service employed a single strand of wire from the central office to the subscriber's set. From that set, a wire went to "ground"—literally; a rod was driven into the earth and a connection made to it, or the ground wire was attached to the underground water pipes. This completed the circuit, and it worked well enough for a few years.

But as early as 1892, the St. Louis *Globe-Democrat* reported that businessmen of that city had found "the telephone and the electric light are inharmonious." They said they couldn't use their phones when lights were on because "a buzzing noise that drowns every other sound" came from the phones. And in 1890, when the Missouri Edison and Municipal Power & Light Company began furnishing commercial electric power, telephone service was disrupted practically everywhere in St. Louis.

Telephone men, "assisted by employees of the Missouri Edison Company"—no mention of involvement by the municipal firm—"worked night and day to provide a common ground system to eliminate the noise." What did they do? They ran an extra wire from the central office along each pole line and connections were made from it to each telephone on that line; the individual wires from the sets to the water pipes or to the earth were disconnected.

Again we read in 1899 that when the electric street railway system began operations in St. Joseph, Mo., that enterprise's ground-return system caused considerable trouble to the telephone people.

As a result of the unwinnable battle with the electric utilities, telephone companies had to double the amount of wire they used to serve their customers. Between the years 1890 and 1900, virtually the entire Bell System exchange wire plant was converted from single-wire to two-wire circuits. (The term "Bell System" includes the four companies which later became Southwestern Bell.)

Pratt, Kan., 1911. A maze of telephone wires covered the town.

St. Louis, 1894. Electric wires made phone service haywire until a common ground system was established.

A Language All Its Own

THE LEXICON of telephone terms can be divided into two sections. One is the formal part, consisting of technical terms and acronyms in quantities enough to overwhelm a newcomer to the business. Perhaps even more extensive, and certainly more entertaining, is the informal part—nicknames telephone people developed as substitutes for official terminology.

Goah Ragsdale, a retiree with forty-plus years of service in the Arkansas plant department, contributed these thoughts about the terms which sprang up like mushrooms after a spring rain. . . .

"The foreman on a construction gang was never referred to as a supervisor, but as the 'boss,' 'pusher' or 'skipper.'

"The foreman's assistant was a 'straw boss.' The source of this title is unknown but perhaps he was being compared to a scarecrow, which often consisted of men's clothing stuffed with straw.

"A lineman was known as a 'clum some.' It's believed that this originated when a young man, when asked if he was a lineman, replied: 'Well, I've clum some.'

"A troubleman was a 'trouble shooter,' a term still in limited use in some areas today. Groundmen were 'grunts' or 'squeaks.' Cable splicers were 'wire tanglers' or 'plumbers,' the latter term being used because in the old lead-sheathed cable days, splicers wiped joints with hot lead in the same way as plumbers did on lead water pipes.

"Main frame workers were

known as 'jumper monkeys.' (Nowadays when women work on main frames they are called 'frame dames.')

"Operators were 'plug shooters' or 'hello girls.'

"Men who drove mule teams on construction jobs were 'mule skinners.'

"Steady workers were called 'home guards' by the 'boomers.' These latter were transient linemen who were hired temporarily because they worked south in the fall and north in the spring.

"Climbers were known as 'hooks' or 'spurs.'

"When a lineman fell off a pole, as they all did occasionally, it was considered a big joke. Everyone laughed and yelled 'Get a ladder!' To call a man a 'ladder lineman' at that time was asking for a fight.

"Telephone humor has changed greatly over the years. For example, in the old days of manual (no dial) service, many people would ask, 'Is this Central?' when the operator answered a signal. If you said, instead, 'Is this the middle?' this was considered screamingly funny."

It probably wasn't all that funny to a busy operator. ∎

Wouldn't It Be Easier To Walk?

TODAY, making a phone call is a matter of touching a few buttons or turning a dial a few times— the other movements we make are so automatic we don't think of them.

It wasn't that easy in 1896. Witness these instructions in a Topeka telephone directory:

"When you wish to call a number, ring the bell by turning the crank to the right of the phone, and at the same time press in on the crank and your

bell will always ring. Now take down the receiver (ear trumpet) and place it against the ear. At the same time press on the lever with elbow of your left arm and you will be ready to talk as soon as you are connected at the central office.

"Do not leave your phone— stay right where you are until you reach who you are after; it takes but a minute or so. Talk into the transmitter or box at the top of the phone with your mouth four or five inches away

in an ordinary tone of voice in clear weather. In cold damp weather, talk close up to the transmitter and quite loud.

"See that the lever or switch on top of the magneto bell is always to the left when you ring or talk. Only turn the switch to the right when you are afraid of lightning."

And what do you suppose was the headline over these instructions?

"TELEPHONING NOT DIFFICULT." ∎

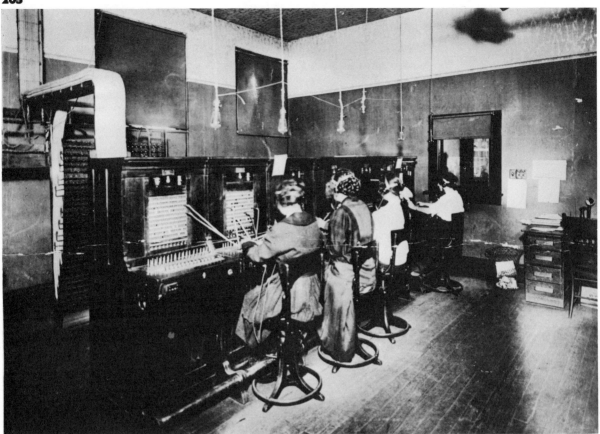

Dallas, 1919. A multiple switchboard.

To the public the change may have been a minor one, although they surely appreciated the fact that transmission was better on the "metallic circuits." But what really made a difference to customers was the gradual replacement of the old, turn-the-crank, "whoop and holler" magneto service with "common battery."

On December 15, 1888, a patent for the common battery switchboard was issued to Hammond V. Hayes of AT&T. In earlier telephone systems, each telephone was equipped with a set of batteries. These had to be frequently tested and replaced at regular intervals. With the common battery switchboard, there was one main battery at the central office which supplied current for all the telephones connected to it.*

Essentially, this principle still holds good today with crossbar or electronic switching systems; the power source is at the central office. However, when Hayes' patent was issued it was intended for application to human switching, by operators. The big difference was that ringing and talking current did not have to be provided by the customer, and it was no longer necessary to turn a crank to "ring up Central." Instead, lifting the receiver off the switchhook lighted an electric signal at her board.

From patent grant to application can take quite a while, however. Apparently it took seven years before the first common-battery switchboard went to work in what would be the territory of Southwestern Bell. Lift-the-receiver service became available in April 1895 for customers served by the central office at Broadway and Collinsville Avenue in East St. Louis, Ill. A similar switchboard was installed in St. Louis in 1898—and, incidentally, it remained in service until 1927.

*In remote rural areas, supplementary batteries were sometimes still required.

In these days, when non-dial telephones are extinct in the United States—Southwestern Bell has been 100 percent dial since 1967—it may surprise some people to learn that a well-maintained and well-operated common battery switchboard provided excellent local service.

Economics, however, is hard to argue with; as the wages of operators improved, automation became increasingly attractive as a way to keep costs down. Also consider this: There aren't enough people in today's national labor pool to handle the volume of calls Americans now place, if those calls weren't dialed.

But let us give due honor to the Bell System's last No. 8 common battery manual switchboard at Caney, Kan. The Missouri & Kansas Telephone Company bought it from Western Electric in 1910, and it served for 54 years before it was replaced by a community dial office May 4, 1964! This was a mere 36 years after Southwestern Bell's first CDO was put in service at Pasadena, Tex.

To the public, the single most noticeable thing about the way their telephone service changed and improved was the development of the instrument itself.

To cite just a few of the stages in this evolution, there was first the large, long wooden box (some called it a "coffin") that had to be mounted on the wall. It had its own power supply, sometimes wet cells, but later almost always dry cells (batteries); a mouthpiece, which today is called a transmitter; an earpiece, today's receiver; ringer bells, usually on top of this array, and a crank on the right to ring up Central. Obviously, the user had to stand at attention while using this intimidating contraption.

In some of the very earliest models the transmitter and receiver were one—no, not a combined handset, but the user took turns listening and talking with the same device. It takes no scientific or mechanical expertise to conclude that the gadget couldn't have been very efficient for either purpose.

These wall units became more compact as the years went on, but the first great step forward was the portable telephone. The bell box remained fastened to the wall but the speaking-and-listening part was a separate unit, connected to the bell box by a four-wire cord. This was the familiar "candlestick" type which has been revived today as a decorator telephone. Its transmitter stands atop a narrow cylinder, and the receiver rests, when not in use, in a switchhook on the side of the cylinder.

When the "202" set, the so-called French telephone, came out in the late 1920s, it was a luxury item. It had the transmitter and receiver combined into a single handset, which rested on a cradle when it was not in use. The demand was so great that telephone companies had to charge a premium, typically 50 cents a month, for the sets until the supply could catch up.

Eventually there were enough 202 sets that everyone could have one, and the premium was eliminated. But many people didn't want to replace their candlestick sets (and pay a changeout charge), so the vintage telephones remained in service well into the thirties.

Next, in 1937, came the 302, the telephone which brought the bell box back into the unit and provided a sturdy base for dialing. (The "French" phone's biggest drawback was the difficulty of holding the handset, steadying the base and dialing all at one time.)

Telephones in the 500 series, introduced in 1950, were technologically a great leap forward but perhaps didn't impress customers much. Their transmission qualities were markedly superior, and the lighter handset made the telephone easier to use for long periods.

Then in 1954 came color! Actually, Western Electric had produced some 202 sets in color in 1927, and a few color 302 sets in 1937, but there was no concerted effort to stimulate demand for them. The story was different in the case of the 500 sets in eight decorator colors. Yes, you could still get black if you insisted; but the telephone company would rather "sell" you a color set.

The extra charge for color created a problem in logic for the telephone companies and their customers. The latter felt, not unreasonably, that if they had paid for a color telephone it was theirs to keep and to move wherever they wanted. The companies felt that since they still had the responsibility of maintaining, repairing and even replacing the set if needed, it remained their property.

These phones show the progression of the instrument. The dates they went into service are, from left: 1878, 1892; 1919; 1927; 1937; and 1954.

The Good Old Days??

TELEPHONE PEOPLE, like soldiers and railroaders, enjoy reminiscing about the start of their careers, and it's fortunate they do. Such memoirs provide a view of the past that seldom gets incorporated in reports by newspapers of the time. Witness the musings of a couple of Texas plant men about telephony in the 19th century.

T. L. Benedict wrote in 1939: "I helped build the Marshall exchange in 1881-1882. Telephones were in their quaint state then. We had to make by hand the greater part of the switchboard. [Customers] had the old magneto telephone with the first Blake transmitter (adjustable) and the three-cell wet LeClanche batteries. The three cells, one standing over and the others underneath the telephone, put it up so high that the bell box was out of my reach.

"When someone would slam a door, it would very often knock the Blake transmitter out of adjustment [and we would have to go out to fix it]. We would no sooner reach the office after adjusting it than we would have to return to go through the same work. All call bells [in the central office] were strung on the wall and there were no drop signals at the switchboard. All ringing was done by hand [crank].

"At this time the first ice plant was installed, and after the exchange was finished two of us, on our own initiative, strung two wires from the office to the ice plant. Then we bolted a magneto to the rafters [at the ice plant] and had a harness maker make us a belt like the one used on a sewing machine. We ran this belt from the magneto to the shaft of the ice plant's engine. Then all we had to do was to press on a button and a bell would ring (almost magic).

"There were no cables of any kind; the iron wires were put through the walls and fastened to a No. 4 knob and then down to the switchboard through 'office wire,' as we called it. This was held in place by wooden cleats. We could not talk but 1½ to 2 miles and very often could not ring that far.

"After the Marshall exchange was finished I went through the woods and connected up an old telephone wire used during the Civil War by the Army, between Marshall and Jefferson. Placing a telephone at Jefferson, I had to go to the Western Union office and telegraph the man at Marshall to get on line. It did not work so well, but after soldering all joints and bridging around the old iron joints, we got to use the line to some extent. This was in 1882.

"Glass insulators were just starting to be used. Before that, what we called 'wooden carbon cups' filled with hot insulation were used. The wooden carbon cup had a zinc top. The brackets were about 16 inches high and 3 inches thick and required 60-penny nails as the weight was about 15 pounds. They were nailed to pine trees."

T. J. Handy of Fort Worth, in an undated memoir, probably prepared in the 1930s, wrote:

"In the fall of 1890, I joined the service of the Southwestern Telegraph & Telephone Company at Dallas. Not long before this, they had taken over the old exchange from the Erie Telephone Company, with somewhere around 500 local subscribers, backed up by our No. 10 iron single toll wires leading out to the nearby towns.

"The company had taken over an awful-looking bunch of junk and was trying to operate with the old magneto system, and the service was very much rotten in comparison with the service of this day. Of course, up to this time the public did not know what good phone service was and did not expect much.

"The plant had been thrown up, and nailed up, in very much of a haphazard way, and it all constituted somewhat a 'whoop and halloo' telephone system. I cannot recall that there was anything to the inside equipment except the old magneto ring-down drop-type boards, with hand generator ringing power.

"The outside plant was what could be termed a jigsaw wonder. Main and Elm streets were lined with low rough-cut native cedar poles, the cross-arms and wires extending down to the old awnings, and usually the old metal awnings were plenty 'hot' from lighting wire contacts. Luckily for us there was no high-powered juice there.

"The old central office pole was a picture for the book. It was a great pine tree, cut from the east Texas forests. It stood up about 75 feet in the air, and if I remember correctly, there were about 60 crossarms on this pole, placed and bisected to all angles of the compass. This was the grand junction where all lines in town headed out from the central office. There was no cable, of course, so they had bundled up a bunch of annunciator wires—the type of wire that was used for wiring call bells—and pulled them in from the pole through a hole behind the window frame."

Handy concluded his detailed account, from which this is excerpted, with this modest disclaimer: "Now, I am hoping that you will be able to pick out an item or two from this little story for your historical work, but I am doubting it; unfortunately, I have not the gift of a writer." Handy was wrong. ∎

It took a long while before an arrangement could be worked out whereby the use of color sets could be transferred from one Bell location to another without a new charge for color; the hang-up stemmed largely from the fact that the charges were included in state tariffs and varied from state to state. And if the customer moved from Bell service to independent service, or vice versa, there was no corporate relationship at all.

The discovery that people would pay extra for extra features in their telephones—including color—encouraged production of other new products they could enjoy. In September 1959 came the Princess® telephone. Next was the Trimline®, which carried the dial or Touch-Tone® buttons right in the handset between transmitter and receiver. This was especially appreciated by users who wanted to make a series of calls without hanging up the set in between calls—for example, those lying down.

Much more than a cosmetic change was involved with the introduction of the Touch-Tone (push-button) telephone in the mid-sixties. First made available November 15, 1963, this set was developed to work with the new electronic switching systems which were not yet in use; the first of these was cut into service at Succasunna, N.J., May 30, 1965. Although it was—and is—possible to use a rotary-dial telephone with electronic central office switching, and even to use a Touch-Tone set with the older electromechanical switches, such hybrid arrangements are naturally not as effective as a pairing up of the right telephone with the right central office equipment. As old-style switching is gradually displaced, the Touch-Tone telephone is destined to become the ultimate telephone—ultimate, that is, until some entirely new concept becomes practical, like the telephones (working, but experimental) which can "dial" a number at the sound of the human voice.

Electronic switching came to Southwestern Bell fairly late. It had first been tried at Morris, Ill., as an experiment starting November 17, 1959. (After the experiment had been pronounced a success, the equipment was taken out of service!) In November 1963, a small ESS for a customer's PBX went into use in Florida; and as stated, the first permanent central office was cut over in New Jersey in 1965.

The Princess phone was introduced in 1959.

But it was February 2, 1969, before Southwestern Bell's first ESS went into service at St. Louis. This was one of the largest ESS conversions in the Bell System up to that time, involving three switching units in the "Evergreen" exchange with about 20,000 main telephones.

Why did all this take so long? After all, the transistor had been invented at the Bell Telephone Laboratories on December 23, 1947. (It was first publicly demonstrated June 30 of the following year). It was, of course, the transistor that created the entire new field of electronics, and the transistor's application to telecommunications, while important, is only part of the way it has transformed our world.

The slow start is easier to accept when one reflects that the ancient Greeks were acquainted with electricity, but it was the 19th century before anyone began to put electricity to practical use. Viewed from that perspective, the development of solid-state electronics, once the transistor principle was discovered, came with breathtaking speed.

Since that cutover at St. Louis, ESS offices have spread throughout Southwestern Bell. By the end of 1982, 70 percent of the company's customers were being served by such offices . . . a percentage that was tops in the Bell System.

The trend is in keeping with Bell scientists' prediction that by the 21st century electromechanical central offices—step-by-step, panel, crossbar and their variations among independent companies—will be found only in isolated communities. Electronic switching is faster, cheaper and easier to maintain.

The ESS provides customers with new services which were impractical before. For a modest additional monthly charge it is now possible to enjoy "Call Waiting"—a signal over a telephone conversation to notify one of the parties that someone is trying to call; "Call Forwarding"—a flexible arrangement for having incoming calls transferred to another telephone, even across the continent; "Speed Calling"—which makes it possible to dial only one or two digits to place a call to a 7- or 10-digit number; and numerous other services just coming off the drawing boards.

The variety of telephone equipment and special services available today has become bewildering to the average person. In the meantime, progress has been going on in other parts of the telephone business, most notably in long distance.

When the first important* long distance line was established in Southwestern Bell territory in 1881, it was a far cry from today's microwave circuits. It joined Little Rock and Hot Springs, Ark., 50 miles apart. The circuit consisted of a single strand of iron wire, tacked to trees, houses and barns along the way whenever possible. If there was no standing structure near the route, the workers cut trees from nearby timber stands for their homemade telephone poles.

*There are reports of earlier short-haul lines such as a 10-mile link between Ashland and Guthrie in central Missouri.

An employee runs mainte-nance checks on an ESS machine.

The Billing Headache and How It Grew

ADVANCES in telephone technology are usually thought of in terms of things the customer can notice—new instruments, faster service, less weather outage and the like. But some of the most striking improvements have taken place in an area of the telephone business that customers don't think about—the way their bills are compiled.

L. A. Lewis, retired from Topeka accounting, saw these changes take place since 1951, when he was transferred from the Commercial Department, and he philosophizes:

"The problem for us was that the engineering technology was ahead of us. We had to invent ways to bill calls that were being transmitted and measured by equipment more sophisticated than anything we had available."

Since Lewis got into the process comparatively late, he doesn't personally recall the earliest days, when every part of the bill was handwritten on a form, from the customer's name to the total amount due. By the time he came aboard, at least the unchanging billing information was printed from Addressograph plates, and the current information was typed in. But it was still a chore. He recalls:

"My first job after six weeks of training was as billing supervisor—getting out the telephone bills, having them printed and mailed. I didn't know how to run the machines, but I learned!—spending my nights and weekends mailing out those lousy bills. Overtime was frowned on; so when we'd get behind schedule, the supervisors had to put in the extra time running those mailing machines. Then, I'd have to take the bills to the post office in the middle of the night."

In 1957 Lewis was transferred from Topeka to Wichita, which was the first IBM-equipped office in Kansas, and he had a new set of skills to master. These were accounting machines, not computers; they used punched cards and printing machines and sorters and calculators.

Then came Direct Distance Dialing, and the telephone engineers had figured out a way to put the records of these customer-dialed calls on wide paper tape. There was just one set of equipment in Southwestern Bell to process this tape, so all DDD offices in the company would ship their tapes to St. Louis by parcel post, or bus or whatever transport was available.

And when the tapes got there, an incredible reverse operation had to take place. The information on the paper tapes was transferred to punched cards, and then the punched cards were used to print paper tickets much like the ones operators had been accustomed to filling out. These paper tickets, then, were bundled up and sent back to the accounting offices in the cities where the paper tapes had originated . . . and there they were processed manually to the billing records.

Just about the time Lewis was transferred to St. Louis, in 1960, the load on that office had become impossible.

Temporary relief came in the form of a new tape-translating office opened in Dallas, which cut the St. Louis workload 50 percent. Meanwhile, for non-DDD calls:

"The company decided they would convert to mark sense tickets, but IBM hadn't yet invented a computer to handle such tickets," Lewis recalls. "So in Southwestern Bell we tried to handle mark sense without computers. It was a disaster!"

"IBM came up with what was called a 607 calculator. We already had the machines that could read the mark sense cards and punch holes in them. The 607 was supposed to do the rating of these things. But the trouble was that we had more rate cards than we had messages. We had to intersperse these rate cards with the punched cards as they went through the calculator.

"It got completely out of hand in the first month, and we had to call a halt to that process until IBM could come up with the 1401 computer. Thank goodness they did, or we'd have been dead."

The mark sense cards Lewis refers to were rectangular IBM-type cards with printed ovals on them relating to the necessary charging information. Operators, instead of writing letters and numbers on a sheet of paper, would "stroke"—draw a pencil line—through the proper ovals, and a machine would "sense" these marks, converting them into punched slots in the card.

Still later came optical character recognition cards. The operators went back to writing letters and digits, and a gifted machine could read the writing (provided it conformed to strict standards). Did the OCR cards make accounting's job easier?

"That created problems for us, too," Lewis says. "Plant and engineering would always invent these good things and then we'd have to figure out a way to administer them.

"Of course now it's practically automatic, with all the billing information moving back and forth over data circuits. It comes right into the accounting office, and you hardly notice what's going on."

Technology, in the end, has triumphed . . . even in the Accounting Department. ∎

It was a halting first step in the fulfillment of Alexander Graham Bell's 1878 prophecy:

"I believe, in the future, wires will unite the head offices of the Telephone Company in different cities, and a man in one part of the country may communicate by word of mouth with another in a distant place."

Three years after the Hot Springs–Little Rock line went into use, international calling (!) was a reality. The fact that the line spanned only a hundred yards or so across the Rio Grande from Brownsville, Tex., to Matamoras, Mexico, should not cause anyone to belittle the event. It was a beginning. Eighty-eight years later—November 7, 1971—it was possible for customers in Southwestern Bell's five-state territory to dial Mexico City directly, without an operator's assistance.

There have been other instances where Southwestern Bell has been involved in important developments in national and international, even extraterrestial telephony.

A few examples from a list that could fill a book:

☐ May 9, 1896—Opening of Kansas City–Omaha long distance lines.

☐ June 24, 1896—Opening of New York–St. Louis long distance line.

St. Louis, June 10, 1915. Business leaders gathered around for the first St. Louis-San Francisco phone call.

☐ November 15, 1898—Opening of Kansas City–New York service.

☐ February 27, 1923—Last gap closed in east-west communications, making it possible to talk from Atlanta, Ga., to Los Angeles directly over a southern transcontinental route. All-copper long distance circuit completed with a link between Big Spring and El Paso, Tex.

☐ December 15, 1926—Chicago–St. Louis telephone cable opened for service.

☐ 1929—Southwestern Bell began five-year project to construct a $45 million long distance cable network connecting the principal cities of Missouri, Kansas, Oklahoma, Arkansas and Texas. Involved about 2,500 miles of cable, much of it underground.

☐ April 1, 1940—First Coastal Harbor Radiotelephone System opened in Galveston to provide the Texas Gulf Coast with ship-to-shore service.

☐ October 9, 1948—Microwave relay transmitters used to carry telecast of the Texas–Oklahoma football game from the Cotton Bowl in Dallas to WBAP-TV, Fort Worth. First intercity microwave relay of a TV signal in Southwestern Bell territory.

Since the list could be continued indefinitely, it might be well to close with one last item . . . about the "longest" long distance call ever made. On July 20, 1969, President Nixon telephoned Apollo II astronauts on the moon. The two-minute call traveled about 290,000 miles each way—from Washington to the moon's Sea of Tranquility.

The call's path began at the White House switchboard and was routed to the Goddard Space Flight Center in Maryland. From there it was switched to the Manned Spacecraft Center in Houston. The call's subsequent path from Houston was to Jamesburg, Calif., thence to Honeysuckle, Australia, and up to the moon.

From that exalted level of communication we can come back to earth to make one final observation about Southwestern Bell's involvement in technology—the pay telephone. True, it was invented in the East, and the first known installation was in Hartford, Conn., in 1889. And the coin telephone that could accept nickels, dimes and quarters in its three slots was first put in use in Manhattan and the Bronx early in 1912.

But the single-slot coin telephone—the one that accepts all three kinds of coins through one slot and distinguishes them electronically—was first manufactured at the Western Electric works in Oklahoma City; and the very first installation of such a set was in downtown Oklahoma City on April 1, 1966. ■

1930. Construction crews bury cable between Kansas City and Joplin.

benefits mean security for Southwestern Bell families

Medical Expense Plan
Summary Plan Description

Long Term Disability Plan (Salaried Employees)
Summary Plan Description

Long Term Disability Plan (Non-salaried Employees)
Summary Plan

Summary of Bell System Voluntary Contribution Plan

Dependent Group Life Insurance Plan

Summary of Bell System Savings Plan for Salaried Employees

Vision Care Plan
Summary Plan Description

Bell System Pension Plan
Summary Plan Description

Summary of plan for group life insurance program

Dental Insurance Protection Plan
Summary Plan Description

Bell System Management Pension Plan
Summary Plan Description

Summary Plan Description of Bell System Savings and Security Plan (Non-Salaried Employees)

 Southwestern Bell

 Southwestern Bell

"A GOOD PLACE TO WORK"

CHAPTER EIGHTEEN

K. G. (RED) SHELL and his wife have good reason to be grateful for the Southwestern Bell benefit program.

Shell, an Oklahoma test desk technician (deskman), retired in May 1981. In a six-month period before and since retirement, he used his benefits for two operations for glaucoma, removal of a cataract, a cornea transplant and removal of a tumor that was threatening the sight of his other (good) eye. In the same period, his wife had her gallbladder removed.

Furthermore, Shell underwent extensive treatment for alcoholism. (He says proudly, "Since the treatment I have not had a drink, nor do I want one.")

All of this cost a lot of money—about $7,000. But Shell had to pay only about $250 of the total; the benefit program picked up the rest.

"And in addition to all these benefits, my pension and Social Security together are paying my wife and me more money than when I was working," he says with a touch of quiet wonder in his voice.

"And of course we have a lot of medication we have to take every day. Our health isn't bad, but we keep it good by following our doctor's directions. Even the medication is paid for.

"I'm thankful for Ma Bell and what she's done for me."

Red Shell's case isn't typical, of course. People's problems don't come in standard packages. In terms of money, many employees have enjoyed even greater benefits. For the vast majority of active and retired Southwestern Bell people, the biggest benefit hasn't been money so much as peace of mind—the secure feeling you get when you know that the program always has been good and constantly is getting better.

When the Bell System Pension Plan was first instituted on January 1, 1913, it guaranteed a minimum monthly payment of $20 at age 65 . . . certainly not a princely sum by today's standards. But when the program was established, it was one of the wonders of the day. (Recall that at this time a typical operator's wage was $5 to $7.50 a week.)

Most employed people in 1913 fully expected to keep on working until they "dropped in the harness," or, if they were lucky, to retire on what they could save from their wages. Small wonder that so few reached the Biblical allotment of three-score and 10 years of life.

So the pension plan was indeed a remarkable institution, setting a new standard of corporate responsibility for its employees. It wasn't intended then—and still isn't today—to supply all the living costs of a retired person. But it provided a stable base on which a provident man or woman could build a happy life in the "golden years."

The plan also introduced compulsory retirement at age 65, a feature that helped ensure a continuing turnover of personnel from operators to president so the organization wouldn't stagnate from lack of new ideas and fresh viewpoints.

Through the years the minimum amount has increased many times, and the compulsory retirement feature has been slightly modified so that most employees can continue working until age 70, if they choose. (However, the average retirement age has been going down, not up, in recent years. The combination of a partial pension and Social Security payments has made it just about as attractive financially to retire early as to keep working until age 65.)

One feature has not changed at all, however: The system is still non-contributory—employees do not pay into the fund, as is done in many other pension plans. Originally, the cost of each year's pensions was taken out of that year's revenues, but on January 1, 1927, pay-as-you-go was phased out in favor of an accrual plan that built up a separate fund similar to depreciation accounting.

At the 1915 meeting of the Telephone Society in Houston, employees received 25-, 30- and 35-year service buttons.

Invisible "Extras" on the Paycheck

ONCE UPON A TIME—and it wasn't so very long ago at that—employee benefits were referred to as "fringes" by personnel departments, unions and employees themselves. That word has become completely outdated.

In the musical comedy "Oklahoma!" there's a song about the surrey with the fringe on top; but if the surrey's fringe had been like today's benefit programs, the driver wouldn't have been able to see where the horses were going.

In fact, in 10 short years, Southwestern Bell's expenditures for benefits just about tripled. In 1972, the company spent about $2,000 per employee; in 1982, this figure was approximately $6,000. Here's how benefit costs added up in 1982:

Funded service pensions
and death
benefits .... $325.2 million
Medical and dental
insurance .... 169.0 million
Savings plan ......38.4 million
Sickness and accident
disability
expenses ...... 30.4 million
Group life
insurance ..... 17.9 million
Disability pensions . 3.3 million
State insurance .... 2.5 million
All other benefit
payments ...... 5.1 million
Total ..... $591.8 million

Besides five distinct improvements in the pension plan since 1972, nine major changes or additions to the benefit program were instituted during this 10-year period. They were:

1976—Long-Term Disability Programs introduced, protecting employees against loss of earned income during extended disability. First available to management employees, the program was extended to non-management employees in 1977.

1976—Dental Expense Plan introduced. It was extended to retirees in 1978, and orthodontic benefits were added in 1979.

1978—Employee Stock Ownership Plan established. Eligible employees are given a share of stock for each $10,000 earned in a year.

1979—Savings and Security Plan for Non-Salaried Employees goes into effect, including a provision for company contributions when employees choose to take part in an investment program. (The corresponding program for management people, already in effect, was further improved in 1979 and 1981.)

1979—Anticipated Disability Program established. Benefits include leave of absence for an anticipated disability such as elective surgery, benefit payments during the disability period and leave of absence to take care of newborn children.

1981—Dependent Group Life Insurance Plan introduced. Allows employees to use payroll deductions to purchase life insurance for husband, wife or dependent children.

1982—A new Medical Expense Plan goes into effect, consolidating three plans which had been administered separately. Plan includes new benefits and improvements in existing benefits.

1982—Voluntary Contribution Plan. Patterned after Individual Retirement Accounts, this program allows employees to use payroll deductions to build a supplemental retirement fund.

1983—Vision Care Plan takes effect, providing partial coverage for eye examinations, frames and lenses for employees and eligible dependents. ∎

Today, the pensions of Southwestern Bell employees are completely funded—enough resources have been set aside so that if the company were liquidated, all pensioners would continue to receive payments as if nothing had happened, and active employees would have amounts credited to their accounts corresponding to their actuarial share of future pensions.

From the beginning, there was more to the benefit plan than pensions, although that was what made news in 1913. The widow of a Dallas employee who died on the job collected the company's first death benefit payment in March of that year. By May 1, 1914, the program was significantly broadened, with the company spelling out a policy that it would pay disability pensions and burial expense payments, too.

Pensions were raised from $20 to $30 a month in 1920 and again to $50 in 1946 as inflation began to erode the dollar's purchasing power. There have been numerous increases since then, so that today a minimum pension is $200, with most retirees receiving considerably more, depending on their length of service and wages while working.

But to speak only of pensions is to overlook a large part of the benefit plan as it stands today. Some of the other features which are figured in the company's total benefit bill include these items:

□ Paid vacations, ranging from a week (for six-month employees) up to five weeks for employees with 25 or more years of service.

□ Group Life Insurance. The company pays the entire premium for the basic insurance, which equals annual basic pay adjusted to the next higher $1,000. (This insurance remains in force for retirees, although its face value is reduced 50 percent over a five-year period, beginning with a 10 percent reduction at age 66 and additional reductions of 10 percent on each of the next four anniversaries of that reduction.)

□ Supplementary Life Insurance. Available to all regular employees under the age of 70 at economical group rates.

□ Medical Expense Plan, which provides medical-surgical coverage to all employees and retirees and certain dependents, with the company paying the entire premium after six months' service. The program has been improved frequently since

Four generations of the Taylor family of Kansas were helped by the benefits program. Seen here, clockwise from the top, are David Taylor Sr., James Taylor, Carla Taylor and David Taylor Jr.

it was instituted and now includes provisions for catastrophic medical or surgical expense—as in the case of Red Shell, mentioned above.

☐ Dental Expense Plan, which provides for routine and special dental care. Again, it is available to both active employees and retirees and certain of their dependents; and again, the company pays the entire premium cost.

☐ Vision Care Plan, effective in 1983, provides for optical examinations, eyeglasses and other necessary care for active employees and their dependents, again with the company picking up the entire premium cost.

☐ Sickness and off-the-job accident benefits, which range from 52 weeks at half pay, for employees with only six months' service, up to 52 weeks at full pay, for those with 25 or more years of service.

☐ Long-Term Disability. When added to other sources of income, this benefit provides 50 percent of base pay when a disability extends past the 52 weeks of sickness benefits mentioned above.

☐ Sickness and off-the-job death benefits—a year's pay to a qualified beneficiary, regardless of the deceased employee's length of service.

☐ On-the-job accident benefits—in the case of total disability, 13 weeks at full pay, and half pay for the duration of the disability, as a minimum. For employees with 25 years of service this is extended to 52 weeks at full pay, and half pay for the duration of the disability.

☐ On-the-job accidental death benefits—three years of pay to a qualified beneficiary.

☐ Survivor's annuity. Under certain circumstances, this amounts to 50 percent of the pension the deceased employee would have received.

Many of these benefits carry over to the retirees, including the death benefits; the entire package is so comprehensive it requires a series of booklets to explain it. But there are at least two other advantages of Southwestern Bell employment which aren't usually lumped in with the benefit plan.

One of these is the tuition plan, which pays the costs of training undertaken by employees at approved educational institutions to improve their career possibilities. The limits are reasonable: An interdepartmental committee must approve the courses as related to the employee's present job or one to which the employee could aspire; and the courses must be completed with satisfactory grades. Many employees have obtained bachelor's or advanced college degrees by means of the tuition plan.

Also not to be overlooked are the various stock purchase plans which are made available from time to time as conditions of the business warrant. As far back as March 1915, Southwestern "System" employees were buying AT&T stock under a payroll deduction plan.* Through this and similar plans, many employees have built up substantial stock holdings.

In July 1969, Southwestern Bell management employees became eligible for the Bell System Savings Plan for Salaried Employees. Those eligible could allocate a small percentage of their salaries to the plan, with the company contributing an additional amount equal to 50 percent of the employee's allotment. (Since it

E.M. "Cap" Cummings was nearly a century old when this photo from SCENE magazine was taken in 1976. His benefits served him well in retirement.

*Then, as now, there were employees inclined to look such "gift horses" in the mouth. Mima Blanchard, the Oklahoma City operator quoted elsewhere, reminisced: "The employees are allowed to purchase AT&T stock on the installment plan. It is whispered that this is a clever way of the company for reducing our pay, and some do not want to buy. I buy one share and keep adding to it each time stock is issued through this plan, until I have 25 shares. The first one cost $89 and all the rest I bought at par ($110). Later I sold them for $135 each." Mima was so enthusiastic about the plan that in 1920 she was put in charge of the local sales drive, and announced with pride, "I personally sold 202 shares."

What About the Mule?

IN ADDITION to the keep-in-touch operation of the Personnel Department's benefits office and the fellowship of the Life Member Pioneers, retired employees are usually assigned a contact who is still active in the department from which they retired.

Henry Altepeter had such an assignment to keep in touch with a construction foreman, one of the first to be retired when the pension program went into effect in 1913. The man lived with his wife on a small farm and apparently at one time raised a few chickens, cattle and the like; but when Henry became acquainted with the couple, they were taking life easy.

When the old-timer passed on, Henry went out to the farm to see if he could help the widow get her affairs in order. She planned to sell the farm, since she didn't want to live there alone. Satisfied that her plans were sound, Henry prepared to leave when the widow asked: "What about the mule?"

Altepeter had seen an old mule in a small pasture on the farm and said: "Well, I suppose you'll have to sell him, too." She demurred: "I can't sell him; that mule belongs to the telephone company."

It turned out that the husband had used a team of mules in construction work and evidently had kept them at his farm when they were not needed on the job. When he retired, he asked what was to be done about the animals and was told to keep them until the company could dispose of them somehow.

Apparently the matter was promptly forgotten. The old gentleman fed and cared for the mules; one of them eventually died of old age, leaving the lone survivor.

"In the telephone business we account for everything," Altepeter points out, "and I assumed it would be a simple matter to 'write off' two mules. I was wrong. Apparently these mules came to us as part of the assets of a company we purchased, and since they had not been specifically identified in the transaction, were never entered on our company's books.

"I finally disposed of the matter, but not until I had driven a few accountants and auditors to desperation by sending them an appropriate form showing two mules as 'found,' one 'retired' by death and another one 'sold' for one dollar, together with a copy of the bill of sale. As far as I know there are no longer any mules on Southwestern Bell's books." ∎

was first introduced, the company's contribution has increased to 66⅔ percent.) Employees taking part now have a choice of investments: AT&T stock, government obligations, a diversified equity portfolio, a guaranteed interest fund or a combination of these. Allotments and company contributions can be withdrawn without penalty after they have been left intact for two years or more through the Periodic Partial Distribution procedure.

Subsequently, the Bell System Savings and Security Plan for Non-Salaried Employees was established so that all Southwestern Bell people now are encouraged to build up a financial backlog, aside from their involvement in the benefit plan.

In addition to all this, an Employee Stock Ownership Plan (ESOP) was established in 1977. Under this plan the vast majority of employees have had shares of AT&T stock assigned to them annually without payment of any kind; the amount they receive depends upon their annual pay. Since divestiture, of course, Southwestern Bell employees no longer are receiving AT&T stock.

Administering all these plans (and others, like the service anniversary gift program, whose effect as a morale-booster is large) is the responsibility of a department that seldom appears in the limelight—the Personnel Department. Besides the staff at general headquarters, there is a similar group in each of Southwestern Bell's five states.

In addition to the benefit program as such, personnel people also are in charge of training programs which affect large numbers of employees, and they administer government policies such as Equal Employment Opportunity and Affirmative Action. Theirs is a complex group of duties, and perhaps unappreciated. Even if employees don't take the benefits themselves for granted, they seldom concern themselves with the question of how they are administered.

At the end of the employee's active tenure, the Personnel Department remains as the principal link with the retiree. Any questions that may arise about retirement benefits are channeled directly to the personnel people. They help in running the Pioneer activities, which become most important for the Life Members—those Pioneers who have retired. Personnel people have a regular calling and visiting program to see that the retirees are getting along all right or to lend assistance when something needs to be done. The Southwestern Bell family never really loses a member.

And yet there is one other "benefit" which might be construed as the best of all. Johnie Pugh, an Amarillo, Tex., telephone repeaterman, summed it up when he was interviewed in 1974:

"We've got something else going for us besides these wages and benefits. That's the fact that the paycheck shows up on schedule every time. A skilled craftsman

A paycheck from 1913.

in another line of business might get a higher hourly rate than I do, but he never knows when the work will stop and the paycheck, too."

Southwestern Bell has good reason to be proud of this record. During the Depression, many employees had to take a reduction in hours and a consequent cut in pay, but hardly anyone lost telephone employment altogether. In the sixties some telephone operating companies found themselves forced to lay off employees because urgent service demands had finally been met and there wasn't enough work for the force. Southwestern Bell's President E. M. Clark considered it one of his proudest achievements that his company didn't have to do this; he had authorized what seemed like extravagant amounts of overtime rather than expanding employment beyond what he felt could be handled when demand slacked off. When the pinch came, this company didn't have to lay anyone off; it just cut out the overtime.

And as the service load declined in Missouri and Kansas during the seventies but continued to boom in Texas and Oklahoma, the company instituted a program of permanent transfers for craftspeople who were willing to move to the Sun Belt. Again, jobs were saved.

When the Missouri Governor's Committee on Employment of the Handicapped named Southwestern Bell as its 1982 "employer of the year," the award was simply for its efforts to hire disabled people—some 11 percent of all those added to the payroll that year. But the company is in the running for "employer of the year" awards in every state, every year. Ask the next employee you meet. ■

Little Rock, 1976. A blind employee is helped by a Braille record system.

A seeing-eye dog waits for its owner, a blind operator.

Year 1885
Lineman —
Mo + Kans Tel Co   Kansas City Mo.

Sherman. Edge

THE
Carpenter
Photographic Rooms.   615 MAIN STREET.   KANSAS CITY.

CHANGING TIMES

CHAPTER NINETEEN

ITEM FROM THE FILES of the Dallas *Herald* for February 18, 1883:

"Some severe criticism has been passed upon the manager of the telephone company in Texarkana for making a Negro the manager of the general office."

The folks at Texarkana weren't greatly different in their attitude from much of the Southwest in 1883. Racial discrimination was a way of life, and probably not too many people (other than those discriminated against) found anything objectionable in the social mores of the time.

And if women were also discriminated against—and they were!—most of them accepted this as the natural order of things. Compare two other news items:

In 1882, an "indignation meeting" of women in the nation's capital formed a group calling itself the Women's National Labor Organization.

What was their beef?

The U.S. Secretary of War and the U.S. Secretary of the Interior issued decrees barring the hiring of women in those departments.

The WNLO declared: "This defeat shall be but the beginning of a warfare that shall never cease until we see the words posted on the gates of this capital and the doors of the departments, 'Equal rights under the American flag to the women of this nation.' "

Twenty-four years after this brave announcement, we read an item in the St. Louis *Globe-Democrat*:

"With school about to open, many mothers are trying to decide what is best for their girls. The general opinion is that the public school studies for children between 12 and 15 are entirely too much given up to arithmetic and kindred subjects that the growing girl finds hard to master without efforts that ruin the health for years to come, if not for life. . . . One continually hears mothers remark that they are willing their girls should continue in school if they could drop arithmetic."

And the next year (July 23, 1907) Secretary of Agriculture James Wilson forbade appointment of females as secretaries in his department. He said that the practice "gives opportunity for confidential relations with the official that may bring the young woman into unpleasant notoriety."

When we consider the subject of early-day discrimination in the telephone business, it's necessary to recognize that Bell and other companies were accepting social attitudes of the day. In fact, they took pride in the fact that they were the nation's largest employer of women. The feeling was that operating a switchboard was a pleasant and psychologically rewarding occupation for which women were peculiarly suited because of their personalities. (Recall that young women replaced boys in such jobs because the boys couldn't get along with the customers.)

And if the truth were told, it was felt that women couldn't handle any of the physically demanding jobs in the business. In other words, sitting at a switchboard for eight hours was felt to be not too different from sitting on a sofa at home and sewing a fine seam.

Pay for switchboard work—for many years, $1 to $1.50 a day—seems incredibly low by today's standards. But everyone's pay was incredibly low in those early days. We note that on November 1, 1902, the Missouri & Kansas Telephone Company came to an agreement on wage demands by inspectors and linemen. The linemen were to get a boost in pay from $2.25 to $2.50 a day. Each inspector—this job appears to have been a "straw boss," not quite management but with more income security than the men paid by the day—got a $5-dollar-a-month raise, to $65. On such a salary a man could support his family, albeit hardly in luxury.

Kansas City, Mo., 1904. Operators' room were strictly the women's domain.

The people who were responsible for such wages could justifiably point out that they were paying the going rates; otherwise there would not be such a demand for telephone jobs. And in later years the benefit programs made such pay scales more attractive.

As for the difference between men's and women's pay, the reply would be: "The men do harder work and, besides, the men have family responsibilities." Indeed, in the early days—even into the 1920s, as one gathers from thumbing through the pages of the *Southwestern Telephone News*—it was taken for granted that when a woman married, she quit her switchboard job.

And those who hired the operators preferred unmarried women who lived at home. Was this a glimmer of social consciousness that even a woman, with her presumed small expenses, might find it hard to pay for a rented room and three meals a day on $6 a week?

World War I made some difference in this attitude. As men left their traditional posts to answer their country's call (that was the prevailing cliché), a great vacuum was created. Occasionally this meant that a woman was able to assume a "man's job" . . . but probably not at a man's normal pay, although no information is available on this point. For instance, "Miss Barndollar" became a local manager at Wellington, Kan., November 1, 1918. She was said to be the first woman to attain such a lofty post.

Dallas, 1919. The score at this testing switchboard was one woman, three men.

Photographs from this period show women working in the Plant Department's test rooms side by side with men, handling customer complaints, reading meters, directing the outside forces in their repair work.

But when the world got back to normalcy, as President Harding put it, so did the job situation. There weren't many supervisory positions open to women, other than such choice assignments as chief operator in traffic or the first-line business office supervisor in commercial.

Then a breakthrough: On April 1, 1966, Polly Paige was appointed the first woman unit manager for Southwestern Bell. (She worked in St. Louis; later she attained increasingly responsible positions in the general Commercial Department at headquarters.)

As for the matter of skin color: There were indeed blacks in the employee body from the earliest days, just as there were black cowboys on the range; but like those cowboys, they seemed to fade out of the tradition preserved in white mem-

Making Room

OFFHAND, one would say that there's no room in the active telephone world for a person who is blind. And probably the same would apply to a person in a wheelchair. And how about someone who doesn't have the use of his or her hands?

Well, there *is* room for the disabled in the Southwestern Bell of today.

True, it wasn't long ago that all prospective employees had to pass a physical exam—pass it with flying colors. But in the last couple of decades there has been a determined effort to reshape the standard telephone jobs to accommodate special needs.

Thus we find blind telephone operators and engineers, relying on Braille printouts and Braille typewriters and special light-sensors to indicate when a signal lamp comes on. One blind woman has successfully handled a job as house service attendant, which involves such chores as mopping floors and dusting walls.

Southwestern Bell takes pride in the fact that the first and second blind telephone operators in the Bell System were Little Rock employees—Ann McDaniel and Belinda Turner.

In 1982, Little Rock's Northgate TSPS unit found a way to accommodate Tina Heath as an operator. Tina's sight is fine, but she can't use her hands and has only limited use of her arms. How could she run a TSPS console, an operation that involves punching various keys?

The answer, for Tina only, was to break a rule. Operators are forbidden to punch the keys with anything but their fingers, because only fingers are sensitive enough to catch and correct a mistake. But Tina can't use her fingers. Her hands are held rigid with metal clamps fastened to her forearms. A pencil tipped with a rubber eraser is inserted in the right clamp. Tina uses that to punch the keys. For anyone else in the unit, pencils are strictly forbidden, but the other operators understand the situation and no one complains.

Tina's boss, Manager-Operator Services Raymond Murry, was concerned about the situation and talked to her about it. "I told her that she was doing very well in training," he said, "but even if her progress was slower than the others', eventually she would have to handle the job as well as anyone else. I explained that we don't have one standard for a person who is disabled and another standard for everyone else."

That was all right with Tina. She told Raymond:

"If I can't do the job well enough to meet the standards, I'll quit. I don't want the other operators picking up extra calls if I can't handle my share."

Tina has proved her ability to handle calls as well as operators with full use of their hands. And her boss observes:

"I've found that a person like Tina, with an outlook like hers, can be one of the best employees you have. She has an extra amount of determination because of the disability she has had to overcome.

"She has shown me that everyone deserves a chance. You never know what people can do until they try." ■

ories. We find references to black linemen and repairmen (the same workmen handled both jobs) in George W. Foster's account of the early days of the Southwestern Telegraph & Telephone Company. The references are always in a patronizing tone which raises the hackles today.

Even in much later periods, black telephone employees seemed to be confined to certain jobs considered more "appropriate" for them. What were these jobs? Well, janitor or "janitress."

It was considered quite a forward step when Southwestern Bell established an all-black business office in the 1940s. The office, in midtown St. Louis, was staffed by six service representatives (female, of course) and a male manager. The rationale for this segregated office was that "our Negro customers will feel more at home dealing with people of their own race."

The rationale was wrong. The customers who were supposed to appreciate this consideration didn't want to be singled out. They continued to come all the way downtown, where they would deal with white people. In the 1950s, management acknowledged its error by closing the all-black office and dispersing the staff into Commercial Department (and public relations) jobs where they worked alongside whites.

There was great apprehension among the management about what would be the effect of this change. Another bad guess: The black employees were accepted into the white work force without incident. After all, they had already proved they could do the work . . . and this always has been the most important consideration for acceptance in the telephone business.

The attitude of the employee body may have been a reflection of what their president, Edwin M. Clark, is unofficially reported to have said: "I don't care whether they're white or black. To me, they're telephone people, and that's what counts." (Clark, incidentally, was a native of Virginia.)

But complete social equality was still down the road a way. Plant Department jobs were generally all-male; commercial and traffic, all-female to the second-line management level. The upper management jobs were exclusively male. Mature,

Oklahoma, 1975. A black switchman is no longer an uncommon sight at Southwestern Bell.

Early telephone workers pursued the great American passion of the day—driving—at the same time they pursued their work.

experienced women in clerical positions understood that a young man, hired fresh out of college into a management job, was to be addressed as "Mister" while he would call them by their first names. This was never written into any practice.

Neither was it written into the practice that when some management person moved out of an office, his last name would be scraped off the glass door with the "Mr." left untouched. This saved labor, since his successor was sure to be another man.

Telephone call slips for office use were printed by the millions with a heading: "Mr. _____/Called by _____." No one noticed the sexist overtone.

The 180-degree reversal of this state of affairs came as a shock to most tele-

In the early days of telephony, plant crews were only for "men's men."

phone people. They knew, since the Supreme Court's 1954 ruling in Brown vs. Topeka Board of Education, that racial discrimination would have to go, and hiring policies would have to be color-blind. Gradually black faces began to appear in the occupational ranks in greater numbers than before, and Hispanics, too, found the job doors opening to them. But it was still the general rule that men got men's jobs, and women got women's jobs.

Then came December 10, 1970. AT&T had asked the FCC to approve an increase in interstate long distance rates to keep up with the continuing march of inflation. But opposition arose from an unexpected quarter. The federal Equal Employment Opportunity Commission asked that the increase be denied until the Bell System ended its alleged discrimination in employment practices.

The next day AT&T Board Chairman H. I. Romnes issued a formal statement terming the EEOC charges "outrageous." He declared that "in the field of equal employment, we have been leaders, not followers."

And a week later, AT&T filed a formal rebuttal. It could have pointed to such incidents as the fact that Robert Blair had just become the first male chief operator in Arkansas. In fact, it could have cited dozens of cases where the System was gradually coming into conformity with the philosophy of the Supreme Court's 1954 ruling. But the EEOC's point was that "gradually" was too slow.

And in the long run, the EEOC triumphed.

There were some mileposts along the way to equality:

On March 16, 1971, businesswoman Frances Jones Poetker was elected a director of Cincinnati Bell—the first woman director of a Bell affiliate.

On April 19, 1972, Catherine B. Cleary, president of the First Wisconsin Trust Company, became the first woman director of AT&T itself.

On August 16 of the same year, Dr. Jerome H. Holland, retiring U.S. ambassador to Sweden, became the AT&T board's first black member.

Other dates in 1972 that were significant specifically to Southwestern Bell: February 21, Liz Tuggle becomes the first woman installation foreman in Dallas history. March 13, Johnnie Wilson, Judy Carpenter and Mary Osborne become the first all-woman frame crew in the Houston area. June 5, Bobbie McCorkle becomes the first female in the Houston area to be a frameman. She eventually became a switchman and finally a frame foreman.

But more formal steps were to be taken. In September, AT&T announced an Affirmative Action program and an Upgrade and Transfer Plan. Both were accepted by the General Services Administration, the federal government's contract compliance agency. And the two programs went into effect October 1.

On January 18, 1973, came another shocker. AT&T, while maintaining that it had never broken any law concerning non-discriminatory hiring or pay, announced that it was going to give $15 million in back pay and $23 million a year in raises to women and minority males. About 15,000 employees shared in this back pay, 36,000 in the raises. This was followed in 1974 by payment of an estimated $7 million in back pay for some 7,000 Bell System management employees.

The dam had not only burst, it had been swept away.

Today it's not uncommon to see women in traditionally male jobs—and vice versa.

Today a formal practice is in existence to make sure that no woman or member of a minority can face discrimination, either in hiring or in promotion. Those who wish to explore other jobs can take advantage of a special practice which keeps them informed of job openings, lets them try out the jobs, and if they find they don't like them, return to their previous positions without penalty.

The changes weren't accepted enthusiastically by all employees. The CWA-CIO, representing most occupational employees, brought suit to stop the "Affirmative Action override," which gave preference to women and minority groups in filling vacancies. This protest was stilled when the U.S. Supreme Court ruled July 3, 1978, in favor of the Bell System.

A century of telephone history when people "knew their place" had come to a formal conclusion. From now on, everybody's place would be everywhere, if he or she could show, through ability, a right to be there.

Even atop a telephone pole. On October 4, 1975, telephone company linemen Ann Smith and Jim Garner exchanged their wedding vows while they were perched on Little Rock pole No. 15. A justice of the peace officiated (on the ground below) while a guitarist serenaded the couple. The pole was decorated with blue and yellow carnations; it also held an ice bucket, a bottle of champagne and two silver goblets. Edward C. Newton, the man who started the first Little Rock telephone exchange, would never have believed it.

The changes which took place in the 1970s in Southwestern Bell social relationships were the kind no one could overlook. But during the period since the turn of the century, other, more subtle forces have been at work, too, and their effects can be seen only when viewed from a perspective of decades.

The nature of this transformation in attitudes can be sensed by comparing the way operators talked to customers—then (about the first 80 years) and now. There was a long, long period when an operator answered a signal with simply, "Operator," or, earlier, "Number, please." If a customer was especially pleased with the service, wanted to write a letter about it and asked the operator's name, he or she would be told, "I'm operator 97" (for instance); no name. Keep it brief, keep it strictly impersonal, keep the calls moving, keep the costs down!

Today the public doesn't have much occasion to exchange words with an operator. But it's not unusual, if you do have a reason to dial "Operator," to hear a pleasant voice say something like this:

"Hi! This is Bill; may I help you?"

And no supervisor is going to tell Bill to cut out the chatter and tend to business.

Times have changed. The Bills (and Charlottes) of the company now have more latitude to be themselves.

No longer does the first-line supervisor expect his crew to follow his orders immediately and unquestioningly. Today the emphasis is on getting things done through leadership, not simply authority.

The telephone manager who sticks to the supervisory technique which personnel specialists call "Theory X"—relying entirely on his rank in the hierarchy—has become an anachronism, if not yet an endangered species. "Theory Y" managers are looked upon with favor for advancement in the company. These are the men and women who have learned to approach every contact with subordinates thinking, "What do they want to get out of the job? How can I persuade them that what I'm asking fits in with those needs?"

It's a much more difficult process than simply saying, "Do it because I say to do it." But today's worker won't accept such "explanations." Higher educational standards, the rise of unionism, greater job pride which comes with greater job skill—all these mandated a new approach to worker-boss relationships.

It wasn't very difficult for the non-management employee to adjust to that new approach. The problem was how to train the managers! Early in the 1950s they began to go back to school to learn a new technique. Formally the instruction went under names like "human relations." Informally, among the student body, the nickname of "charm school" was popular. (And the student comment most often heard was: "I wish my boss would take this course!")

The curriculum was laid out by the company's Personnel Department, but that organization couldn't provide enough teachers to create the necessary faculty. Consequently, instructors were drafted from the operating departments.

There were at least three good reasons to do it this way:

□ They spoke the language of the people they were instructing;

□ Since giving the training occupied only a few months for each subject, it wasn't necessary to build a permanent staff; and

□ It was good for the teachers themselves, applying a well-known pedagogical principle: "You never really know a subject until you've taught it a few times."

This off-job instruction usually occupied only a few days for each student. Sometimes a manager would be pulled off his or her job until the course was completed; more often the training would be spaced out over a period of time, for example, six consecutive Fridays.

The training was aimed primarily at first- and second-line supervisors, but those who had attained third-line (district-level) positions were also brought in for the course. Only in these cases there was a conscious effort to groom the students for still higher ranks.

Even department heads have been given training, although in their case it usually takes the form of off-job college training in modern business techniques.

And all this training is aside from what is needed to teach the skills of modern technology, which can range from a few days devoted to hands-on study of new equipment to several weeks at a Bell System electronics engineering school or a stay at the Bell Telephone Laboratories.

More recently, Southwestern Bell has instituted a series of Corporate Policy Seminars in St. Louis. Managers are brought in from all parts of the company for several days' intense study of a single business-related theme. Outside speakers as well as members of the company's top management discuss the issues involved.

In one of the most recent of these seminars, managers are beginning to explore "Theory Z" management, which takes the approach that manager and worker are both part of the same team, motivated by the same things—a concern for quality, pride in a job well done. The "Quality of Work Life" program is an attempt to incorporate this idea into the Southwestern Bell approach to management.

Gone are the days when a manager could feel that school was out for good. Today the bells are constantly ringing, calling him or her back to the classroom. Being a telephone manager today calls for skills that must be constantly sharpened and modernized. ■

Rosenberg, Tex., 1973. The gender barrier fell as males became directory assistance and TSPS operators.

Southwestern Bell
Telecom

 Southwestern Bell
Mobile Systems

 Southwestern Bell
Corporation

 Southwestern Bell
Publications

Southwestern Bell
Telephone

*new general headquarters
building*

THE ROAD AHEAD

CHAPTER TWENTY

WHEN THE American Telephone & Telegraph Company announced January 8, 1982, that it had agreed to break up the Bell System as the Justice Department demanded, the news came with the force of a thunderbolt to most of the System's 992,000 employees.

After all, here was an organization that had served the United States well for more than a century. It was recognized internationally as a model of efficiency and progress as well as a mainstay of national defense. Many observers were shocked that the venerable Ma Bell would agree to break up the family and kick the kids out the door, as one magazine described the situation. So why did it happen?

Different people will interpret the facts in various ways. But one point can't be denied: The Bell System's once unchallenged sway over much of the nation's communications* had been seriously curtailed. Regulatory and judicial rulings had whittled away its ability to protect its business, starting with the Carterfone ruling of 1968. That ruling was the first breach in a wall of Bell System principle erected decades before—"You can't hang your washing on our clothesline."

The little crack in the wall became a gap, and through that gap gushed a wave of competition. The most lucrative portion of the telephone business is long dis-

*It should not be overlooked that one-sixth of the nation's telephones have been served, and served well, by 1,459 independent companies; and that those 35 million independent telephones were in 11,086 exchanges covering more than half the geographic territory of the country. The 1982 modified Consent Decree does not apply to those companies, but they will inevitably be affected since they have had a close working relationship with the Bell System.

A Decade To Remember

AS THE new Southwestern Bell Corporation plunges into the uncertain waters of corporate financing, it can point to an outstanding management performance achieved before it became independent.

In the last 10 years alone, the company has been reshaped in service and personnel almost as if divestiture could have been foreseen. Consider these advances:

Ten years ago service, although good, was not good enough to brag about. There were severe problems in some cities, especially in Houston. People waited unconscionably long periods to get telephones in the Rio Grande Valley. Today there are no KSI (Key Service Indicator) weak spots. Service is at its best level ever.

The number of electronic central offices has risen from 15 to 390. Nor have these locations been chosen by accident; every ESS has been installed where it would do the company and its customers the most good.

Management has been largely reshaped. No corporate officer is in the same position as a decade ago, and the average age of these leaders is only 52—young for such positions of authority.

The board of directors has been almost entirely renewed. It consists largely of outstanding corporate leaders whose names are well known throughout Southwestern Bell territory.

Net income has improved an average of more than 10 percent a year.

The year 1982 provides an example of how well Southwestern Bell has done. Operating revenues were up 13.7 percent, to $7.7 billion; operating expenses were up 16.5 percent, to $5.2 billion; and net income increased 10.6 percent, to $864 million. However, President Zane

Barnes was not satisfied with two measures of rate of return—12.05 percent on average common stock equity (until divestiture, all Southwestern Bell stock was held by AT&T) and 10.12 percent on average total capital.

During 1982, Southwestern Bell led the 22 operating companies in residence revenues, directory sales and percent of business customers with higher technology services and systems. Despite the recession, demand for Southwestern Bell products and services increased. The company had 2 percent more access lines in service, and this

figure represented 17 percent of the total line gain for the entire Bell System.

It may be especially significant to prospective investors that 60.13 percent of capital requirements was generated internally during 1982. This was a substantial improvement over the three previous years; it's good news in a period when external financing becomes increasingly costly, as government and business vie for available financial resources. Southwestern Bell's goal was to increase this figure to 75 percent in 1983, and eventually to 100 percent. ■

tance service; for decades, operating companies had used their share of long distance revenues to make up for losses in providing local service. Now an incredible "cream-skimming" operation began.

Using Bell telephones as their terminal points, and choosing the profitable high-volume routes for their service offerings, the competitors could charge less than "Ma Bell" and still do well, for the AT&T rates were based on nationwide average costs and included subsidy for the local service provided by operating companies, Bell and independent alike. (Bell was not challenged on serving the unprofitable routes, which government regulation required it to do.)

As long as this trend continued—and there was no reason to think it would not continue—the traditional telephone business was being bled of its financial strength.

At the same time, Bell was fenced in by restrictions which actually forbade it to benefit from the technological breakthroughs it had achieved. The transistor was a Bell invention; three Bell Laboratories scientists shared a Nobel Prize for their discovery. Yet AT&T had to make its patents available to all comers and was not allowed to use them in the kinds of products other firms were manufacturing and selling.

"Competition," it seemed, was a one-way street. Other companies could use Bell facilities and discoveries to run their businesses. But AT&T was forbidden to start any new enterprise which might be construed as taking advantage of its size, skill and know-how.

In retrospect, the decision to cut the System's losses and come to some kind of terms with the U.S. Department of Justice may have been inevitable, although it was a decision deeply regretted by most telephone people. Whether the public will also come to regret that decision, time will tell.

As the agreement was finally worked out (after changes insisted on by federal Judge Harold H. Greene) AT&T—"Ma Bell" to millions—had to turn out her 22 children (the operating companies) to fend for themselves. That historic event took place January 1, 1984.

The new American Telephone & Telegraph Company comprises these elements: its administrative staff, based in New York and New Jersey; AT&T Communications (long distance), with six regional offices around the country; AT&T Information Systems, equipment suppliers; and AT&T Technologies, which is composed of AT&T Bell Laboratories and what formerly was called Western Electric, the manufacturing arm of the old Bell System. AT&T also continues to operate the overseas group, known as AT&T International.

Thus AT&T retains most of the Bell System's long distance network, its manu-

Washington, D.C., January 8, 1982. Department of Justice official William Baxter, left, and AT&T Chairman Charles Brown announce the signing of the Consent Decree.

facturing arm (which is now free to sell to all customers, rather than being restricted to supplying Bell operating companies), and the pool of technical brilliance which made the System the envy of the world. It can use these resources to become a formidable entry in the new communications enterprises now springing up like mushrooms after a spring rain.

What about the BOCs (Bell operating companies)? They lose the financial "umbrella" of being a part of the Bell System. They also lose most of the revenue from long distance, which was an important part of their rate structure.

But the BOCs are not without resources. In a revision of the preliminary Consent Decree, it was agreed that the BOCs would continue to issue the telephone directories, including the Yellow Pages—the money-making part of the directory business. This will help.

They also have some long distance revenue from calls placed within LATAs in their territory. A LATA (local access and transport area) is a grouping of present telephone exchanges that serves a metropolitan area and surrounding cities and towns. Charges on calls within a LATA belong entirely to the BOC. Calls between LATAs involve a long distance supplier, whether AT&T or some other firm. This supplier pays the BOCs for the privilege of connecting to their local network. As initially planned, there will be 25 LATAs in Southwestern Bell—two in Kansas, two in Oklahoma, three in Missouri, three in Arkansas and fifteen in Texas.

The BOCs' loss of a major portion of long distance revenue has created a problem. This revenue historically has been used to hold down the cost of local service. Now that it's gone, it has to be made up in some other way.

Even as this book was being printed, that issue hadn't been resolved. At first, the Federal Communications Commission ruled that the cost of local service gradually would be transferred to the local customer over a period of seven years. That's what the FCC's access charge plan is about, and it was supposed to go into effect January 1, 1984, the same day divestiture officially occurred.

Congress, however, got jittery about the plan, and late in 1983 bills were proposed in both the House and the Senate to modify it. Then on October 18, the FCC announced that it was delaying the kickoff date for access charges until April 3. The FCC suggested that between January 1 and April 3, the telephone industry should continue to operate under historic, complex formulas for determining costs and dividing revenues between local companies and long distance carriers.

The Justice Department, however, pointed out that if divestiture really took effect, the formulas couldn't work because the system they were built on (the Bell System) wouldn't exist.

Talk about being left in the lurch! Well, on to other matters.

Re-creating some of the advantages which existed under a unified Bell System, regional holding companies of BOCs now own and operate a central services organization (located in New Jersey) which provides network planning, software development service and non-technical administrative, training and support services.

The divested companies are permitted to offer new customer premises equipment and, with certain restrictions, to enter other lines of business besides local exchange telephone service. They have kept about 75 percent of total Bell System assets, including but not limited to such things as transmission and switching equipment, land and buildings, motor vehicles and other work equipment, materials and supplies.

The seven regional holding companies:
1) *Southwestern Bell Corporation*
2) *Pacific Telesis*
3) *US West*
4) *BellSouth*
5) *Ameritech*
6) *Bell Atlantic*
7) *NYNEX*

Steps on the Road to Divestiture

1968, JUNE 26—The Carterfone Decision. The Federal Communications Commission strikes down existing interstate telephone tariffs which prohibit "foreign attachments." This term has been used to designate any equipment or device not supplied by the telephone company. Previously, connecting such equipment to the public telephone system was forbidden; now the FCC rules that it is permissible under certain circumstances. Decision is outcome of a suit filed October 20, 1966, by Carter Electronics of Dallas, which wanted to connect its private mobile radio systems to the nationwide telephone network.

1969—The FCC authorizes MCI, a competing long distance carrier, to build and operate private line facilities between St. Louis and Chicago.

1971, January 22—FCC announces it will conduct a comprehensive investigation of AT&T, covering these subjects: rate of return on investment, cost increases, role of Western Electric in the corporate enterprises, and price structures for services.

1971—FCC authorizes specialized common carriers to use telephone company local exchange facilities in completing private line services.

1971, June 11—AT&T files tariff changes with the FCC, providing for interconnecting customer-furnished terminal equipment and systems with most voice grade private line services. Proposed new tariff calls for protection devices supplied at the point of interconnection.

1972—FCC authorizes domestic communications satellite carriers to provide private line services.

1974, June 13—AT&T established "hi-lo" rates for private line voice grade circuits. In effect these recognize that System policy of charging uniform rates by distance has left room for competitors to undercut the rates on heavy-usage, economical routes.

1974, November 20—U.S. Justice Department files civil antitrust suit against AT&T. Charges monopolization, and conspiracy to monopolize, the supply of telecommunications service and equipment.

1975—FCC bars MCI's "Execunet" service because it is similar to regular long distance service, rather than the private line service the FCC authorized in 1969.

1976—Consumer Communications Reform Act introduced in the U.S. House of Representatives. As first drafted, it affirms universal service as a national telecommunications goal and sets tests for competitive entry into the industry.

1976—FCC initiates the Second Computer Inquiry to consider merging telecommunications and computer technologies.

1977—FCC establishes a program allowing "registered" non-Bell telephone equipment to be connected to the telephone network without protective connecting devices.

1978, January 17—U.S. Supreme Court refuses to review, and thus leaves standing, a decision by the U.S. Court of Appeals in Washington that overrules the FCC in the *Execunet* case.

1978—HR 13015 introduced in U.S. House of Representatives. Described as a rewrite of the Communications Act of 1934.

1979—Congress considers new bills and House Interstate and Foreign Commerce Committee reports out HR 6121. (Bill died as session ended.)

1980—In Second Computer Inquiry, FCC rules that enhanced network services and terminal equipment will be detariffed. AT&T may provide them only through an unregulated separate subsidiary. Effective date of change set at March 1, 1982 (later postponed to January 1, 1983).

1981—AT&T files for the organization of a separate subsidiary as required by the FCC. (Originally named "American Bell," later renamed "AT&T Information Systems.")

1981—FCC orders resale and sharing of WATS service.

1981—HR 5158, the Telecommunications Act of 1981, introduced in House. Hearings set for February 1982.

1982, January 8—Consent Decree announced. AT&T agrees to divest itself of 22 operating telephone companies, including Southwestern Bell. In return, Department of Justice agrees to drop its antitrust suit brought in 1974.

1982, July 20—Efforts to act on HR 5158 abandoned after bill's chief sponsor concedes impossibility of passage.

1982, August 24—Federal Judge Harold H. Greene approves the Consent Decree agreed to by AT&T and the Justice Department.

1982, December 16—AT&T files Plan of Reorganization with Judge Greene. This plan spelled out the details of the Bell Systems breakup.

1983, August 4—Company President Zane E. Barnes announces the name of the firm's holding company—Southwestern Bell Corporation.

1983, August 5—Judge Greene approves the Plan of Reorganization, thereby clearing the way for divestiture.

1984, January 1—Southwestern Bell begins its new life as a stand-alone company, totally independent from AT&T. ∎

Left: The Southwestern Bell headquarters building stood proud and tall when completed in 1926. Above: The building will be overshadowed by the new headquarters building, scheduled for completion in late 1984.

...And One Last Look Back...

Although this chapter deals primarily with the future, a letter from Mildred Holley of Austin, Tex., seems to fit in here as a reminder that "the good old days" were, indeed, very good for a lot of telephone people. The letter, only slightly edited, follows.

▌READ RECENTLY that [AT&T] Chairman Charles Brown hopes to do away with the "Ma Bell" image, and I understand his objections to the derogatory implications. Still, I might take issue with this, for this is a nurturing, compassionate giant—much more than a corporation, truly approaching a family situation.

In the early 1900s my mother, Bess Millard, was one of the younger children of a large Houston family, the daughter of a Southern Pacific engineer. One day this shy, obedient young lady decided that the family's financial situation required improvement because she and her sisters had only one flounced petticoat each! On that day, without receiving customary permission, she got herself a job at the Telephone Company. She was the first woman in the family to ever "work"—although the large families of that day kept all the ladies *working* at home. She was soon to be assistant chief operator and stayed on for 13 years.

All calls were manually connected in those days, and customers came to know and appreciate their operators. As foreign as any technical equipment was to young ladies at that time, my mother learned to "jiggle" the ringing equipment when it didn't work properly, and to recognize various TAT (trouble at times) situations in the old cord switchboards. These years were a happy memory for her to the end of her life.

I went to work for Southwest-ern Bell in 1941, after graduation from high school, and many of the people who had worked with and for my mother were still there. We were soon to be in World War II (my mother had worked through World War I), and it was a busy, growth period, with rapid advancement.

In 1943 I married Martin Holley, who had gone from school to the Toll Test Room, with its Wheatstone bridge, open wire and cumbersome patch cords. Later that year he went into the service, knowing that he had a job waiting for him when the "big one" was over. There aren't words to describe what that knowledge, and the letters from his boss and co-workers, meant to a lonely boy overseas.

Austin, Tex., 1965. Holley family members included Martin Jr. (now chief accountant for the state of Texas); Mildred; Kevin (who may someday work at Bell Laboratories); and Bess Breakfield, the boys' grandmother who worked for the company in the early 1900s.

While my husband was stationed at various locations in the States, we visited telephone companies—and were always at home. I worked in Sacramento, Calif., and St. Louis, Mo., transferring and welcomed; and again, it's hard to express how wonderful it felt to have a job waiting, a sense of security in those frightening times. We met so many wonderful people and have kept in touch with a number of them throughout all these years. If the concern and caring that we encountered wasn't "mothering," then it certainly came close.

After the war we returned to Houston, where I was a commercial instructor, South District, until I left to raise our two sons. My husband recently retired with over 40 years' service in toll plant; he had been in Austin, Tex., since 1959. Together, we had almost 50 years with the company, and I hope we made some contribution, because, through it, ours has been a good life.

We almost had a third generation employee early last year. After receiving his master's degree at the University of Texas, our younger son, Kevin, was invited to Bell Laboratories in New Jersey and offered a research position there. He decided to accept a scholarship for doctoral study at the University of Maryland instead, because a Ph.D. in his research field will be of inestimable value. Mr. Kennedy, personnel director at Bell Laboratories, wrote Kevin that they'll look forward to seeing him again when he has received his doctorate. We'll look forward to that, too, for there is no place we would rather see our son devote his time, training and talents.

Where else are 40-plus-year careers so numerous; are miracles so ordinary and performed daily; is loyalty of employees so general; is devotion of retirees so visible in organizations such as the Pioneers; do company stock and decisions have the confidence of its holders, both employees and non-employees, to such a total degree?

We were privileged to be with the company during very interesting times for us, the company and the nation. Future changes will come faster and be even more fantastic. I hope some things won't change—I hope it can always be thought of as "Ma Bell." ∎

BOCs will have a small psychological advantage in state commission rate cases that they didn't have before. No longer can their adversaries cite AT&T profits to justify making an operating company do without an adequate profit of its own.

Most of all, however, the operating companies have an asset which can't be priced on a balance sheet—*people*: their employees, their customers. Removing Ma Bell's apron strings won't change that warm relationship, which has grown over the years. It's conceivable that in some quarters the feelings of loyalty may become even stronger than they have been. The vast majority of employees stayed in their current jobs with their current companies.

And Southwestern Bell is a special case among these children being put out of the house. The 22 companies have been grouped into regional entities, large enough to be financially viable even though they can no longer call on AT&T's resources. There are seven of these groupings, most comprising several BOCs.

Southwestern Bell is different. As 10 percent of the Bell System, it's large enough to stand alone. It is a regional entity in itself.*

Divestiture—the formal term for the breakup—proceeded as planned. And Southwestern Bell found the planning easier and faster than most of the other companies.

That's not to say it hasn't been a mammoth task. The entire organizational structure of Southwestern Bell was re-examined in light of the new responsibilities the company faces alone. Boundaries of local exchanges had to be reviewed. Pricing structures for local delivery of long distance calls had to be worked out, and those schedules had to win the approval of state commissions. A new regional staff has been established at the St. Louis headquarters to take over services currently provided by AT&T (financial) and Western Electric (supplies management).

For many Southwestern Bell customers the changes are bringing a novelty: outright ownership of their telephones. Although it has been possible for several years for customers to buy their own telephone sets, and many have done so, this will become much more widespread in the future.

Some of the new products being offered by Southwestern Bell Telecom, the corporation's equipment subsidiary established November 9, 1983.

*All 22 operating companies involved in the decree were wholly owned subsidiaries of AT&T. Each AT&T share owner holds the same number of shares in the new AT&T as before; in addition, most share owners received shares in each of the seven regional holding companies. (Those with fewer than 10 AT&T shares received cash instead of additional stock.)

Leasing of equipment, in the traditional manner, is on the way out for business customers, who will be expected to own and maintain their own phones, PBXs and similar hardware. Many of them are already doing just that.

Residence customers, according to present plans, will have the option of continuing to lease their equipment for the time being. However, over the years it can be anticipated that more and more residence customers will come to accept the idea of owning their own telephones just as they own their own electric lamps, gas-fired water heaters and plumbing.

The situation as it stands today can be well summed up in statements by two Southwestern Bell officials.

In 1981, Paul Roth, Southwestern Bell's vice president of revenues and public affairs in Texas, told a public utilities conference in Dallas:

"The Justice antitrust suit hangs over us like a black cloud, and it could result in the dismemberment of the Bell System."

About a year later, President Zane E. Barnes told the same group:

"It's time—it's long *past* time—to get out from under that black cloud. We've reached the point where it's more important to get the rules of the game clarified than to hold out for our choice of a perfect solution. . . . We've come to accept that a radical change in our structure is inevitable."

And a few months after that, Barnes told 100,000 Southwestern Bell employees through the pages of the company magazine, *SCENE:*

"After divestiture, Southwestern Bell's destiny for the first time will be entirely in our hands. That's fine with me. If anybody can get the job done, we can."

This book, which looks back a little more than a century, shows that history fully supports Barnes' confidence in the people who built this company. The next hundred years should be exciting, too. ■

APPENDIX

THE TELEPHONE PIONEERS OF AMERICA

HENRY W. POPE couldn't have dreamed what he was starting that day in 1910. Out of a casual proposal to compile a list of people who had been in at telephony's beginnings arose an organization which today embraces 569,000 members in the United States and Canada— employees and retirees of Bell companies and independent companies, including some run by the Canadian government.

Pope was a special agent of the American Telephone & Telegraph Company. He made his suggestion, so the accepted story goes, to another man in the office, Charles R. Truex. The list-making pastime became so absorbing that they called in a helper, Thomas B. Doolittle. Doolittle, a famous inventor of the time, was retired; he added a few more names. Then the list was mailed out to everyone named, with a challenge to add still other entries, and the list grew again.

Pope and Truex presented the "Roll of Honor" to Theodore N. Vail, AT&T president. Vail was impressed. He suggested that it might be mutually enjoyable and instructive if the veterans named were brought together for a meeting—and thus, to make a long story short, the Telephone Pioneers of America was born.

In the beginning, the requirement for membership was 25 years of service in the industry. But this was promptly reduced to 21 years, partly because at the time 21 years was the legal age of majority. (Only since 1974 has the minimum requirement been reduced to 18 years, conforming to the lowering of the voting age in the United States. The change, of course, has had the effect of adding substantially to the potential membership.)

The first meeting of the Pioneers took place in Boston, convenient for Alexander Graham Bell to attend. Theodore Vail was elected the association's first president, and was re-elected each year until his death in 1920.* W. T. Gentry, president of the Southern Bell Telephone & Telegraph Company, was elected vice president. Henry Pope—who by coincidence celebrated his 63rd birthday during the meeting—was chosen as secretary and treasurer.

At the time of the 1911 meeting, there were 52 charter Pioneer members in what is now Southwestern Bell territory.

---

*Traditionally, international presidents of Pioneering have been presidents of AT&T or operating companies. Two Southwestern Bell presidents have been so honored—Eugene D. Nims in 1929 and A. B. Elias in 1933.

Seven of them attended the Boston meeting: H. J. Curl, W. W. Johnson and C. W. McDaniel of Kansas City; J. E. Farnsworth and M. F. Thomas of Dallas; J. K. Wass of St. Louis; and P. Kerr Higgins of Oklahoma City.

At that first meeting, probably reflecting the social mores of the day, there were no women members (although some men brought members of their families with them, and a few daring females eschewed the session of poetry-reading provided to entertain them in favor of eavesdropping on the meeting).

By the second meeting, held in New York City, there were women members in the audience, and they have been an integral part of the membership ever since.

Although the Pioneers continued to grow in members during the early years, the rate of increase was slowing. There were no binational sessions in 1917, 1918 or 1919, and the next general session in 1920 (in Montreal) attracted 500 members and guests—the same number that had attended the 1912 affair. At this crucial point the idea of "chapters" arose.

Pioneers in Chicago held a get-together just before Christmas 1920, and the gathering adopted

DINNER

Given by

MR. H. J. PETTENGILL

President of the
Southwestern Bell Telephone Co.

TO THE EMPLOYEES IN
THE ST. LOUIS TERRITORY
WHO HAVE BEEN IN THE
SERVICE OF THE COMPANY
FOR MORE THAN TWENTY
YEARS

Saint Louis:
MERCANTILE CLUB
January twenty-fourth
1917

a resolution that the annual international meetings did not provide "sufficient opportunity for association and fellowship among the Pioneers." The resolution went on to recommend creation of local units which could provide "more frequent and more accessible assembly."

Similar informal groups were coming into being in other cities, and the officers of Pioneering responded to the members' wishes. But to set up such smaller units, the organization's constitution had to be completely revised. This revision was adopted at the annual meeting in St. Louis, October 24-25, 1921. There were many extensive changes, but the most significant was the authorization for local chapters.

By the time the executive committee met July 7, 1922, 12 local groups had applied for recognition as chapters. All were chartered on the same day, with numbers assigned in arbitrary sequence. Chicago received Charter No. 1 and chose the name "Vail." The Southwestern contingent was assigned No. 11 and named the chapter after George F. Durant, the man who brought the telephone to St. Louis.

Originally, the Durant chapter represented Pioneers in what is known today as "Region Four"— Missouri, Kansas, Arkansas, Oklahoma and Texas. Its domain also included a small area of Illinois, across from St. Louis, which at that time was served by Southwestern Bell.

Obviously, the original chapter's territory was too far-flung to meet the members' needs, and other chapters were soon carved out of this territory. Today the George F. Durant group shares responsibility for Region Four members with eight other chapters, generally corresponding to Southwestern Bell operating areas as they stood in the mid-seventies. These are the other chapters: Charles S. Gleed (Kansas City and much of Missouri); Sunflower (Kansas); Arkansas; Oklahoma; Lone Star (Dallas); Alamo (San Antonio); San Jacinto (Houston) and Thunderbird (employees of the Western Electric manufacturing unit in Oklahoma City).

The activities of the chapters, which at first were primarily social in nature, have broadened greatly in recent years. Pioneering has a threefold objective— fellowship, loyalty and service. Service (to the community) is being stressed much more than in the early days. Besides formal meetings (at least two each month) there are such activities as rolling bandages for hospital patients; helping autistic children; distribution of radio sets to the blind so they can receive special broadcasts programmed for their interests; manufacturing talking dolls which stimulate retarded children; distribution of the "beeper ball," which makes it possible for blind children to play a version of softball; repairing and testing of tape recorders and small phonographs used by shut-ins; staging "Pioneer Days" programs aimed at all employees regardless of membership, and a multitude of other activities.

No Telephone Pioneer can justifiably complain that "there's nothing to do" in spare time. The question is how deeply one wants to be involved. And for Pioneer Life Members—those who are active members during working years and are now retired—Pioneering can turn the "sunset years" into "golden years."

The chapter setup has expanded further. Chapters now include smaller groups called "councils" and these councils in turn are often broken into "clubs," providing manageable units and a chance to develop leadership at the grass-roots level. Each of these groups has its slate of officers.

As mentioned earlier, the chapters in Southwestern Bell territory are embraced in a larger unit known as "Region Four," one of 13 such units in the Pioneers. The head of each region is a vice president in the overall organization.

This seems a fitting place to recognize the region and chapter leadership since that first (Durant) chapter was chartered in 1921. Space restrictions unfortunately make it impossible to recognize the thousands of others who have contributed to the organization's growth and achievements.

Region (initially Section) Vice Presidents

1936: Edwin T. Mahood
1937: Harry I. McCall
1938: Carrie Werner
1939: A. C. Bookhout
1940: Sewell W. Black
1941: Eugene L. Smith
1942-43: J. Allen Armstrong
1944-45: Carl E. Garrett
1946-48: A. I. Wissman
1948-50: Lucretia Jones
1950-52: C. G. Wassall
1952-54: Arthur M. Rubeck
1954-56: Colby R. Hamilton
1956-58: M. J. Stooker
1958-60: Robert J. Farmer
1960-62: Eleanor Ervin
1962-64: Harry T. Dougherty
1964-66: William J. Hancock
1966-68: Sam E. Holcomb
1968-70: James M. Crump
1970-72: Etta M. Cranor

St. Louis, 1936. The "Silver Jubilee" of the Telephone Pioneers.

1972-74: Curtis T. Mallory
1974-76: Robert M. Arms
1976-78: Francis H. Brockman
1978-80: Jack A. McQueen
1980-82: Earl D. Lander
1982-84: Bettye Knight

The chapter presidents are listed in the order in which chapters were chartered.

George F. Durant Chapter (chartered July 7, 1922)

1922-23: H. J. Pettengill
1923-24: J. K. Wass
1924-25: F. P. Sherwood
1925-27: O. W. Ficklin
1927-28: Percy Redmund
1928-29: C. E. Zahm
1929-30: F. J. Brandle
1930-31: C. W. Harrison
1931-32: W. W. Hall
1932-33: J. M. Judge
1933-34: J. M. Gammons
1934-35: W. D. Keniston
1935-36: J. P. Anderson
1936-37: J. G. Bain
1937-38: F. J. Hagedorn
1938-39: George H. Quermann
1939-40: Robert B. Deason
1940-41: C. B. Allen
1941-42: G. F. Jordan
1942-43: Shields R. Smith
1943-44: Charles B. Crabbe
1944-45: A. I. Wissman
1945-46: E. J. McNeely
1946-47: J. R. Peterson;
　　　　　W. O. Lacey
(Peterson was loaned for government service in Washington and had to resign.)
1947-48: S. J. Ewald
1948-49: C. E. Duke
1949-50: T. P. Halley
1950-51: H. L. Foerstner
1951-52: John T. Dwyer
1952-53: W. J. Casey
1953-54: M. H. Stiegemeier
1954-55: L. D. Harrison
1955-56: Max W. Newby
1956-57: Harry Walter

1957-58: Marge Biermann
1958-59: W. L. Redmond
1959-60: B. Roger Robards
1960-61: W. F. Pilliard
1961-62: D. Nelson Bentrup
1962-63: Maurice Cleaver
1963-64: D. H. Miller
1964-65: L. G. Fligor
1965-66: Etta M. Cranor
1966-67: H. H. Elbert
1967-68: Harold C. Roedemeier
1968-69: Morris W. Betts
1969-70: Ben Smith
1970-71: Rosalie M. Frillman
1971-72: George M. Willard
1972-73: Edward C. Heilman
1973-74: Robert G. Bannecker
1974-75: Francis H. Brockman
1975-76: M. James Grimes
1976-77: Agnes Gillespie
1977-78: Ray E. Durand
1978-79: Ralph G. Kramer
1979-80: Thomas E. Arnold
1980-81: Betty Pallardy
1981-82: Robert Hollocher
1982-83: Ronald D. Sczepanski

Lone Star Chapter (chartered June 5, 1923)

1923-24: J. E. Farnsworth
1924-25: J. F. Henderson
1925-26: J. G. Maben
1926-27: F. M. Rounds
1927-28: J. W. Ezelle
1928-29: R. W. White
1929-30: Fred Linington
1930-31: J. S. Trapp
1931-32: A. L. Edmondson
1932-33: E. L. Smith
1933-34: D. M. Parkinson
1934-35: H. I. McCall
1935-36: H. G. Brickhouse
1936-37: W. H. Duls
1937-38: H. N. Calhoun
1938-39: H. E. Brashear
1939-40: J. F. Seibert
1940-41: A. L. Brown
1941-42: W. B. Kellogg
1942-43: N. H. Moore

1943-44: A. H. Tuttle
1944-45: E. R. Culver
1945-46: Ray Jackson
1946-47: P. J. Trieller
1947-48: W. L. Prehn
1948-49: Julius Amann
1949-50: Robert R. Farmer
1950-51: Victor Tinsley
1951-52: Bert W. Shaffer
1952-53: R. E. Felix
1953-54: Guy H. Hearon
1954-55: W. H. Melbern
1955-56: Eula M. Reynolds
1956-57: T. G. Brown, Jr.
1957-58: R. A. Goodson
1958-59: P. E. Porterfield
1959-60: R. W. Huff
1960-61: A. J. Solcher
1961-62: O. M. Crouch
1962-63: W. Gordon Young
1963-64: J. W. Straiton
1964-65: J. H. Wishcamper
1965-66: Morris Appell
1966-67: H. H. Redding
1967-68: W. K. Wilkinson
1968-69: C. H. Word
1969-70: K. W. Mitchell
1970-71: J. E. Smith
1971-72: R. M. Arms
1972-73: Jack D. Howard
1973-74: Bea Clary
1974-75: Les Millison
1975-76: Betsy Green
1976-77: Charles Bridges
1977-78: Betty Burke
1978-79: Janice Palmeri
1979-80: W. T. Hall
1980-81: Jack Powell
1981-82: Edith Rutledge
1982-83: Bobbie Price

Charles S. Gleed Chapter (chartered July 15, 1926)

1926-27: Phillip H. Hopkins
1927-28: Val B. Mintun
1928-29: John B. Doolittle
1929-30: E. T. Mahood
1930-31: J. A. Armstrong
1931-32: J. A. Leen

1932-33: C. L. Jeffries
1933-34: J. W. Easley
1934-35: Thomas J. Collins
1935-36: Edwin L. Barber
1936-37: Martin J. Ziegler
1937-38: Harry A. Smith
1938-39: J. F. Frazier
1939-40: Edward J. Ryan
1940-41: Rex P. Hughes
1941-42: Willard S. Scherff
1942-43: Harry A. Miller
1943-44: Clarence Weiser
1944-45: F. O. McKinney
1945-46: L. H. Schultz
1946-47: H. L. Enoch
1947-48: M. J. Stooker
1948-49: Karl D. Patnott
1949-50: Alice Walker
1950-51: K. C. Hollingsworth
1951-52: T. R. Smither
1952-53: F. S. Manaugh
1953-54: R. B. Collins
1954-55: H. E. Hendron
1955-56: M. H. Pettit
1956-57: W. K. Myers
1957-58: Marie Hagerty
1958-59: E. E. Buckner
1959-60: O. T. Stueck
1960-61: G. O. Ison
1961-62: E. A. Abend
1962-63: D. C. Williams
1963-64: C. W. Floyd
1964-65: T. C. Robinson
1965-66: Friday Shipman
1966-67: Ben Brackman
1967-68: D. W. Yerke
1968-69: Anna Green
1969-70: Stanley Arnold
1970-71: Melvin Kleppas
1971-72: William Mulvihill
1972-73: Robert Ichin
1973-74: William Gampher
1974-75: Elizabeth Hall
1975-76: Ray Moffatt
1976-77: Robert Beckstead
1977-78: Roosevelt Curren
1978-79: Jim Johnston
1979-80: Earl Lander
1980-81: Ross Dyer

1981-82: Roger Cozart
1982-83: Carl Miller

Oklahoma Chapter (chartered March 17, 1931)

1931-32: L. M. Jones
1932-33: O. N. Dailey
1933-34: E. B. Jennings
1934-35: J. W. Ross
1935-36: M. A. Sanders
1936-37: A. C. Bookout
1937-38: Robert Burns
1938-39: Clarence Oliver
1939-40: Jasper M. Allen
1940-41: R. E. Howard
1941-42: R. B. Kramer
1942-43: C. B. Fariss
1943-44: C. O. Barnes
1944-45: L. J. Bullis
1945-46: O. E. Hopkins
1946-47: E. B. Jeffrey;
     C. E. Zahm
(Zahm took over when Jeffrey retired March 14, 1947.)
1947-48: J. H. Almond
1948-49: R. B. Shoemaker
1949-50: H. W. Nation
1950-51: H. H. Wortman
1951-52: Paul E. Gentry
1952-53: Coy Smith
1953-54: Chester B. McCloud
1954-55: Paul H. Berry
1955-56: M. R. Peterson
1956-57: Clifford H. Sherrod
1957-58: Harold N. Magruder
1958-59: A. L. Cathey
1959-60: Harry L. Dougherty
1960-61: Roy L. Jones
1961-62: Emmeh Hall
1962-63: John Wegner
1963-64: Bob Jarrell
1964-65: Dorothy Kyle
1965-66: Eric Just
1966-67: Dale Nowlin
1967-68: Bill Wells
1968-69: Gladys Bryant
1969-70: Stan Olejnik
1970-71: Bob Goldman
1971-72: D. A. Taylor

1972-73: Anastasia Lane
1973-74: Jim Morrison
1974-75: George Orcutt
1975-76: John W. Boren
1976-77: William G. White
1977-78: James D. Hall
1978-79: Bob Howard
1979-80: Peggy Trezise
1980-81: Bob White
1981-82: Bettye Knight
1982-83: Dwayne Thornton

Arkansas Chapter (chartered December 29, 1938)

1939-40: Roy Munn Porter
1940-41: F. A. Tillery
1941-42: T. B. Kelly
1942-43: J. W. Gause
1943-44: Roy C. Echols;
     W. E. Nelson
(Echols transferred to Indiana Bell)
1944-45: P. P. Cheatham
1945-46: W. E. Gosdin
1946-47: Fred J. Uppinghouse
1947-48: R. P. Miller
1948-49: S. C. Ragle
1949-50: Grace Brown
1950-51: A. M. Rubeck
1951-52: T. S. Hall
1952-53: Leland Krugh
1953-54: Susie Oliver
1954-55: C. T. Hubbard
1955-56: J. W. Harrington
1956-57: C. R. Wharton
1957-58: Margaret Pachl
1958-59: Olin Smiley
1959-60: Haynes Jacoway
1960-61: Euel Forrest
1961-62: Robert F. Farrell
1962-63: Jack Wells
1963-64: Inez Lusby
1964-65: Bert W. Shaffer
1965-66: Ed Campbell
1966-67: Bruce Crume
1967-68: C. T. Mallory
1968-69: Virginia Davis
1969-70: John M. Ostner
1970-71: Cecil P. Boaz, Jr.

1971-72: Hugh Atwood
1972-73: Eula Ruth Harrison·
1973-74: Jack Bouldin
1974-75: Janie Reed
1975-76: Mildred Aldridge;
      Leonard C. McBryde
(Aldridge died in office.)
1976-77: Leonard C. McBryde
1977-78: Wendell Workman
1978-79: Hal Price
1979-80: J. C. A. Flath
1980-81: Bill Jones
1981-82: Royce Tester
1982-83: Don Wade

Sunflower Chapter
(chartered March 9, 1951)

1951-52: Stanley Skinner
1952-53: M. J. Stooker
1953-54: Byron Wolcott
1954-55: S. M. Hardaway
1955-56: M. M. Christensen
1956-57: John W. Walker
1957-58: W. J. Hancock
1958-59: Wanda Palmer
1959-60: Earl Knock
1960-61: L. E. Driver
1961-62: Colby Hamilton
1962-63: Herman Dixon
1963-64: Jesse Edwards
1964-65: Lillian Eis
1965-66: M. H. Ladd
1966-67: Chet Flory
1967-68: Glenn O. Ison

1968-69: C. L. Todd
1969-70: Clara Schwartz
1970-71: A. G. VanNortwick
1971-72: Carl O. Smith
1972-73: Margaret Kauffman
1973-74: W. T. Dinwiddie
1974-75: Mary Barron
1975-76: Paul D. Howland
1976-77: Chester L. Andres
1977-78: Hope Cheeseman
1978-79: Clara I. Haynes
1979-80: George Mistler
1980-81: George Storey
1981-82: Esther Sinclair
1982-83: Dean R. Little

San Jacinto Chapter
(chartered as "Lone Star
South" chapter February 21,
1961)

1961-62: Owen F. Haynes
1962-63: R. M. Bishop
1963-64: Sam E. Holcomb
1964-65: George Hughes
1965-66: Harold Miller
1966-67: J. M. Crump
1967-68: Burt F. Goldman, Jr.
1968-69: C. Woodrow Petty
1969-70: J. E. Tuffly
1970-71: Ruth Foley
1971-72: Jack P. Chance
1972-73: Leonard Woods
1973-74: Wayne N. Williams

1974-75: Elmer S. Ingle
1975-76: Curtis E. Parkerson
1976-77: Howard H. Burney
1977-78: Johnnie Steele
1978-79: William P. Lodge
1979-80: John Tipple
1980-81: Archie Rife
1981-82: Pat Burroughs
1982-83: Lynn W. Zimmerman

Alamo Chapter
(chartered September 13,
1968)

1969-70: George Smith
1970-71: Sibyl Rushing
1971-72: Bill Haehnel
1972-73: Tom Davis
1973-74: Jack McQueen
1974-75: Pete Morrow
1975-76: Gertie Grosskopf
1976-77: Jim Beal
1977-78: Jim Kendrick
1978-79: Don Shaffer
1979-80: Lorraine Fuqua
1980-81: Sonny Farley
1981-82: Alton Linder
1982-83: Hazel Bernhard

Thunderbird Chapter
(chartered July 1, 1979)

1979-80: Dick Baikie
1980-81: Dorothy Schwaniger
1981-82: Joe Hustak
1982-83: Jackie Dunbar

BEYOND THE CALL OF DUTY

CONCERN FOR OTHERS, help in emergencies, willingness to go the extra mile . . . these have been characteristic of telephone people since the earliest days. The reasons are twofold.

In the first place, the business itself creates a feeling of responsibility and involvement—the public depends on the telephone in the small and large crises of life. In the second place, people who care are naturally attracted to telephone work as a career. It has a peculiar psychological similarity to working in a hospital or with the fire or police forces.

This is not to suggest that all telephone people share this dedication to public service, but their proportion in the total is larger than the law of averages would call for.

To recognize and honor such selfless service, the Bell System established the Vail Awards in 1920, shortly after the death of AT&T President Theodore N. Vail. The Vail Memorial Fund issues three principal types of awards: gold, silver and bronze medals. There are also special plaques and, for the first five years the fund operated, "national awards" were issued as well.

The medals are accompanied by cash grants, which have been increased from time to time. Since January 1981, a gold

medal has meant $10,000, a silver medal $5,000, and a bronze medal $2,000.

It is not surprising that Southwestern Bell people have won more Vail Medals than employees of any other company, inasmuch as Southwestern Bell has represented approximately 10 percent of the Bell System for many years. The proud total through the end of November 1983 was 292 medals in all categories, broken down as follows:

Gold	1
Silver	25
Bronze	266

including group awards.

The top award, which implies that the recipient knowingly risked his or her life to serve others, is a rare one; through 1983, only 20 gold medals had been awarded. Southwestern Bell's winner was Charles Erwin Rider, station installer of Guthrie, Okla., who was singled out for the top honor in 1924.

The act which won the gold

Vail Medal for Rider becomes all the more noteworthy when one learns that at the time he was 52 years old, in failing health and under doctor's orders not to expose himself to wind, cold, dust or fatigue.

It was the morning of June 5, 1923, when a freight train toppled off a bridge across the Cimarron River near Guthrie. The train consisted of tanker cars full of oil. They exploded, setting the bridge on fire and turning the river into a sea of flames. The heat melted the wires on the old north-south toll lead—a major link providing long distance service between Kansas and Missouri on the north, Oklahoma and Texas on the south.

Rider took charge. He rowed a small boat out into the blistering heat, not once but dozens of times, and never stopped until he had restored 15 circuits across the blazing river so that emergency calls could go through.

Rider's proudest possession was the gold Vail Medal he received the following year. He cherished it so much that, at his request, the medal was inset in the tombstone over his grave when he died five years later, at the age of 57. Charley Rider, man of courage, had finally lost his fight against cancer.

Rider's brave act is a striking illustration of what the Vail

Southwestern Bell's only gold Vail Medal winner, Charles Erwin Rider of Oklahoma, asked that the medal be inset in his tombstone. Rider received his medal for an act of heroism performed June 5, 1923.

Medals are all about. In 1920 the National Committee of Awards issued a statement of their purpose:

"Hardly a day has passed since the organization of the Bell Telephone System that did not record somewhere in the companies some act that strikingly illustrated the loyalty and devotion of telephone employees. This thought of 'service first' is more than devotion to an organization. . . .

"It comes from a sense of individual responsibility (and) from intelligent recognition of the vital importance of telephone service . . . to the safety and well-being of the community."

Silver medals have gone to 13 men and 12 women who worked in Southwestern Bell territory—not all of them were Southwestern Bell employees, as the Vail Awards go to deserving people who are engaged in telephone service, regardless of their employers. Thus PBX operators, and employees of independent telephone companies or of "agency offices," are also eligible for such awards.*

The silver medal winners' names, places of employment and the years when the medals were issued are listed herewith:

1920 Kate Day
Dallas, Tex.; Dallas Telephone & Telegraph Company.**

1920 Charles Nesbit Cox
Harlingen, Tex.

1921 Verda Ray Townley
Freeport, Tex.

*An agency office, an arrangement no longer in effect, was a location of telephone company switchboard equipment in a building, usually a private home, not owned or leased by the company. The switchboard was operated by someone, typically a housewife, under a contract agreement. PBX operators, of course, are employees of private or public enterprises and operate the switchboards for those enterprises.

1921 Lillian Elizabeth Barry
St. Joseph, Mo.

1922 Cleve Floyd
Little Rock, Ark.

1922 Doris Howard
San Saba, Tex.

1923 Myrtle Ethel Hadley
Snyder, Okla.

1925 Ruby Laverne Wilson
Washington, Ark.#

1927 William Foster Owens
Rock Springs, Tex.; Rock Springs Telephone Company**

1929 Myrtle Dorothy Dull
Elmdale, Kan.##

1932 Irene Regina Duncan
St. Joseph, Mo.

1932 Lila Cook Gaddy
Streetman, Tex.; Three States Telephone Company**

1933 Manley Adrian Norlin
Independence, Mo.

1933 Charity Blackburn
Port Isabel, Tex.; Rio Grande Valley Telephone Company**

1936 Robert Hilderbrand
Fulton, Mo.

1938 Jerry Frank Kincannon
Miami, Okla.

1966 Glen Dale Beauchamp
Waco, Tex.

1967 Theodore Dannecker
Oklahoma City, Okla.

1968 John W. Ranallo
Spiro, Okla.

1968 Janie Barron
Taylor, Tex.

1969 Harry Burttschell
Houston, Tex.

1971 Mary Kathryn Schwaninger
San Antonio, Tex.; PBX operator.+

1971 Michael Bray
Dallas, Tex.

1971 Errick Wayne Mackey
Dallas, Tex.

1972 Russell A. Wyatt
Moore, Okla.

NOTE: Of the listed silver medal winners, seven were not Southwestern Bell employees, as indicated by the marginal symbols:
**Employee of independent telephone company
+PBX operator
#Agency operator
##Agency chief operator.

These symbols also apply to the listings of bronze Vail Medal winners.

Since the Vail Awards were instituted in 1920, only two years have passed (1975 and 1977) without the award of least one bronze medal to a telephone person in the five states served by Southwestern Bell. The names of the bronze medal winners follow in alphabetical order:

Jim Arthur Ables,
Oklahoma City, Okla.

Stacy Lee Adams,
Port Arthur, Tex.

H. A. Alexander,
Beeville, Tex.

Jere Marie Alexander,
Malvern, Ark.

Jessie Louise Alexander,
Dewar, Okla.

Virgie Ruth Alexander,
Marietta, Okla.

Garnett Helen Alley,
Derby, Kan.**

Robert D. Ballew,
Dallas, Tex.

Charles Bankey,
Augusta, Kan.

Joseph Elmer Bauer,
Mehlville, Mo.

Lloyd Lawrence Bauer,
Springfield, Mo.

Bird McGuire Bennett,
Tulsa, Okla.

Arla Bettis,
Marlow, Okla.

L. R. Bishop Jr.,
Houston, Tex.

Jack H. Blythe,
Kansas City, Mo.

Virgil G. Bond,
Cushing, Okla.

M. T. Booher,
Greenville, Tex.

James L. Bowdy,
Kansas City, Mo.

Dale Edwin Boyer,
Springfield, Mo.

Harold Frederick Boyer,
St. Louis, Mo.
(two awards, 1935 and 1946)

Clifton T. Boyter,
Oklahoma City, Okla.

Louise Howerton Bradley,
Miami, Okla.

William A. Bray Jr.,
Dallas, Tex.

H. F. Brenner,
Houston, Tex.

Bedford Mack Brewton,
Longview, Tex.

B. G. Brightwell,
St. Louis, Mo.

Frances Marie Brock,
Bentonville, Ark.

Val G. Brooks,
Wichita, Kan.

Jerry L. Brown,
Leavenworth, Kan.

Hazel May Bull,
Burlington, Kan.**

Lottie Burge,
San Antonio, Tex.

John W. Byers,
Little Rock, Ark.

Charles Cecil Campbell,
Oklahoma City, Okla.

Oscar J. Castillo,
Anadarko, Okla.

Ada Mae Chapman,
Belleville, Ill.

Carleton King Cheek,
Kansas City, Mo.

Junie Chubb,
Burlington, Kan.**

Louis Ray Clardy,
Eagle Pass, Tex.

William Fred Cochran,
Pawnee, Okla.

R. R. Collins,
Tulsa, Okla.

Arthur John Conway,
Topeka, Kan.

Mary L. Cook,
Shamrock, Tex.

Jasper N. Cosby,
Little Rock, Ark.

Frank R. Costello,
St. Louis, Mo.

Harold Don Couch,
Oklahoma City, Okla.

Sue E. Crockett,
Stephens, Ark.##

Hershel L. Crone,
Hot Springs, Ark.

David Cuevas,
Corpus Christi, Tex.

Floyd E. Davis,
Tulsa, Okla.

Frank Edward Davis,
Tulsa, Okla.

Lloyd F. Davis,
Dallas, Tex.

William Harold Davis,
New Braunfels, Tex.

Eugenia R. Delezen,
Camden, Ark.

Charles Edwin Disser,
St. Louis, Mo.

Bertha Dobbs,
Madill, Okla.

Warren J. Dockery,
St. Louis, Mo.
(two awards, 1958 and 1967)

Houston, 1971. Bronze Vail Medal winner Frank Brenner is hugged by Jodie Phillips, the 13-year-old he saved from drowning.

D. C. Donelson,
Midland, Tex.

Walter E. Donis,
St. Louis, Mo.

Margret Ann Dorton,
Jonesboro, Ark.

Joe E. Eakin,
Dallas, Tex.

Elizabeth Earhart,
Hazen, Ark.**

Gordon L. Ebright,
Dallas, Tex.

Anna Sophronia Edmundson,
Oklahoma City, Okla.

Joseph C. Engelman,
Kansas City, Mo.

Richard R. Etzel,
Topeka, Kan.

Robert A. Evans,
Kansas City, Mo.

Kenneth W. Fancher,
Topeka, Kan.

Frieda Farquhar,
San Antonio, Tex.

Roland Fishel,
Oklahoma City, Okla.

Eugene Flanagan,
El Reno, Okla.

Paul Fleming,
Forrest City, Ark.

Andrew D. Forgione,
Enid, Okla.

Henna Marie Frazier,
Weleetka, Okla.

Carl J. Fridrich,
Altus, Okla.

Joseph E. Froehle,
Tulsa, Okla.

E. G. Fuller,
Amarillo, Tex.

Albert B. Gale,
Little Rock, Ark.

James Emmett Garland,
St. Louis, Mo.

Tanner Gary,
Little Rock, Ark.

David Gayner,
Topeka, Kan.

Chassie Glass,
Wolfe City, Tex.##

Wilbur Bascon Glenn,
Tulsa, Okla.

Grace Pearl Gracey,
Leeds, Mo.

Van Graham,
Little Rock, Ark.

Joseph H. Grieshammer,
St. Louis, Mo.

Audrey Groves,
McPherson, Kan.

E. A. Grubbs,
Pryor, Okla.

Percy V. Harris,
Kansas City, Mo.

H. E. Hart,
Dallas, Tex.

Billy R. Hartt,
Beeville, Tex.

Jesse L. Head,
Brownwood, Tex.**

Lloyd B. Hedrick,
Fenton, Mo.

Henry Charles Herrington,
Houston, Tex.

Ethyl Jean Hill,
El Dorado, Ark.

Lester William Holden Jr.,
Topeka, Kan.

Rupert A. Holland Jr.,
Little Rock, Ark.

Julia E. Holly,
Dallas, Tex.

James D. Holt,
Jonesboro, Ark.

Thelma Holtmann,
Belleville, Ill.

Floyd R. Horton,
Coffeyville, Kan.

Zula Fay Howard,
Hutchins, Tex.**

James H. Howe,
Oklahoma City, Okla.

O. W. Hudson,
Fort Worth, Tex.

Mrs. Bob Huff,
Dewar, Okla.

John Westley Hunsaker,
St. Louis, Mo.

Herman Guy Hunter,
Oklahoma City, Okla.

Robert Jackson,
Houston, Tex.

Margaret Celestia Jansenius,
Clifton, Kan.**

W. Spencer January,
Dallas, Tex.

Goldie Maud Jenkins,
Mathis, Tex.##

Helen Lillie Mae Jenkins,
Ardmore, Okla.

Arthur Ray Johnson,
Big Spring, Tex.

Ida Mary Johnston,
Marietta, Okla.

Loman Johnston,
Uvalde, Tex.

Darlis May Jones,
Dewar, Okla.

Edna Mae Jones,
Cherokee, Okla.

Margaret Mae Kelley,
Coweta, Okla.

Ruth Kennedy,
St. Louis, Mo.

E. L. Kinkead Jr.,
Dallas, Tex.

Roy Langford,
St. Louis, Mo.

William Lee,
Moberly, Mo.

Marie A. Lester,
Little Rock, Ark.

John Morgan Leverett,
Hobart, Okla.

Debra Ann Linker,
Enid, Okla.

Charles Alfred Lorenz,
Houston, Tex.

Harry J. Madden,
St. Louis, Mo.

Raymond John Mahoney,
St. Louis, Mo.

Jesus Maldonado,
Corpus Christi, Tex.

Ila Mae Mann,
Hamburg, Ark.##

Emma Alvina Marquardt,
Bartlett, Tex.

Pearl Inez Martin,
Dublin, Tex.

Monroe Lee Mayer,
Harlingen, Tex.

William Andrew McAllester,
Little Rock, Ark.

Marguerite Elizabeth
McCallion,
Burlington, Kan.**

Rose Marie McCallion,
Burlington, Kan.**

Dale McConnell,
Fort Smith, Ark.

Ruth Ann McElroy,
Malvern, Ark.

James E. McGriff,
Pine Bluff, Ark.

V. I. McKee,
Topeka, Kan.

Harry J. McMackin Jr.,
St. Louis, Mo.

Oma Pearl McNair,
Shamrock, Okla.##

Gertrude Medford,
Aledo, Tex.

Mrs. D. W. Medford,
Aledo, Tex.

George Mertens,
Arkadelphia, Ark.

Blanche Claudia Miller,
Bonner Springs, Kan.**

Richard W. Miller,
Topeka, Kan.

Ray Mireles,
Laredo, Tex.

Nina Jean Mixon,
Sand Springs, Okla.

Lee Powell Montgomery,
St. Louis, Mo.

Georgia Lee Moon,
Hugo, Okla.

Leo R. Moore,
Coffeyville, Kan.

George M. Morrison,
Wichita, Kan.

Stanley A. Morrison,
St. Louis, Mo.

Willard Murawski,
Carthage, Mo.

John A. Muth Jr.,
Wichita, Kan.

Cora B. Myers,
Worth, Mo.**

Robert Lee Napier,
Little Rock, Ark.

B. H. Neal,
Altus, Okla.

Burle C. Neely,
Coffeyville, Kan.

Stanley O'Brien,
Port Arthur, Tex.

Ruby E. Bennett O'Dell,
Nowata, Okla.

John M. Ostner,
Little Rock, Ark.

Betty Carol Pace,
Sedalia, Mo.

Lydia Annie Park,
Caddo, Okla.##

Mayme Hardy Payne,
Cleveland, Okla.

Gertrude Minnie Peanick,
Gray Summit, Mo.**

C. B. Phillips,
Topeka, Kan.

Elsie Polzine,
Tulsa, Okla.

Bessie May Potter,
Burlington, Kan.**

Jim C. Powers,
Tulsa, Okla.

Lawrence L. Pruett,
Brownwood, Tex.**

Thomas Everett Quick,
Brookfield, Mo.

Donald A. Ranallo,
Muskogee, Okla.

Blanche Irene Reeves,
Lincoln, Kan.**

Royce B. Reeves,
San Antonio, Tex.

Richard Edgar Reid,
Little Rock, Ark.

Byron A. Rexroth,
Enid, Okla.

Wilbur B. Roberts,
Victoria, Tex.

Donald Robinson,
Springfield, Mo.

Juan Rodriguez,
Corpus Christi, Tex.

Daisy Dorcas Rogers,
Hobart, Okla.

John Alexander Ross,
Fort Worth, Tex.

Frank William Sanders,
Fort Smith, Ark.

Lucinda Sanford,
Belleville, Ill.

Gary W. Savage,
Houston, Tex.

Walter J. Schubert,
St. Louis, Mo.

Charles I. Scott,
Little Rock, Ark.

Weda Idena Sesler,
Waller, Tex.**

Franklin M. Sexton,
Harlingen, Tex.

Michael A. Shearer,
Tulsa, Okla.

Billy J. Shuffield,
Little Rock, Ark.

R. F. Sides,
Dallas, Tex.

Frank Adolph Sievers,
St. Louis, Mo.
(two awards, 1937 and 1946)

Jimmy D. Smith,
Longview, Tex.

Joe S. Smith,
Drumright, Okla.

Thomas Clifford Smith,
Rockwall, Tex.

Aubrey L. Spence,
Austin, Tex.

Weldon Horace Spray,
Dallas, Tex.

Daniel E. Stanley,
Greenville, Tex.

Edward M. Stark,
Moberly, Mo.

Bert Arthur Storm,
Wanette, Okla.

Myrtle L. Story,
Cherokee, Okla.

Jay B. Strain,
Springfield, Mo.

Thomas E. Sweaney,
Eldon, Mo.

A. R. Taylor,
Jonesboro, Ark.

Troy G. Taylor,
Houston, Tex.

Avis Brooks Thompson,
Galveston, Tex.

M. A. Thompson,
Kansas City, Mo.

Homer Carl Todd,
St. Louis, Mo.

O. E. Tomme,
Odessa, Tex.

Edward Oliver Townsend,
Wichita, Kan.

Albert Amos Tuggle,
Tulsa, Okla.

Herman Lee Turney,
Weleetka, Okla.

Wallace Tuttle,
St. Louis, Mo.

John D. Waddle,
Little Rock, Ark.

Bertha Nell Walker,
Spur, Tex.

Frank Walker,
Springfield, Mo.

Dexter Hill Walters,
Corsicana, Tex.

Donald E. Wardlaw,
Florissant, Mo.

Clinton Rosler Watson,
St. Louis, Mo.

Floyd L. Weaver,
Nowata, Okla.

David J. Wells,
Arkansas City, Kan.

W. E. Wiggins,
Fort Worth, Tex.

Hazel Lee Williams,
Spur, Tex.

James Leroy Williams,
Little Rock, Ark.

Luther H. Wilson,
Fort Worth, Tex.

Robert Vincent Wilson,
St. Louis, Mo.

W. A. Wilson,
St. Louis, Mo.

Joe M. Woods,
Paris, Mo.

Margaret Lucille Woolsey,
Chautauqua, Kan.#

Paul H. Worley,
Topeka, Kan.

Rosa Belle Yates,
Trenton, Tex.##

Stephen E. Ziarniak,
Houston, Tex.

William E. Zmeskal,
Corpus Christi, Tex.

GROUP AWARDS

Work force at Hobart, Okla.
  Edith Ball,
  Leroy Woodson Elkins,
  Hugh Alfred Fry,
  John Morgan Leverett,
  Ruby McGee,
  Daisy Dorcas Rogers,
  Herman Wilks Weaver,
  Anna Pearl Woods

Traffic force at Isabel, Kan.
  Alberta Irine Puder,
  Helen Lucille Puder**

**Traveling construction crew,
Lawrence, Kan.**
  C. Albert Theis,
  F. A. Springer,
  L. Gilbert Parker

**Operating force,
New Madrid, Mo.**
  Emma Powell,
  Katherine Corinna Baehr,
  Frances Myler,
  Minnie Elizabeth Gaines#

Operating force, Maysville, Okla.

Work force, Washington, Kan.
  Merle Lenora Meitler,
  Mary Esther Thomas,
  Frances Una Smith,
  Julian Earl Perkins**

**Work forces, Lawrence and
Topeka, Kan.**
  Daisy Marie Cagle,
  Charles Willis Kassinger,
  Maxwell Lawrence Hilliard,
  Louis Edwin Blair,
  Joseph Bradley Reed

**Work forces, Picher and
Miami, Okla.**
  Jeannette Edwards,
  Otis Lee Saunders,
  Curtis Walling,
  Joe Cornelius Atkins,
  Henry William Hinkle

Work force, Merriam, Kan.
  Floyd Franklin Davis,
  Miles Williams Clark,
  Charles Earl Myers,
  Will Dinges Nyhart,
  Mildred Esta Davis,
  Martha Matilda Case,
  Doris Gertrude Cathey,
  Anna Mae Houlehan

Traffic group, Marion, Kan.
  Elizabeth R. Grubb,
  Lillie D. Keazer,
  Winifred Meierhoff

**Plant and traffic group,
St. Louis, Mo.**
  Howard E. Compton,
  Madalon R. Herron,
  Florence C. Leitner,
  Gertrude A. Meyers,
  Ruth E. Mischke,
  Aurelia M. Munier,
  Helen M. Nicholas,

Doris V. Redfield,
Evelyn M. Reesor,
Constance M. Schack,
Fordney B. Smith,
Antoinette E. Stoll,
Maxine J. Warfel,
Susan N. Warner,
Ruth M. Welz,
Dorothy V. Young

**Employees at Woodward, Okla.
(April 1947)**

Traffic group, Shawnee, Okla.
Reta Mae Wright,
Dorothy Irene Richardson,

Winona Louise Stephenson,
Mary Jane Robinson

Plant group, Topeka, Kan.
Howard Franklin Drayer,
Marvin B. Wieligman,
Dale Edward Gideon

**Westport traffic group,
Kansas City, Mo.**
Catherine Alliett,
Mary Wise Miller,
Mary Ellen Pierce

Traffic group, Lawton, Okla.
Marion Cowley,
Lavonna John,
Beulah Wood

Traffic group, Duncan, Okla.
Elizabeth Byford,
Elizabeth Winfield,
Ollie Wininger

**Employees who served during
Hurricane Carla, September
1961**

**Employees who served during
Hurricane Beulah, September
1967**

Plant group, St. Louis, Mo.
James Cook,
Thomas Nogalski,
Theodore Sundays ■

SOUTHWESTERN BELL'S FAMILY TREE

As WITH MANY, if not most, of today's corporations, the developmental history of Southwestern Bell Corporation is incredibly complex. In the first 100 years, telephone operations in the five states involved—Arkansas, Kansas, Missouri, Oklahoma and Texas—began as a series of small-town enterprises, developed into intercity networks (both electrical and corporate), merged, went out of business or changed hands several times.

In the early days quite a few of the exchanges now served by Southwestern Bell had competing telephone systems—two or even three companies seeking to serve the same population. The Bell company didn't always come out on top. Sometimes it sold out or simply shuttered its doors. Sometimes, even when there was no competition, the revenue just wasn't sufficient to keep going, and operations were discontinued.

Even as late as 1918 and 1919, the Bell interests sold out to other enterprises serving Dallas and Kansas City. These two territories were later reacquired, of course (in 1925 and 1927 respectively). Other exchanges, such as Jefferson City, Mo., were relinquished, and there has been no effort to reclaim them. "Independent" (the Bell word for "non-Bell") compa-

nies are serving these exchanges today and serving them well.

One analysis of Southwestern Bell's roots (illustrated on the facing page) depicts "20 Original Ancestors" of the company. In chronological order, they are as follows:

American District Telegraph Company
St. Louis, April 1878;

Kansas City Telephone Exchange
Kansas City, May 1879;

T. B. Anderson
Pettis County (Sedalia), Mo., May 1879;

A. B. Homer
Austin, Tex., July 1879;

Little Rock Telephone Exchange Company
January 1880;

Atchison (Kan.) Telephone Exchange,
March 1880;

J. B. Burson & Company
(Part of Illinois), March 1880;

Hot Springs Telephone Company
June 1880;

J. R. Mulvane
Topeka, October 1880;

Hannibal (Mo.) Telephone Company
1879;

M. H. Insley
Leavenworth, Kan., December 1880;

E. A. Woelk
Springfield, Mo., December 1880;

Loomis & McDaniel
Southwest Missouri, February 1881;

Southwestern Telegraph & Telephone Company
Arkansas and Texas, March 1881;

T. P. Parry
Mexico, Mo., May 1881;

J. A. Glanden
Columbia, Mo., September 1881;

Roberts & Palmer
Jefferson City, Mo., October 1881;

Clark & McDaniel
Moberly, Mo., November 1881;

C. R. Lingle
Clinton, Mo., December 1881;

Pioneer Telephone & Telegraph Company
Oklahoma Indian Territory and part of Kansas, February 1904.*

Without belittling the other 16, certainly the four enterprises in extra bold type were the most significant. They, or their direct descendants, became the Big Four which were finally united in April 1920 to form today's Southwestern Bell Telephone Company. Even earlier, as of 1912, the four operated with a single general staff and were

*The Pioneer company was not an original, however; it was created by merger of three independent companies already existing in the territory.

SOUTHWESTERN BELL'S FAMILY TREE*

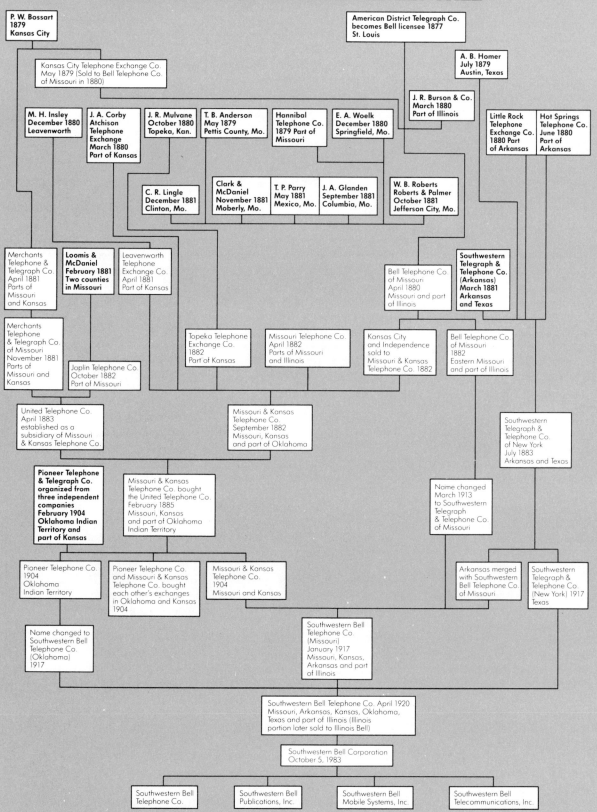

*The 20 original ancestors of Southwestern Bell are indicated in bold type.

known as the "Southwestern Bell Telephone System."

The **Kansas City Telephone Exchange** was a Western Union subsidiary organized in 1878 and opened for business in 1879. A few months later, the property was taken over by the Merchants Telephone & Telegraph Company, and this in turn was succeeded by the Missouri & Kansas Telephone Company, incorporated in 1882. The M&K is the official corporate parent of Southwestern Bell. (See pages 267-270.)

American District Telegraph Company, which originated telephone service in St. Louis under George Durant's direction, picked up the Burson company across the Mississippi River in Illinois, as well as the Kansas City exchange. The enterprise then took the name of Bell Telephone Company of Missouri, a name used from April 1880 to March 1913. After it sold back the Kansas City and Independence exchanges to the Missouri & Kansas Telephone Company in September 1882, Bell of Missouri operated principally in a small part of eastern Missouri and two counties in Illinois.

The Southwestern Telegraph & Telephone Company was created in March 1881 from a number of exchanges in both Arkansas and Texas. It was formally reincorporated as a New York concern a little more than two years later. In 1917, as the eventual character of the "Southwestern System" became clearer, the Arkansas exchanges were separated from SWT&T and assigned to Bell of Missouri for administration. SWT&T, then, became a wholly Texas operation for three more years until the final merger.

Pioneer Telephone & Telegraph Company in Oklahoma, serving the state which was the last of the five to attain full statehood, had a less involved

background. Early on, it swapped its Kansas exchanges with the Missouri & Kansas company, receiving the latter's Oklahoma exchanges in return. Pioneer then remained essentially unchanged, as far as corporate structure is concerned, until the year 1917.

This was the year that formal name changes acknowledged the reality of the working relationship among the Big Four. Pioneer was renamed Southwestern Bell Telephone Company (Oklahoma). Bell of Missouri, which had been renamed Southwestern Telegraph & Telephone Company of Missouri in 1913, brought along its new acquisition of the Bell exchanges in Arkansas and merged with the Missouri & Kansas company. The merger was named "Southwestern Bell Telephone Company (Missouri)." The Texas operation continued to be known as Southwestern Telegraph & Telephone Company for the time being.

Finally, in April 1920, the three remaining Bell companies in the five-state territory were united under the name already carried by the Missouri-Kansas-Arkansas operation.

In 1923 Southwestern Bell purchased the Kinloch Telephone System, which had been a major competitor in the city of St. Louis—one of the last remaining cases of competing telephone companies in a United States metropolis. In 1925 the company reacquired the Dallas exchange from the Dallas Telephone Company, and in 1927 it bought back the exchanges of the Kansas City Telephone Company, which had been an independent since 1918. In 1929, the company sold 23 of its Missouri exchanges to the Southeastern Missouri Telephone Company. (It brought the latter company back into the fold in 1951.)

In a wave of acquisitions in

the mid-thirties, Southwestern Bell bought a number of small companies in Kansas and Texas, principally because they were about to go under during the Depression. Perhaps the most important of these was the United Telephone Company of Kansas—no connection with the present, prosperous independent.

Largely as a result of state commission insistence, Southwestern Bell has also acquired or divested itself of numerous individual exchanges where it appeared the public interest would be served by such tradeoffs. All these transactions have taken place with government (state and federal) approval and in accord with the Kingsbury Commitment (see Chapter 12).

Two more major changes should be noted. Both were occasioned by a Bell System program to bring each company's operations within its state boundaries—a program that affected many companies besides Southwestern Bell.

As far as Southwestern Bell is concerned, these are the results: Southwestern Bell exchanges in the Illinois counties of Madison and St. Clair were sold to Illinois Bell Telephone Company, and the El Paso County, Tex., operations were purchased from Mountain Bell Telephone Company. This change took place January 1, 1982.

The latest change has come about because of the breakup of the Bell System. In 1984, the company will do business as Southwestern Bell Corporation, and the telephone company will be a subsidiary of the corporation.

Other subsidiaries include Southwestern Bell Publications, Inc., which will publish Yellow Pages and other publications; Southwestern Bell Mobile Systems, Inc., which will provide cellular mobile phone service; and Southwestern Bell Telecommunications, Inc., which will sell and lease customer premises equipment.

Involved and probably confusing as this account may be, it is a drastic simplification of telephone corporate history during the first 100 years in the five Southwestern states. To recite all the changes in detail would require all the space in this book.

Perhaps it is simpler to come away with a few basic ideas:

□ Telephone corporate history in the five states involved began in St. Louis in 1878. Telephone service of a rather primitive type was available at some localities in four of the five states by 1880, a little later in Oklahoma.

□ Through a series of mergers, four Bell-affiliated operating units evolved. These were Bell of Missouri, serving essentially the St. Louis-East St. Louis territory; Missouri and Kansas, serving most of Missouri and all of Kansas; Southwestern Telegraph and Telephone, serving Arkansas and Texas; and Pioneer, serving Oklahoma. There were and are, of course, many independent telephone companies operating in these states in locations where Bell did not have a franchise.

□ The Big Four were grouped into the "Southwestern System" in 1912.

□ The "System" formally became the Southwestern Bell Telephone Company in 1920.

□ For 1984, a new Southwestern Bell Corporation has been formed. The telephone company is now one of four subsidiaries of the corporation. ∎

DAVID VS. GOLIATH

THE STRUGGLES between the early Bell interests and the Western Union Telegraph Company took some surprising twists and turns in the early decades of telephony. In the beginning, the giant Western Union threatened to wipe out the Bell interests altogether. Later Bell had become so substantial that it actually bought a controlling interest in Western Union and reported that firm's financial statements in its combined annual report. Threatened with federal antitrust action in 1913 (which would not have been possible in 1878, when Western Union first tried to defeat Bell), AT&T agreed to divest itself of its holdings in the rival enterprise.

A history of Southwestern Bell compiled in 1940 sums up the first stage of the struggle this way:

"When [Theodore N.] Vail took hold as first general manager of the Bell Telephone Company, that embryo industry was threatened by a corporate giant, the Western Union Telegraph Company. In 1876-77, the telephone had been offered to that management, but Western Union had refused to buy, for the telegraph was working successfully, while the telephone was regarded as a scientific toy. But

in 1878, when Hubbard's private telephone lines and early exchanges had replaced several Western Union lines, and a number of brokers' offices had knocked out a ticker or printing telegraph service, the great corporation came to life.

"The printers and tickers were operated by a subsidiary called the Gold & Stock Telegraph Company. Western Union reorganized this to include telephone service and also organized the American Speaking Telephone Company as a sort of parent company to its telephone lines.

"The Western Union companies opened telephone offices, using apparatus manufactured under patents taken out by Elisha Gray, Thomas Edison and others. All these patents infringed upon the Bell patent, but at the moment that fact was worth as little as a claim of right-of-way after an automobile collision.

"The Bell companies were faced with fierce competition in all cities where they were operating. . . . Prospective licensees were frightened out of entering towns in which Western Union managed to establish first exchanges. In some cases, notably Philadelphia, the telegraph officials used influence with city

politicians to hamper Bell men by refusing permission to string wire and so on. Also, Edison devised a carbon transmitter that "talked" more clearly than Bell's and that began to win subscribers from the Bell service.

"The overall effect of this competition was favorable, however. Businessmen argued that if Western Union thought the telephone practicable, it must be a coming thing after all. . . .

"After suit had been filed against Western Union for infringement, the new general manager [Vail] stiffened the backbones of wavering telephone managers and license-holders until they gave blow for blow in the matter of establishing and maintaining exchanges."

The battle ended on November 10, 1879, when the two parties reached an agreement under which Western Union gave up "all its patents, claims and facilities in the telephone business," as John Brooks puts it in his book *Telephone: The First Hundred Years*. Brooks reports that Western Union surrendered a network of 56,000 telephones in 55 cities. In return, it received 20 percent of telephone rental receipts during the 17 years that the Bell patents were effective. ∎

THE COMPANY CHARTER

As described in some detail on pages 262-265, today's Southwestern Bell Telephone Company, now a subsidiary of Southwestern Bell Corporation, is a tapestry woven of many separate strands. The company today, however, operates under a charter first issued to the Missouri & Kansas Telephone Company in August 1882. The charter has been modified several times with the last significant change taking place in February 1921, when the company head-quarters was moved from Kansas City to St. Louis, where it has been ever since.

Selections from the original charter of incorporation and significant changes since are shown here. The originals are on file with the Missouri Secretary of State in Jefferson City.

KNOW ALL MEN BY THESE PRESENTS:

That we, the undersigned, hereby associate ourselves for the purpose of forming a corporation under the provisions of Article V, Chapter 21, of the Revised Statutes of the State of Missouri.

The name of this corporation shall be "The Missouri and Kansas Telephone Company."

Second.* The amount of the capital stock of the Company shall be One Million Dollars, divided into ten thousand shares of One Hundred Dollars each. The same has been bona fide subscribed.

Third. The business of the corporation shall be managed by a Board of seven directors, and the location of the principal office or place of business of said company shall be at Kansas City, Jackson County, Missouri.

Fourth. The number and names of the subscribers to the stock of said company, and the number of shares of stock taken by each subscriber are as follows, to wit:

Names of subscribers	No. of shares.
1. E. T. Gilliland	9,815
2. John R. Mulvane	25
3. M. H. Insley	40
4. George R. Peck	20
5. C. D. Crandall	20
6. E. L. Smith	40
7. George L. Beetle	40

Fifth. The name of the authorized agent of said company at Kansas City is George L. Beetle.

In Witness Whereof, we have hereunto set our hands and seals on this 23rd day of August, 1882.

[Signed by the seven subscribers named above]

*The charter shows no article labeled "First." It must be assumed that the article designating the name is the first article.

STATE OF MISSOURI

No. 2008.

CERTIFICATE OF CORPORATE EXISTENCE.

Whereas, E. T. Gilliland, George L. Beetle, C. D. Crandall and others have filed in the office of the Secretary of State Articles of Association or Agreement, in writing, as provided by law, and have, in all respects complied with the requirements of law governing the formation of private corporations for telegraph and telephone purposes.

Now, Therefore, I Michael K. McGrath, Secretary of State of the State of Missouri, in virtue and by authority of law, do hereby certify that said parties, their associates and successors, have become a body corporate and duly organized under the name of "The Missouri and Kansas Telephone Company," and have all the rights and privileges granted to telegraph and telephone corporations under the laws of this state. And that the amount of the capital stock of said corporation is one million dollars.

In Testimony Whereof, I have hereunto set my hand and affixed the Great Seal of the State of Missouri. Done at the City of Jefferson, this twenty-fourth day of August, A. D. eighteen hundred and eighty-two.

[signed by McGrath]

STATE OF MISSOURI

DEPARTMENT OF STATE

NO. 2008

Whereas, on the 14th day of September, 1899, there was filed in the office of the Secretary of State, as required by law, a certificate of

"The Missouri and Kansas Telephone Company" (a corporation organized and existing under the laws of the State of Missouri), accepting the provisions of the general laws of said state relating to corporations, and extending the time of duration of said corporation 100 years from the 6th day of July, 1899, and said corporation having complied with the law authorizing the the extension of time of duration of private corporations:

Now, Therefore, I, Alexander A. Lesueur, Secretary of State of the State of Missouri, in virtue and by authority of law, do hereby certify that the time of duration of

"The Missouri and Kansas Telephone Company"

is extended to 100 years from the 6th day of July, 1899.

In Testimony Whereof, I hereunto set my hand and affix the Great Seal of the State of Missouri. Done at office in the City of Jefferson, this 14th day of September, A.D. 1899.

[signed by Lesueur]

AFFIDAVIT OF CHANGE OF NAME

State of Missouri,)
) ss.
City of St. Louis   )

Mr. H. J. Pettengill, President of the Missouri and Kansas Telephone Company, a corporation duly incorporated under the laws of the State of Missouri, being duly sworn upon his oath states that at a meeting of the stockholders of said corporation duly called and held on the 29th day of December, 1916, the name of said corporation was by a vote of its Stockholders cast as its by-laws direct changed from The Missouri and Kansas Telephone Company to Southwestern Bell Telephone Company.

H. J. Pettengill,
President

Subscribed and sworn to before me, a Notary Public within and for the City of St. Louis, State of Missouri, this 2nd day of January 1917.

Witness my hand and notarial seal the day and date last above written.

John M. Moran
Notary Public

My Commission expires the 3rd day of October, 1920. Filed for record and duly recorded in my office this 3rd day of January, A. D. 1917, at 9 o'clock, 32 minutes, a.m.

P. H. Bowler, Recorder
by J. R. Morrison, Deputy

State of Missouri,)
) ss.
County of Jackson.)

I, P. H. Bowler, Recorder of Deeds within and for the County of Jackson aforesaid, do hereby certify that the above and foregoing is a full, true and complete copy of the affidavit and note of record thereon of change of name as the same appears of record in my office in Book Series B 1767, page 275, and following.

In Testimony Whereof, I hereunto set my hand and affix the seal of said office at Kansas City, Missouri, this 3rd day of January, A.D. 1917.

(Seal)

P. H. Bowler, Recorder
by John T. Dwyer, Deputy

Filed and copy issued January 3, 1917

Cornelius Roach
Secretary of State

OFFICE OF THE RECORDER OF DEEDS

City of Saint Louis, Missouri   Charles F. Joy
                                                   Recorder

Affidavit Changing Location

State of Missouri,)
) ss.
City of St. Louis   )

E. E. Nims, President, and **J. P. Crowley,** Secretary of the
Southwestern Bell Telephone Company, a corporation duly
incorporated under the laws of the State of Missouri, located at
Kansas City, Missouri, being duly sworn, upon their oaths state
that at a meeting of the Stockholders of said corporation duly
called and held at the office of said Company at Kansas City,
Missouri, on the 1st day of February, 1921, the Articles of
Association were by unanimous consent of the Stockholders
amended by changing the location of said corporation from
Kansas City, Jackson County, Missouri, to the City of St. Louis,
Missouri.

[The affidavit is notarized in St. Louis by A. C. Hoffmeister,
Notary Public, February 11, and recorded by Charles H. Moore,
Recorder of Deeds (John T. Dwyer, Deputy) in Jackson County
February 17. It is then re-recorded by Mrs. Charles F. Joy,
Recorder for the City of St. Louis, April 6, and finally filed by
Charles U. Becker, Secretary of State, April 12, 1921.]

Numerous other charter amendments during and after this
period deal with increases in capital stock and changes in the
number of directors. As of December 1983, these items stand at
$1.54 billion capital stock and 17 directors for the telephone
company. ■

THE TOP 10

SOUTHWESTERN BELL has had 10 presidents since the "Southwestern Bell Telephone System" was created in 1912. (The final consolidation took place in April 1920.) These are the 10:

Heman Judson Pettengill,
March 18, 1912-September 12, 1919.

Eugene Dutton Nims,
September 12, 1919-March 25, 1930.

Albert Barnes Elias,
March 25, 1930-March 23, 1937.

Albert Clinton Stannard,
March 23, 1937-December 31, 1946.

Victor Edward Cooley,
January 1, 1947-March 28, 1950.

James Leslie Crump,
March 28, 1950-June 30, 1951.

Edwin Montilla Clark,
July 1, 1951-June 30, 1965.

Richard Allen Goodson,
July 1, 1965-April 1, 1970.

Angus Sorenson Alston,
April 1, 1970-October 16, 1973.

Zane Edison Barnes,
October 16, 1973, to present.

H. J. Pettengill was one of the last of the old-time telegraph men to enter the telephone business. Born in Brunswick, Maine, April 8, 1851, Pettengill got his first communications job as a telegraph messenger, and in 1867—at the age of 16!—he was made manager for the telegraph company in Lewiston, Maine. He "entered the service of the Bell

Heman Judson Pettengill

System May 8, 1899," according to his sketchy official biography. This apparently refers to his service as vice president of the Glidden chain of companies using Bell patents. On March 11, 1902, he became a director of the Texas-Arkansas company, the Southwestern Telegraph & Telephone Company. He remained a director of this company when he later joined the other boards as well, serving until January 1931. From September 12, 1919, to June 30, 1927, he was chairman of the combined board.

Pettengill's first presidency was of the Southwestern Telegraph & Telephone Company, a post he assumed December 31, 1904. Without relinquishing this title, he added three more presidencies in March 1912: Bell of Missouri, Pioneer, and M&K. In effect, then, he was president of Southwestern Bell eight years before it became a corporate unit. In September 1919, at the

age of 68, he retired from the presidency, but kept involved with the business for another dozen years.

Eugene Dutton Nims

Succeeding Pettengill as president was Eugene D. Nims, a colorful early entrepreneur who was instrumental in creating the Arkansas Valley Telephone Company of Perry, Okla., in 1897. Nims came to Oklahoma as a lumber salesman; his father owned mills in Wisconsin, and there was a booming demand for lumber to build houses and business establishments in the territory newly opened to American settlers.

When the Arkansas Valley firm was merged into the Pioneer Company in 1904, Nims became Pioneer's president. In 1912, as Pettengill took over the quadruple presidency, Nims became first vice president and treasurer of the Southwestern System. He became president September 12, 1919, and held this post until retirement March 25, 1930.

Albert Barnes Elias

A. B. Elias, a native of Spring Brook, Pa., studied electrical engineering and traveled throughout the Western Hemisphere installing and overhauling terminal equipment. His Bell System career started in 1900 with a job as a galvanometer tester for the New York Telephone Company. In 1913 he was sent to Dallas as general plant superintendent for the Texas operation, and four years later became general manager. He came to St. Louis in 1919 as second vice president of the System, became first vice president of Southwestern Bell in 1926, and was elected president in 1930 when Nims retired. Elias retired from the presidency in March 1937 and served a year as board chairman before leaving active service in October 1938.

Albert Clinton Stannard

The next Southwestern Bell president, A. C. Stannard, was a native of Greenfield, Mass. His first telephone job was operating a switchboard in 1899 for AT&T Long Lines in Springfield, Mass.

His career steps included New England Telephone Company, Southern Bell, AT&T again, Pacific Telephone, and Chesapeake & Potomac of Baltimore and Washington. He had been general traffic manager in both San Francisco and Washington, and came to Southwestern Bell in St. Louis with that same title in 1921. In 1928 Stannard was made vice president, then in 1935 he became first vice president. He was elected president March 23, 1937, and retired December 31, 1946.

Victor Edward Cooley

Another "traffic man," Victor Cooley, succeeded Stannard. Cooley, a native of Cloverdale, Calif., got his first telephone job as a clerk with the Pacific Company in 1911. He came to Southwestern Bell in 1921 as general toll traffic engineer. Later he became traffic superintendent for the Texas area. He was brought to the New York Telephone Company for assignments in the Commercial Department and became their vice president-public relations in 1929. In 1943 he returned to Southwestern Bell as first vice president and succeeded Stannard in the presidency January 1, 1947, retiring March 28, 1950.

J. L. Crump, a native of Fulton, Mo., started as a laborer with the M&K Company at Winfield, Kan., in 1905. His biographical outline shows a patient climb up the ladder—installer-repairman, wire chief,

central office installer (for Western Electric), field engineer for Southwestern Bell, division

James Leslie Crump

plant superintendent and the like—until he became general plant manager at St. Louis in 1936. In those 21 years he worked in 13 different Southwestern Bell cities. He became first vice president in 1947, president in 1950 and retired 15 months later.

Edwin Montilla Clark

Up to the present, Edwin M. Clark has had the longest term as Southwestern Bell president—14 years. Clark, a native of Danville, Va., taught mathematics for a year after graduation from college, then started with Western Electric in New York as an installer in June 1923. A year later he became a student engineer for Bell of Pennsylvania and held various plant and engineering titles with that company until he became vice president-operations in March 1949. He came to Southwestern Bell with the same title in April 1950 and succeeded Crump in July 1951. After his retirement from the presidency in June 1965, he remained with the board of directors until June 1968.

Richard Allen Goodson

Clark's successor was R. A. Goodson, a native of Jacksonville, Tex. He worked as a sales clerk for a Houston oil company for nine months after he graduated from college. Then he caught on as a traffic assistant with Southwestern Bell in Dallas March 12, 1928. From then on his career was a steady climb through traffic and general operations ranks, interrupted by a year in 1963-64 when he went from vice president-Texas to vice president-operations for AT&T in New York. He became Southwestern Bell vice president-operations June 1, 1964, and president July 1, 1965. He moved up to chief executive officer April 1, 1970, and formally retired in October of that year.

Goodson's successor, Angus Alston, is the only Southwestern Bell president whose career was shortened by death. Alston, a native of Salt Lake City, Utah, started out as a coin box collector in that city March 2, 1936. His early career was with Mountain Bell in Utah, Colorado and Arizona. He became a vice president and general manager for Bell of Pennsylvania in 1962, and went from there to AT&T in New York for a six-year period during which he rose to executive vice president. He came to Southwestern Bell as president April 1, 1970. In 1973, like Goodson before him, he moved up to chief executive officer and was replaced as president by Zane E. Barnes. As Alston's health continued to fail, he confined his activities to serving as chairman of the board, and he died January 12, 1975, at the age of 60.

Barnes, the current president, had his first telephone job as a plant craftsman; he "broke in"

Angus Sorenson Alston

with Ohio Bell in his home town of Marietta, Ohio, in 1941. His telephone activity was interrupted by service in the Navy in World War II, after which he returned to college, then came

Zane Edison Barnes

back to Ohio Bell. His first management job was plant supervisor in Columbus. His career path took him to AT&T for two years, 1960 and 1961, back to Ohio Bell, to Pacific Northwest Bell, back to Ohio Bell again, and then to Pacific Northwest Bell once more. He became president of PNB in April 1970, leaving the post for the presidency of Southwestern Bell October 16, 1973. On December 2, 1974, he also assumed the title of chief executive officer of the company. In the new Southwestern Bell chief executive officer. On October 14, 1983, he became chairman of the board, president and chief executive officer of Southwestern Bell Corporation. ∎

SOUTHWESTERN BELL CORPORATION LEADERSHIP

As of January 1, 1984, there were 17 directors on Southwestern Bell Corporation's board. This board also serves as the board of Southwestern Bell Telephone Company.* The directors' names, principal business or other affiliations and beginning of terms of office on the telephone company board follow alphabetically:

Louis C. Bailey
executive vice president and chief financial officer, Southwestern Bell Corporation; executive vice president, Southwestern Bell Telephone Company; March 4, 1970

Clarence Barksdale
chairman of the board and chief executive officer, Centerre Bancorporation and Centerre Bank, St. Louis; March 26, 1982.

Zane E. Barnes
chairman of the board, president and chief executive officer, Southwestern Bell Corporation; president and chief executive officer, Southwestern Bell Telephone Company; September 28, 1973.

John W. Bates Jr.
chairman of the board and chief executive officer, Reading & Bates Corporation, Tulsa, Okla.; March 22, 1974.

*Morris Tanenbaum, executive vice president-AT&T, was elected to the telephone company board July 30, 1982. He continued to serve on the telephone company board through 1983 but was not part of the corporation board.

Jack S. Blanton
chairman of the board and chief executive officer, Scurlock Oil Company, Houston, Tex.; April 15, 1977.

Henry W. Bloch
president and chief executive officer, H&R Block, Inc., Kansas City, Mo.; September 28, 1979.

Lloyd S. Bowles Sr.
chairman of the board and chief executive officer, Dallas Federal Savings & Loan Association, Dallas, Tex.; September 12, 1968.

August A. Busch III
chairman of the board and president, Anheuser-Busch Companies, Inc., St. Louis; November 21, 1980.

George H. Capps
president, Capitol Coal and Coke Company, St. Louis; March 22, 1974.

Ruben R. Cardenas
partner, Cardenas & Whitis, McAllen, Tex.; October 30, 1975.

Herschel H. Friday
senior partner, Friday, Eldredge & Clark, Little Rock, Ark.; May 30, 1980.

Tom C. Frost
chairman of the board, Cullen/ Frost Bankers, Inc., and senior chairman of the board, Frost National Bank, San Antonio, Tex.; March 22, 1974.

Joe H. Hunt
executive vice president, Southwestern Bell Corporation; executive vice president and chief

operating officer, Southwestern Bell Telephone Company; June 24, 1977.

Charles F. Knight
chairman and chief executive officer, Emerson Electric Company, St. Louis; March 22, 1974.

William W. Martin
president and chief executive officer, Martin Tractor Company, Inc., Topeka, Kan.; March 22, 1974.

Haskell M. Monroe Jr.
president and professor of history, University of Texas at El Paso; March 26, 1982.

Howard T. Tellepsen
chairman of the board, Tellepsen Construction Company, Houston, Tex.; December 19, 1958.

Besides these individuals, 73 persons have served on the Southwestern Bell board since it became a unified corporation in 1920. They are listed alphabetically herewith, with their terms of office.

Angus S. Alston, 1970-1975

Robert B. Anderson, 1952-1953

Charles R. Anthony, 1949-1972

Thomas H. Barton, 1949-1959

John M. Black, 1951-1964

Edgar S. Bloom, 1925-1926

William C. Bolenius, 1956-1964

Thomas E. Bolger, 1974-1979

Dutton Brookfield, 1959-1979

Vincent M. Carroll, 1939-1944

Maurice R. Chambers, 1973-1980

Edwin M. Clark, 1950-1968

Victor E. Cooley, 1945-1953

Cleo F. Craig, 1946-1951

James L. Crump, 1947-1954

Russell L. Dearmont, 1958-1964

John D. deButts, 1966-1972

James E. Dingman, 1964-1966

J. F. Downing, 1920-1926

Hal S. Dumas, 1951-1956

Albert B. Elias, 1925-1939

Robert W. Ferguson, 1976-1977

Ned N. Fleming, 1955-1974

Roy Furr, 1961-1975

Walter S. Gifford, 1925-1935

C. S. Gleed, 1920

R. A. Goodson, 1964-1974

Edward G. Greber, 1965-1970

E. K. Hall, 1920-1925

Frank H. Hamilton, 1920-1931

Fred M. Hoag, 1931-1938

William L. Holley, 1938-1945

Charles L. Holman, 1920-1925

D. F. Houston, 1926-1927

Charles E. Hugel, 1979-1982

Andrew C. Jobes, 1920-1933

Edwin S. Jones, 1971-1982

Robert McK. Jones 1920-1940

M. A. Low, 1920-1921

William McDonnell, 1949-1973

Powell B. McHaney, 1951-1957

Charles Nagel, 1932-1940

Eugene D. Nims, 1920-1951

Harold F. Ohlendorf, 1959-1980

Cornelius W. Owens, 1972-1974

Earl H. Painter, 1944-1951

Guido Pantaleoni, 1920-1942

Heman J. Pettengill, 1920-1930

Preston B. Postlethwaite, 1940-1956

Frank C. Rand, 1940-1949

Harry H. Ranson, 1967-1976

Alfred L. Shapleigh, 1940-1945

Ethan A. H. Shepley, 1955-1973

George W. Simmons, 1920-1925

Marvin E. Singleton, 1926-1938

Tom K. Smith, 1938-1940

Walter W. Smith, 1942-1949

Kenneth A. Spencer, 1949-1958

Edwin J. Spiegel, 1954-1967

Albert C. Stannard, 1931-1951

Robert G. Storey, 1949-1973

Edward F. Swinney, 1934-1946

Jay Taylor, 1956-1959

H. B. Thayer, 1920-1925

Harold E. Thayer, 1973-1982

Charles A. Thomas, 1950-1974

Theodore N. Vail, 1920

Harry B. Wallace, 1946-1955

Frank O. Watts, 1920-1946

Charles P. Whitehead, 1953-1974

Eugene S. Wilson, 1927-1935

Howard I. Young, 1940-1965

Richard A. Young, 1966-1971

As Southwestern Bell Corporation began its life as an independent company on January 1, 1984, these individuals were in top management positions:

SOUTHWESTERN BELL CORPORATION OFFICERS

Zane E. Barnes
chairman of the board, president and chief executive officer

Louis C. Bailey
executive vice president and chief financial officer

Gerald D. Blatherwick
vice president-public relations

James F. Haake
vice president-personnel

John E. Hayes Jr.
vice president-revenues and public affairs

Joe H. Hunt
executive vice president

Edgar Mayfield
vice president and general counsel

Robert G. Pope
vice president-corporate development

R. McRae Geschwind
vice president-finance and treasurer

Ann Goddard
secretary

SOUTHWESTERN BELL TELEPHONE COMPANY OFFICERS

Zane E. Barnes
president and chief executive officer

Louis C. Bailey
executive vice president

Gerald D. Blatherwick
vice president-public relations

James F. Haake
vice president-personnel

John E. Hayes Jr.
vice president-revenues and public affairs

Joe H. Hunt
executive vice president and chief operating officer

Edgar Mayfield
vice president and general counsel

Robert G. Pope
vice president-corporate development

Kenneth R. Bender
vice president-information systems

James C. Denneny Jr.
vice president-marketing

Charles E. Foster
vice president-staff

R. Alden Pendery
director-centralized services

Robert N. Schoonmaker
vice president-comptroller and treasurer

Ross H. Spicer
vice president-network

William C. Sullivan
vice president and associate general counsel

Arkansas

James B. Nichols
vice president-Arkansas

Kansas
Edward E. Whitacre Jr.
vice president-Kansas

Missouri
Randall D. Barron
vice president-Missouri

J B. Kibler Jr.
vice president-customer services

James E. Taylor
general solicitor-Missouri

Oklahoma
John R. Parsons
vice president-Oklahoma

Texas
James R. Adams
vice president-Texas

John W. Anderson
vice president-customer services
(Texas)

W. Herbert Bowen Jr.
vice president-customer services
(Texas)

Ghyrane A. Davidson
director-comptrollers operations

Ford W. Hall
general solicitor-Texas

Harold Holigan
vice president-centralized services

Roy L. Moskop
director-public relations

Paul F. Roth
vice president-revenues and public
affairs (Texas)

Chester L. Todd
vice president-customer services
(Texas)

OTHER SUBSIDIARY HEADS
*Southwestern Bell Mobile
Systems, Inc.*
James W. Callaway
president and chief executive officer

*Southwestern Bell
Telecommunications, Inc.*
R. Scott Douglass
president and chief executive
officer

Southwestern Bell Publications, Inc.
A. C. Parsons
president and chief executive officer

SOME NOTABLE SOUTHWESTERN ALUMNI

A REVIEW of the list of Southwestern Bell's 10 presidents discloses that only three of them—Nims, Crump and Goodson—can be considered "home grown." The others came from Maine, Pennsylvania, Massachusetts, California, Virginia, Utah and Ohio and began their communications careers elsewhere. (And although Nims first entered the telephone business in Oklahoma, he came to Oklahoma from Wisconsin as a lumber dealer.)

The diversity of origins reflects a policy of choosing the best available person for a job at the time an opening occurs. It's obvious that most Southwestern Bell presidents were carefully groomed and tested before they were given the top responsibility.

The process worked both ways. People with part or most of their careers in Southwestern Bell held corresponding high office in other Bell companies, including the parent AT&T. (A vice presidency in the AT&T headquarters office is generally recognized as equivalent to the presidency of an operating company.)

No fewer than 18 persons who worked for this company (or its predecessors) at some time have gone on to the top spots in other Bell companies. Here are their names, companies and terms of office:

Edward M. Block
vice president-public relations, AT&T, 1975 to present.

Edgar S. Bloom
president, Central Union, Ohio and Indiana Bell Telephone Companies, 1919-1921; vice president, AT&T, 1922-1926; president, Western Electric, 1926-1939.

Edwin F. Carter
president, Ohio Bell, 1926-1930; vice president, Western Electric, 1926-1937.

Roy C. Echols
vice president, AT&T, 1958-1960; president, Indiana Bell, 1960-1968.

Randolph Eide
president, Ohio Bell, 1930-1952.

F. Mark Garlinghouse
vice president, AT&T, 1965-1979.

Edward G. Greber
vice president, AT&T, 1970-1976.

Harold B. Groh
president, Wisconsin Bell, 1963-1973.

Floyd O. Hale
president, Illinois Bell, 1930-1938.

William A. Hughes
president, New Jersey Bell, 1948-1958.

Jasper Keller
president, New England Telephone, 1910-1912.

Franklin P. Lawrence
executive vice president, AT&T Long Lines, 1940-1954.

William L. Lindholm
president, C&P Telephone, 1965-1970, vice president, AT&T, 1970-1972; vice chairman, AT&T, 1972-1976; president, AT&T, 1976-1977.

Charles Marshall
vice president and treasurer, AT&T, 1976-1977; president and CEO, Illinois Bell, 1977-1981; vice president, AT&T, 1981-1983; chairman, AT&T Information Systems, 1983 to present.

Eugene M. McNeely
president, Northwestern Bell, 1949-1952; vice president, AT&T, 1952-1961; president, AT&T, 1961-1964.

Lloyd Miller
vice president, AT&T, 1960-1968.

John Robinson
president, New England Telephone, 1934-1944.

Henry B. Stone
president, Chicago Telephone Company and Central Union Telephone Company, 1890. ∎

SOUTHWESTERN BELL EXCHANGES

THE FOLLOWING EXCHANGES were operated by Southwestern Bell Telephone Company as of December 31, 1983. The most recent addition was El Paso, Texas, acquired from Mountain Bell on January 1, 1982.

In telephone parlance, an "exchange" is a geographical area provided with local telephone service. The word does not refer to either telephone numbers or telephone equipment. (Telephone people call the first three digits of a telephone number the "prefix," and the telephone switching equipment and building serving an exchange may be called either a "central office" or a "wire center," depending on circumstances.)

ARKANSAS

Altheimer	Dermott	Little Rock	Rogers	Andale
Arkadelphia	Earle	Lonoke	Searcy	Anthony
Arkansas City	El Dorado	Lonsdale	Smackover	Arkansas City
Ashdown	Eudora	Luxora	Springdale	Atchison
Batesville	Eureka Springs	Macedonia	Stamps	Attica
Bauxite	Fayetteville	Magnolia	Stephens	Atwood
Beebe	Forrest City	Malvern	Strong	Baileyville
Benton	Fort Smith	Marianna	Swan Lake	Basehor
Bentonville	Grady	Marion	Tupelo	Belleville
Black Fish Lake	Gravette	McGehee	Turrell	Beloit
Black Rock	Greers Ferry	McNeil	Urbana	Bird City
Blytheville	Grubbs	Mena	Van Buren	Blue Rapids
Bodcaw	Gurdon	Monticello	Village	Bucklin
Brinkley	Hamburg	Moro	Walnut Ridge	Burns
Calion	Harrisburg	Morrilton	Warren	Caney
Camden	Heber Springs	Mount Holly	Watson	Canton
Cash	Helena	Nashville	West Memphis	Cedar Vale
Cave City	Hickory Ridge	Natural Dam	Wilmar	Chanute
Center Ridge	Hindsville	Newark	Wilson	Chapman
Cherry Valley	Hope	Newport	Wynne	Chase
Chidester	Hot Springs	Norphlet		Cheney
Cleveland	Hughes	Oil Trough	**Total Arkansas telephone access lines: 621,173**	Cherryvale
Concord	Huttig	Osceola		Chetopa
Conway	Jessieville	Paragould		Clay Center
Crawfordsville	Joiner	Parkin		Clinton
Crystal Springs	Jonesboro	Paron	**KANSAS**	Coffeyville
Dell	Jones Mills	Pine Bluff	Abilene	Colby
	Lake Village	Portland	Almena	Coldwater

Concordia
Cottonwood Falls
De Soto
Dodge City
Douglass
El Dorado
Ellsworth
Emporia
Enterprise
Erie
Eudora
Eureka
Florence
Fort Scott
Fowler
Frankfort
Garden City
Garden Plain
Goodland
Great Bend
Greensburg
Gypsum
Halstead
Hamilton
Hanover
Harper
Hartford
Hays
Herington
Herndon
Howard
Hoxie
Humboldt
Hutchinson
Independence
Iola
Jewell
Kansas City
Kingman
Kinsley
La Crosse
Larned
Lawrence
Leavenworth
Leon
Liberal
Lincoln
Lindsborg
Lyons

Manhattan
Mankato
Marion
Marquette
Marysville
McDonald
McPherson
Meade
Medicine Lodge
Minneapolis
Minneola
Moline
Mount Hope
Neodesha
Newton
Nickerson
Norcatur
Norton
Oakley
Oberlin
Ottawa
Paola
Parsons
Pawnee Rock
Peabody
Penalosa
Phillipsburg
Pittsburg
Plains
Plainville
Pratt
Protection
Reading
Sebatha
St. Francis
St. Paul
Salina
Scandia
Scott City
Sedan
Seneca
Severy
Smith Center
Solomon
Spivey
Stafford
Stockton
Sublette
Tonganoxie

Topeka
Towanda
Washington
Waterville
Wellington
Wichita
Williamsburg
Winfield
Yates Center

**Total Kansas
telephone
access lines:
937,089**

MISSOURI
Adrian
Advance
Agency
Altenburg-Frohna
Antonia
Archie
Argyle
Armstrong
Ash Grove
Beaufort
Bell City
Benton
Billings
Bismarck
Bloomfield
Bloomsdale
Bonne Terre
Boonville
Bowling Green
Brookfield
Camdenton
Campbell
Cape Girardeau
Cardwell
Carl Junction
Carrollton
Carthage
Caruthersville
Cedar Hill
Center
Chaffee
Charleston
Chesterfield
Chillicothe

Clarksville
Clever
Climax Springs
Deering
De Kalb
Delta
De Soto
Dexter
Downing
East Prairie
Edina
Eldon
Elsberry
Essex
Eureka
Excelsior Springs
Fair Grove
Farley
Farmington
Fayette
Fenton
Festus-Crystal City
Fisk
Flat River
Frankford
Fredericktown
Freeburg
Fulton
Gideon
Glasgow
Grain Valley
Gravois Mills
Gray Summit
Greenwood
Hannibal
Harvester
Hayti
Herculaneum-
    Pevely
Higbee
High Ridge
Hillsboro
Holcomb
Hornersville
Imperial
Jackson
Jasper
Joplin
Kansas City

Kennett
Kirksville
Knob Noster
Lake Ozark-
    Osage Beach
Lamar
La Monte
Lancaster
Leadwood
Lilbourn
Linn
Lockwood
Louisiana
Macks Creek
Malden
Manchester
Marble Hill
Marceline
Marionville
Marshall
Marston
Maxville
Meta
Mexico
Moberly
Monett
Montgomery City
Morehouse
Neosho
Nevada
New Franklin
New Madrid
Nixa
Nixa-South
Oak Ridge
Old Appleton
Oran
Pacific
Patton
Paynesville
Perryville
Pierce City
Pocahontas-
    New Wells
Pond
Poplar Bluff
Portage des Sioux
Portageville
Puxico

Qulin
Republic
Richmond
Richwoods
Risco
Rogersville
Rushville
St. Charles
St. Clair
Ste. Genevieve
St. Joseph
St. Louis
St. Marys
San Antonio
Scott City
Sedalia
Senath
Sikeston
Slater
Smithville
Springfield
Stanberry
Strafford
Trenton
Tuscumbia
Union
Valley Park
Versailles
Vienna
Walnut Grove
Wardell
Ware
Washington
Webb City
Wellsville
Westphalia
Willard
Wyatt

Total Missouri telephone access lines: 1,786,270

OKLAHOMA
Ada
Afton
Alex
Allen
Alluwe

Altus
Alva
Anadarko
Antlers
Ardmore
Atoka
Bartlesville
Bennington
Bessie
Billings
Binger
Blackwell
Blair
Bokoshe
Boswell
Braggs
Breckenridge
Bristow
Byars
Cache
Caddo
Calvin
Carney
Carrier
Cashion
Cement
Chandler
Chelsea
Cherokee
Chickasha
Claremore
Cleveland
Clinton
Coalgate
Collinsville
Commerce
Copan
Cordell
Coyle
Cromwell
Cushing
Davis
Delaware
Depew
Dewey
Drumright
Duncan
Durant
Eldorado

Elk City
El Reno
Enid
Eufaula
Fairland
Fairmont
Fairview
Forgan
Fort Cobb
Fort Gibson
Fort Towson
Glencoe
Granite
Grove
Guthrie
Harrah
Hartshorne
Headrick
Healdton
Henryetta
Hillsdale
Hitchcock
Hobart
Holdenville
Hooker
Hugo
Idabel
Indiahoma
Ketchum
Kiefer
Kingston
Konawa
Kremlin
Lawton
Lone Wolf
Luther
Madill
Mangum
Marietta
Marland
Marlow
Maud
McAlester
Medford
Meridian
Miami
Minco
Morrison
Muldrow

Mulhall
Muskogee
Newkirk
Noble
Nowata
Oilton
Okemah
Oklahoma City
Okmulgee
Olustee
Oolalgah
Pauls Valley
Pawhuska
Pawnee
Perkins
Perry
Picher
Pocasset
Pocola
Ponca City
Pryor
Quapaw
Ralston
Rattan
Red Rock
Ringling
Ripley
Rocky
Roff
Rush Springs
Ryan
Sallisaw
Sayre
Seminole
Shawnee
Skiatook
Soper
Spiro
Stigler
Stillwater
Stratford
Tahlequah
Talihina
Tishomingo
Tonkawa
Tulsa
Tupelo
Vinita
Walters

Wanette
Wapanucka
Waukomis
Waurika
Weatherford
Weleetka
Wellston
Westville
Wetumka
Wewoka
Wilburton
Wilson
Woodward
Wynnewood
Yale

Total Oklahoma telephone access lines: 1,272,967

TEXAS
Abilene
Adamsville
Albany
Alice
Allen
Allison
Alpine
Alvarado
Alvin
Amarillo
Angleton
Anna
Anson
Asherton
Atlanta
Aubrey
Austin
Bandera
Bartlett
Bastrop
Batesville
Bay City
Bayside
Beaumont
Beeville
Bellevue
Bellville
Belton
Benavides

Big Spring	Deweyville	Hillsboro	McCamey	Richmond-
Big Wells	Donna	Hondo	McKinney	Rosenberg
Borger	Eagle Lake	Honey Grove	McLean	Rio Hondo
Bowie	Eagle Pass	Houston	Medina Lake	Roby
Brackettville	Eastland	Huntsville	Mercedes	Rockdale
Breckenridge	Edcouch	Iowa Park	Meridian	Rockport
Brenham	Edgewood	Iraan	Mexia	Rockwall
Bridge City	Edinburg	Italy	Midkiff	Roscoe
Brownsville	Edna	Itasca	Midland	Rotan
Bruni	El Campo	Jacksboro	Midlothian	Royse City
Buna	Elgin	Jasper	Mineola	Runge
Burkburnett	El Paso	Jefferson	Mineral Wells	Sabinal
Calvert	Encino	Jewett	Mission	Sabine Pass
Cameron	Ennis	Karnes City	Monahans	San Antonio
Campbellton	Evadale	Kenedy	Moulton	San Augustine
Canadian	Falcon Heights	Kermit	Mt. Pleasant	San Benito
Canyon	Falls City	Kingsville	Nacogdoches	San Diego
Carrizo Springs	Fannett	Kirbyville	Nederland-Port Neches	Sealy
Carthage	Farmersville	Kountze	New Braunfels	Seguin
Castroville	Flatonia	La Belle	Nordheim	Seminole
Catarina	Floydada	Lacoste	Odessa	Shamrock
Celina	Forney	Ladonia	Oglesby	Shiner
Center	Fort Davis	Lake Belton	Omaha	Silsbee
Childress	Fort Stockton	Lampasas	Orange	Sinton
Chillicothe	Fort Worth	La Pryor	Owentown-Winona	Skellytown
China	Freeport	Laredo	Pampa	Skidmore
Chireno	Freer	Lefors	Paris	Slaton
Christine	Frisco	Liberty	Pearsall	Smithers Lake
Cisco	Gainesville	Liberty Hill	Pharr	Smithville
Cleburne	Galveston	Lindale	Pinehurst	Snyder
Cleveland	Garwood	Liverpool	Pipe Creek	Sour Lake
Clute-Lake Jackson	Goldsmith	Lockhart	Pittsburg	South Vidor
Colorado City	Goliad	Lockney	Plainview	Splendora
Columbus	Gordon	Longview	Pleasanton	Spring
Combine	Graham	Los Fresnos	Port Arthur	Spurger
Corpus Christi	Granbury	Lubbock	Port Bolivar	Stamford
Corrigan	Grandfalls	Luling	Port Isabel	Stanton
Corsicana	Greenville	Lumberton	Poteet	Stinnett
Cotulla	Gruver	Lytle	Pottsboro	Strawn
Crandall	Hale Center	Madisonville	Prairie View	Sullivan City
Crane	Hallettsville	Marathon	Princeton	Sweetwater
Crystal City	Hamlin	Marfa	Prosper	Taylor
Cuero	Harlingen	Marion	Pyote	Teague
Cypress	Hearne	Marlin	Quanah	Temple
Dallas	Hebbronville	Marshall	Ranger	Terminal
Dayton	Hempstead	Matagorda	Rankin	Terrell
Deadwood	Henrietta	Mathis	Reagan	Texas City-
Denison	Hereford	Mauriceville	Red Oak	La Marque
Devine	Hermleigh	McAllen	Refugio	Timpson

Tomball
Troy
Tyler
Uvalde
Valley Lodge
Vernon
Victoria
Vidor
Waco
Waller
Warren

Waxahachie
Weatherford
Westbrook
Westbury
Wharton
Wichita Falls
Wildwood
Wills Point
Wink
Wolfe City
Woodsboro

Woodville
Wortham
Yoakum
Yorktown
Zapata

**Total Texas
telephone
access lines:**
5,671,026

NOTE: Telephone access line
figures are as of October
1983.

CHRONOLOGY

THE HISTORY SUMMARY that follows is as accurate as could be achieved at the time this book was compiled. Some of the surviving records of early days are in contradiction, and at this late date there seems to be no practical way to reconcile them.

Furthermore, it is human nature for people in and out of the telephone business to claim the instance they know about is the "first" in any new development. Such claims are hard to refute, but they can often be viewed with skepticism.

With these reservations, then, we present an overview of events during the first 100 years of Southwestern telephone history:

1874
George F. Durant becomes manager of American District Telegraph Company in St. Louis.

1877
November—American District Telegraph Company becomes licensee of Bell Telephone Company.

1878
February 23—James Hamblet demonstrates first telephone in Arkansas, at Little Rock.

March 18—A. H. Belo has private telephone line hooked up between his home and the office of the Galveston *News*.

April 19—St. Louis Telephonic Exchange opens with 12 customers.

1879
May 12—Western Union opens first telephone exchange in Kansas City, using Edison equipment.

August 21—Western Union opens exchange in Galveston.

September 11—Western Union opens exchange in Topeka.

Month uncertain—Charles W. McDaniel opens exchange in Hannibal, using Bell patents.

November 1—First exchange in Arkansas opened in Little Rock by Edward C. Newton of Western Union Company.

December—Western Union telephone operations in Kansas City taken over and operated under Bell patents.

Month uncertain—Telegraph line constructed by U.S. government from Fort Reno to Fort Sill, in what is now Oklahoma. Line, about 70 miles long, was used intermittently for telephone communication and may be considered the first telephone line in Oklahoma.

1880
June 5—First commercial long distance telephone line in Southwest goes into service. Built by Western Union from Little Rock to Hot Springs, Ark., a distance of 50 miles.

Month uncertain—Exchange built at Springfield, Mo., by Edward Welk. (Purchased by Missouri & Kansas Company in 1882.)

1881
February 5—Colonel Logan H. Roots and Jasper N. Keller organize the Southwestern Telegraph & Telephone Company, with head-quarters in Little Rock. They obtain exclusive rights to use of Bell patents in both Texas and Arkansas.

June 1—Southwestern Tel & Tel buys Western Union's Little Rock exchange for $3,585.13.

June 1—Southwestern Tel & Tel opens Dallas exchange at 224 Elm Street with 40 subscribers.

June 17—Southwestern Tel & Tel opens San Antonio exchange.

June 24—Southwestern Tel & Tel opens exchange at Austin.

September 1—Southwestern Tel & Tel opens Fort Worth exchange with about 40 subscribers.

October 1—Southwestern Tel & Tel opens Waco exchange with 45 subscribers.

1882
August—Missouri & Kansas Telephone Company incorporated. It takes over Kansas City property. Purchases 11 exchanges, two in Missouri and nine in Kansas, from the Merchants Tel & Tel Company.

Fall—M&K Company granted license by Bell Telephone Company in exchange for stock valued at $350,000.

1883
February 26—Service established across the Mexican border between Brownsville, Tex., and Matamoras.

March 31—Southwestern Tel & Tel opens first exchange in Pine Bluff, Ark.

April 4—United Telephone Company organized. Purchases

"the rights and privileges of the Merchants Telephone & Telegraph Company" in Kansas; also the "rights and privileges" of the Joplin (Mo.) Telephone Company.

May 22—Erie Telephone Company (Lowell Syndicate) organized. Along with other properties in the Southwest, takes over operation of the Southwestern Telegraph & Telephone Company.

1885

February 25—M&K Company purchases entire property of United Telephone Company for $210,000.

1886

August 26—First commercial telephone line in Indian Territory completed. Connects Tahlequah, Fort Gibson and Muskogee. Promoted, built and financed by Cherokee Indians in Tahlequah.

December—M&K Company institutes toll charges between its Joplin, Webb City, Carthage and Galena, Mo., exchanges. Joplin exchange closed because of loss of business due to toll charges.

1889

June 1—M&K closes exchanges at Webb City, Carthage and Galena.

1891

March 10—Patent issued for a machine-switching system to Almon B. Strowger, Kansas City funeral director. The Strowger system was the first to use the ideas that led to step-by-step switching systems.

1893

June 15—M&K Company opens its first Oklahoma telephone exchange in Oklahoma City.

1894

Strowger Automatic Telephone System introduced at Hannibal, Mo., but proves to be a failure. (See 1896 item concerning Clinton, Mo.)

Month uncertain—First nickel pay telephone in Little Rock installed in Capitol Hotel.

1895

Month uncertain—Little Rock Telephone Company, a competitor to Southwestern Tel & Tel, organized with 300 subscribers.

1896

First telephone lines opened from Kansas City to St. Louis (date not recorded) and from Kansas City to Omaha, Neb. (May 9).

Clinton, Mo., changed from automatic to manual (operator-handled) service.

June 24—St. Louis–New York long distance line opened.

1897

September 8—Arkansas Valley Telephone Company organized at Perry, Okla.

December 14—Muskogee (Okla.) National Telephone Company incorporated.

1898

November 15—Kansas City–New York long distance line opened.

1899

February 8—First common battery (no magneto-cranks) service in use at Dallas. First such installation south of St. Louis, where similar service was installed a year previously.

Month uncertain—First telephone system opened for service in Tulsa, Okla.

1900

Erie Telephone Company dissolved. Property in Arkansas and Texas turned back to the Southwestern Telegraph & Telephone Company.

1901

"The Long Distance Telephone Company" incorporated at Shawnee, Okla.

1902

February 17—Name of Arkansas Valley Telephone Company, Perry, Okla., changed to the Pioneer Telephone Company, with no change in management.

1903

January 16—Exchange at Tulsa purchased by the Indian Territory Telephone Company, headquartered in Vinita.

1904-11

M&K buys 18 telephone companies and Pioneer buys seven. Pioneer also acquires (June 1, 1905) all Oklahoma properties of M&K. Both companies also open new exchanges in various communities to bring their holdings to approximately 60 Missouri and 70 Kansas exchanges for M&K and 30 Oklahoma exchanges for Pioneer.

1904

April 1—Kansas City Home Telephone Company, a competitor to M&K, opens for business with 6,500 subscribers.

1909

Functional organization—the "three column" principle—introduced in the four companies of the Southwestern System. Duties and responsibilities redistributed among the working force to create three departments—plant, traffic and commercial. (Engineering at this time was a department only at the staff headquarters level.)

1910

April 1—Southwestern Tel & Tel sells the El Paso exchange to the Tri-State Telegraph & Telephone Company of Colorado.

1911

Bell System announces plans to consolidate its associated operating companies into statewide or territorial units—the beginning of the present group.

July 3—Southwestern Tel & Tel buys the Pine Bluff (Ark.) Telephone Company.

July 21—Southwestern Tel & Tel buys the Texas Telegraph & Telephone Company. Includes six Texas exchanges.

December 1—Southwestern Tel & Tel buys property of the Southern Telephone Company of Fordyce, Ark. Includes 68 exchanges and 9,000 subscribers in Arkansas and Louisiana. Also included in the sale is the Pan

Electric Telephone Company's exchange at Fort Smith, Ark.

1912

Little Rock Telephone Company, only remaining competition in the city, sold to Southwestern Tel & Tel.

November-December— Cleburne, the first automatic telephone exchange in Texas, declared a failure; the plant is disassembled and the poles chopped down. Troubles blamed on climatic conditions and the wearing effect of dirt and dust on the delicate machinery.

1913-20

During this period a series of corporate rearrangements took place, ending with a single company—Southwestern Bell Telephone Company—operating Bell exchanges in five states. (See pages 262-265.)

1913

January 1—Plan for employee pensions and death and disability benefits inaugurated in AT&T and the Bell operating companies.

December 13—The "Kingsbury Commitment": Nathan C. Kingsbury, vice president-AT&T, writes U.S. attorney general committing AT&T to dispose of its holding in Western Union stock, to provide connection of Bell System long distance lines to independent telephone systems—where there is no local competition—and not to purchase any more independent companies without Interstate Commerce Commission approval.

1918

July 16—Congress adopts joint resolution providing for federal control of the nation's telephone companies during the rest of World War I. Control took effect at midnight July 31, 1918.

August 1—Kansas City Telephone Company is formed, merging Southwestern Bell operations in Kansas City with the Kansas City Home Telephone Company. SWB sells all its prop-

erty with the exception of its toll plant and the telephone building at 11th and Oak streets.

August 1—Arkansas Valley Telephone Company merged with Southwestern Bell. SWB gained 11 exchanges and 8,000 subscribers in 28 Kansas counties.

October 1—Southwestern Tel & Tel sells Dallas exchange to Dallas Automatic Telephone Company. Name of latter changed to Dallas Telephone Company.

1919

July 31—Federal control of telephone companies terminated at midnight.

1921

Three Dallas central offices convert to dial switching—the "X" office, the "2" office, and the "Woodlawn" office. (The Woodlawn office was owned by the Dallas Telephone Company; at the time, Dallas had two competing telephone companies.) Cutover of the "2" office July 30 was the first in the nation using Western Electric equipment installed by Bell System employees.

1922

January 28—Oklahoma City gets first dial service when machine switching equipment is cut into service at the "Northwest" central office.

June 17—First Southwestern Bell "panel" dial system installed at Kansas City "Victor" office.

August 19—First dial service in Little Rock. City's numbering plan changed, with five digits assigned to most stations.

November 25—First dial system in Kansas when 28,000 Topeka telephones are cut over.

1923

February 27—All-copper long distance circuit completed between Big Spring and El Paso, Tex. Makes it possible to talk from Atlanta, Ga., to Los Angeles directly over a southern transcontinental route instead of

diverting traffic through Amarillo or Denver.

March 1—Southwestern Bell takes over Kinloch Telephone System in St. Louis. Purchase includes five central offices in St. Louis, six Illinois exchanges, six exchanges in St. Louis suburbs and the Sedalia exchange in central Missouri. SWB also takes over property of the Kinloch Long Distance Company.

June 21—President Warren G. Harding delivers radio address from St. Louis (first broadcast by a U.S. president).

1924

November 1—Entire city of Tulsa cut to dial at once; 23,561 stations involved. Conversion from old to new system takes three minutes and 50 seconds, with no service interruption.

1925

January—Southwestern Bell authorized by the city of Kansas City to operate the Kansas City Telephone Company. (Takes formal title in 1927.)

October 1—SWB purchases Home Telephone Company of Joplin, Mo., including eight southwest Missouri exchanges.

October 1—SWB purchases Dallas Telephone Company and city once more has single-company service.

1926

New-style directory tried at Topeka and Houston. All advertising eliminated from the alphabetical section and larger type used for listings. Yellow Pages include a new method of indexing and grouping of business listings, as well as improved display ads and type.

March 6—First telephones cut to dial in St. Louis (Laclede-Prospect office).

December—Company headquarters administration building completed at 10th and Pine streets in St. Louis.

December 15—Chicago–St. Louis telephone cable opened for service.

1927

"Jackson" central office in Kansas City moved 15 feet in order to widen the street.

1928

May 7—Equipment installation begun for first CDO—unattended dial exchange—in Southwestern Bell's Pasadena, Tex., office.

July 1—Southwestern Bell buys the Pecos and Rio Grande Telephone Company territory known as "Big Bend." Five exchanges.

1929

Southwestern Bell begins five-year project to construct $45 million long distance cable network connecting the principal cities of Missouri, Kansas, Oklahoma, Arkansas and Texas. About 2,500 miles of cable, much of it underground.

National trademark service started in directories. Dealers listed under brand names.

January 22—Formal opening of new Dallas administration building, which cost more than $5 million. Ceremonies attended by 3,500 people.

February 9—Formal opening of Oklahoma City's new 16-story administration building. Ceremonies attended by 4,000 people.

June 1—Southwestern Bell sells 23 exchanges in southeast Missouri to the Southeast Missouri Telephone Company.

June 27—Formal opening of 28-story Kansas City telephone building, with 6,650 guests present. (The building was not entirely new, but 14 floors had been added to the original structure.)

September 3-5—Four-story building housing Dallas "2" office moved 18 feet so Akard Street could be widened. No interruption of service, and people inside the 4,200-ton building were not conscious of the movement.

December 1—Southwestern Bell buys four exchanges south of St. Louis from the Scotia Telephone Company.

1930

March 1—Wichita, Kan., converted from manual to dial; 32,000 telephones.

April—Teletypewriters used in St. Louis to transmit service orders between the assignment bureau, the Directory Department, the installation office at the pole yards and three central offices. First installation of its kind in Southwestern Bell.

1931

January—St. Louis toll building at Olive and Beaumont streets completed.

1932

April 1—Southwestern Bell buys Creve Coeur Telephone Company and Ballwin Mutual Telephone Company, operating in St. Louis suburbs.

1933

Service representative job title established in Commercial Department.

1937

Combined handset telephone introduced.

1940

April 1—First Coastal Harbor Radiotelephone System in Southwestern Bell territory becomes operative in Galveston. Serves most of the Texas Gulf Coast.

1941

September 29—First installation of No. 1 crossbar equipment in Southwestern Bell territory: St. Louis Lockhart office.

December 7—Japanese attack on Pearl Harbor affects the telephone system of the United States by causing tremendous traffic peaks in all cities, and 100-400 percent increases in long distance telephoning—already at a record high.

1942

July 30—First "K" carrier system in Southwestern Bell completed

between Dallas and San Antonio, a distance of 275 miles.

1943

May 24—Southwestern Bell joins other Bell companies in having toll operators ask long distance users to limit their calls to five minutes because of war conditions. Request made only on circuits where calls were being delayed. New plan put into effect first in St. Louis, Kansas City and Dallas; other cities added later.

July—Badges made available for Southwestern Bell people to show that the wearer was in an industry essential to the war effort. Badge is square red, white and blue ribbon with a small handset telephone printed in the center.

1945

April—More than 205,000 applicants in SWB territory on lists to get telephone service. Communications equipment being manufactured goes to meet demands of armed forces.

December 17—First public use of rural power-line carrier, at Gordon Nelms' general store, Brookland, Ark.

1946

March 18—Test of mobile telephone service in St. Louis; station W9XAY is first in Bell System program.

June 17—First commercial installations of "telephone on wheels" in United States. Two St. Louisans are first customers: Monsanto Chemical Company and Henry L. Perkinson, building contractor.

August 24—About a third of Beaumont, Tex., telephones changed to dial operation. First major dial conversion in SWB territory in more than five years, and one of the first in the nation since the war.

1947

April 7—First nationwide strike in telephone history begins. Lasted 44 days and at one time or another involved all but five operating companies and some 370,000 employees.

1949

July 2—Houston telephone numbers changed from one letter and five figures to two letters and four figures (Metropolitan Numbering Plan). Largest simultaneous number change in company history; affects 250,000 numbers.

August 20—East St. Louis, Ill., cut to dial. One of largest dial conversions ever made at one time in Southwestern Bell history; replaces one of the largest Bell System manual exchanges in the country.

September—Biggest telephone order system west of the Mississippi installed by Famous-Barr Company of St. Louis: a 60-position number 6A automatic call-distributing system.

October 1—Waco exchange, largest remaining manually operated telephone system in Texas, cut to dial. Nearly 26,000 telephones involved. Dial equipment alone cost more than $1 million.

October—SWB begins selling residence extensions again for the first time since World War II.

1950

April 15—First No. 5 crossbar switching office in Southwestern Bell territory cut into service at Granite City, Ill.

April 17—Southwestern Bell reorganized on a state basis. Each state has its own general manager and all department heads in that state report to the general manager instead of reporting to general headquarters in St. Louis. Arkansas becomes a separate area, with state headquarters at Little Rock.

November 9—Dedication of first A4A toll switching system in Southwestern Bell territory at Kansas City, Mo. Operators use push buttons to ring telephones on long distance calls.

1951

January 1—Merger of South-east Missouri Telephone Company and Southwestern Bell: 46,000 telephones involved.

November 24—Operator long distance dialing becomes available in Texas. A4A toll switching system installed in Dallas to serve 15 cities.

1952

December—St. Louis and Kansas City, Mo., change from 5-cent to 10-cent coin phones.

1953

January 1—Operations of Southwest Telephone Company and Southwestern Bell merged. Involves 10 Kansas exchanges.

October—Ozark Central Telephone Company (south-central Missouri) merged with Southwestern Bell.

November—First 4A card translator equipment in Southwestern Bell installed at Dallas. Translators—metal cards with holes in them—direct light rays to activate phototransistors. These, in turn, operate relays which advance the call.

December 5—Suburban districts adjacent to St. Louis converted to two-five numbering plan. Several dial conversions at same time.

1954

Portrait of "Spirit of Service" on directory covers replaced by local area scenes.

Color TV network begins serving the Southwest—St. Louis, Kansas City, Tulsa, Oklahoma City, Dallas, Fort Worth, Houston, Austin, San Antonio, Galveston and Topeka.

"B" wire for rural construction introduced in SWB. Consists of plastic-covered copper wire pairs twisted together.

April 3—St. Louis proper converted to two-five numbering plan. (Also in 1954, San Antonio, Wichita and Little Rock were converted to such numbers.)

1955

February 6—Harlingen becomes first city in Southwestern Bell

to have DDD (customer long distance dialing, also called direct distance dialing). Customers can dial station-to-station calls directly to 13 towns in Rio Grande Valley.

April 17—4A crossbar system cut into service at St. Louis.

1956

New "L3" carrier system for coaxial cable, one of the first of this type in the country, put into operation between San Antonio and Corpus Christi.

New Automatic Message Accounting Center, first in Southwestern Bell, goes into service in St. Louis. It processes Braille-like tapes which record billing information on customer-dialed calls.

1957

First Braille PBX switchboard in SWB territory installed in office of the Little Rock Packing Company.

1958

Topeka becomes first city in Southwestern Bell to use outdoor reporting telephones for police and fire emergencies

Southwestern Bell's first dial exchange on wheels goes into use, serving about 500 customers in the Lumberton area near Beaumont, Tex.

1959

March 16—Four-party service eliminated in Oklahoma's Shawnee and Muskogee districts. First districts in Southwestern Bell to eliminate four-party service.

South Texas area created.

1960

All-Number Calling—seven-digit telephone numbers—introduced at Wichita Falls, Tex., first Bell System exchange to make the change.

1961

During this year a number of new services and products were offered to the public:

Telpak, a private-line service for business customers offering broadband communications channels.

WATS (Wide Area Telephone Service), permitting customers to call long distance as often as they want at a set monthly rate.

Home interphone, farm interphone, Bell Chime and Dataphone® introduced.

July 26—Mr. and Mrs. Hugh T. Polson of Wichita become two-millionth AT&T share owners. (Millionth stockholder celebration May 15, 1951, honored Saginaw, Mich., family).

August 31—Nationwide teletypewriter exchange service (TWX) converted from manual to dial. All TWX users now able to dial direct to any other TWX station in the United States.

Southwestern Bell purchases Farmers Mutual Telephone Company at Weatherford, Okla. Weatherford was the last town in Southwestern Bell territory to have competing local phone companies.

1962

Indexes introduced in Yellow Pages.

July 25—TWA inaugurates Bell System's "Skyphone" air-ground public telephone service for commercial airline use. Trial is on flights between St. Louis, Chicago and the East Coast.

September 17—First Centrex installation in Southwestern Bell territory is at the Humble Oil and Refining Company's headquarters building in Houston. Direct Inward Dialing (DID) is one of the big features.

1963

Panel phone introduced.

Operators start mark-sensing computer cards instead of writing out toll tickets manually.

February 15—Federal Telecommunications System (FTS) goes into service. Initially includes six cities in Southwestern Bell territory—St. Louis, Kansas City, Oklahoma City, Dallas, Fort Worth and Hous-

ton—and one central office at Hillsboro, Mo.

1964

March 2—First nationwide private switched service telephone network other than for the U.S. government installed for General Electric Company.

May 4—Last No. 8 common battery switchboard in the Bell System is replaced by a 990-line community dial office at Caney, Kan. The manual-type switchboard was purchased by the M&K Company from Western Electric and served for 54 years.

December 6—Expanded Direct Distance Dialing (EDDD) goes into service in Springfield, Mo. First in Southwestern Bell, third in the nation. Enables customers to dial long distance calls they could not dial before, such as collect, person to person, credit card calls and calls from coin phones. Made possible by introduction of company's first TSP (Traffic Service Position).

1965

February—Mechanized intercept service begins in St. Louis. First of its kind in the world.

October—Houston area headquarters building completed.

1966

January—Touch-Tone telephones begin trial in Enid, Okla. First in Southwestern Bell.

January 17—Traffic Service Position System (TSPS) No. 1 installation begins in the Beaumont-Port Arthur-Orange area of Texas. First to be installed in SWB and second in the Bell System. Scheduled for service in late 1967.

April 1—New single-slot coin telephone's first installation in downtown Oklahoma City.

June 1—National INWATS bureau, only one of its kind in the country, goes into service at East St. Louis, Ill. Bureau is the information and assistance center for Inward Wide Area Telephone Service (also known as "800" Service).

August—First convictions under federal fraud-by-wire statutes. In Oklahoma City federal court, defendants found guilty on all counts of using electronic "blue boxes" to defraud telephone company.

October 1—SAM (Service Attitude Measurement) plan starts in North Texas area—first in Southwestern Bell. Program is designed to help determine what customers think of their telephone service, on theory that service can be considered good only if the customer thinks it is good. (Originally conducted by personal interviews, plan was later revised to use telephone interviews and re-christened TELSAM.)

1967

February—ECS (Emergency Call System) cut over in Wichita.

March—Arkansas customers become first in company to drop area code on long distance calls if called party has same area code as the caller ("1-plus calling").

September 1—Marketing Department created in North Texas area—first in Southwestern Bell.

October 17—COLETS (Central Oklahoma Law Enforcement Teletype System) goes into operation at Oklahoma City, Del City, Shawnee and Edmond.

1968

June 26—Carterfone decision. FCC strikes down interstate tariffs which prohibit attachment or connection to the public telephone system of any equipment or device not supplied by the telephone companies. Suit was brought October 20, 1966, by Carter Electronics of Dallas, which wanted to interconnect private mobile radio systems with the nationwide network.

Summer—Operators begin using phrase "Directory Assistance" instead of "Information."

October 1—San Antonio area becomes operational.

December—Southwestern Bell's first "911" Emergency Number Service inaugurated in Alva, Okla.

1969

MCI authorized to operate long distance service between St. Louis and Chicago.

February 2—SWB's first ESS goes into service in St. Louis. Evergreen 1, 3 and 5 central offices cut over to electronic switching, with approximately 20,000 main telephones. One of the largest ESS conversions in the Bell System so far.

July 12—Oklahoma's first ESS, and the first 101 ESS in SWB territory, goes into operation at Western Electric's Oklahoma City plant.

October 1—Missouri area splits, becoming St. Louis area and Kansas City area. Thus Kansas City once more becomes an area headquarters city.

1970

March 30—Southwestern Bell's first CRB (Customer Records and Billing) system goes into effect in Illinois district.

December 10—Equal Employment Opportunity Commission asks FCC to deny AT&T pending interstate rate increase until company ends alleged discrimination in employment practices.

1971

Lightweight headsets for operators introduced in SWB St. Louis area.

January 22—FCC announces comprehensive investigation of AT&T in connection with interstate rate request—rate of return, cost increases, Western Electric and service pricing.

April 1—Western Union Corporation's telegraph subsidiary completes acquisition of the TWX service operated by AT&T and several independent operating companies. Sale does not include AT&T's private line teletypewriter service or the machines used by AT&T's Dataphone® customers.

November 7—Direct Distance Dialing inaugurated to Mexico from SWB five-state territory.

1972

March—New Arkansas headquarters building at Little Rock occupied.

March—A 50-cent charge is established for non-published numbers in Illinois.

July 15—Cutover of second-largest Centrex in the U.S.— McDonnell Douglas, St. Louis, 6,900 lines.

September 19—General Services Administration, federal government's contract compliance agency, announces it has approved AT&T's Affirmative Action Program and Transfer and Upgrade Plan.

October 1—Transfer and Upgrade Plan goes into effect.

December—Bell System's first T-2 carrier system, which electronically compresses 96 voice channels on each pair of wires, goes into use between Dallas and Terrell, Tex.

December 1—A $1 a month charge is instituted for non-published numbers in Missouri.

1973

January—Topeka headquarters building dedicated.

January 18—OCR (optical character recognition) goes into effect in Springfield, Mo. First in Bell System; means the end of mark sense. Operators fill out toll ticket billing information in longhand and machine reads their writing.

January 18—AT&T agrees to give $15 million in back pay and $23 million a year in raises to women and minority males against whom it had allegedly discriminated. About 15,000 employees share in back pay and 36,000 in the raises. Technically, settlement does not constitute an admission by the Bell System that it had ever broken any law concerning non-discriminatory hiring or pay.

1974

March 6—New high-capacity underground coaxial cable system, called L-5, placed in service between St. Louis and Pittsburgh. The 823-mile stretch of cable can carry 108,000 simultaneous conversations— more than three times the capacity of the System's largest previous cable.

May 30—An estimated $7 million in back pay for some 7,000 Bell System management employees is approved by the U.S. circuit court in Philadelphia, under provisions of an agreement between AT&T and the federal government.

November 20—Justice Department files a civil antitrust suit against AT&T, charging monopolization and conspiracy to monopolize the supply of telecommunications service and equipment, and asks the separation of Western Electric from the Bell System. The suit also asks the court to order separation of some or all of the Long Lines Department and perhaps other parts of the Bell System. Besides AT&T, Western Electric and Bell Laboratories are named as defendants.

1977

Joplin, Mo., directories used in Bell System experiment. White pages divided into two sections, one for residential and one for business customers. In residential listings, each surname is printed only once. Also new to Joplin is a separate blue pages section for government, public and private school listings.

IDDD (International Direct Distance Dialing) introduced in metropolitan Kansas City. Customers can dial overseas calls directly to 36 foreign countries.

June 6—Ann McDaniel, 21, becomes nation's first blind long distance operator. Works with a Braille console at Little Rock's South I TSPS unit. Console converts standard 82 TSPS buttons into 12-character Braille symbols.

April 20—2,512 attend AT&T share owners' annual meeting, held in Kansas City at the H. Roe Bartle Exposition Hall.

May 1—General headquarters operations staff reorganized into two departments: customer services and engineering, and network services. These changes are first in a reorganization plan to eliminate the historic Plant, Traffic and Commercial departments.

May 16—First Dimension PBX in SWB territory cut into service at J. C. Penney Regional Distribution Center in Lenexa, Kan.

September 17—First No. 3 ESS in SWB territory cut into service at Tonganoxie, Kan.

1978
First bank in the United States to install a Dimension 2000 is the First National Bank in Kansas City, Mo.

January 1—The Accounting Department's name is changed to the Comptrollers Department.

January 17—U.S. Supreme Court refuses to review lower court decision that a microwave communications operator can compete with AT&T's long distance service by hooking into local telephone lines at each end of the call.

April—Teletypewriter service for the deaf put into operation in Little Rock–North Little Rock metropolitan area, providing deaf customers a means to discuss their phone bills, repair needs or other service problems. First service of its kind in SWB territory.

May—Southwestern Bell installs its 15-millionth telephone. First of the operating companies in the Bell System to reach this mark.

June—Conversion of coin telephones to "Dial Tone First" begins in St. Louis.

October—First coinless public telephones installed at Fort Riley, near Manhattan, Kan.

November—Operators in St. Louis start using their names instead of phrases like "Operator" or "Number, please."

December 1—Southwestern Bell begins reorganizing along marketing lines. Operating units restructured into three segments: business, residence and network.

1979
First sale in SWB territory of an "electronic blackboard" made to the U.S. Defense Department in St. Louis.

April—Second-largest Centrex II system in the world is installed at the Department of Defense office in St. Louis; 8,000 Touch-Tone stations. Second only to Centrex at the Pentagon.

1982
January 1—Southwestern Bell acquires El Paso, Tex., exchange from Mountain States Telephone Company.

January 8—Consent Decree. AT&T agrees to divest itself of local operating companies, including Southwestern Bell. In return, U.S. Department of Justice agrees to drop its antitrust suit of November 20, 1974.

December 16—AT&T files plan of reorganization in Judge Greene's court.

1983
August 4—Southwestern Bell Corporation, a holding company, announced. The corporation will constitute one of seven regional organizations into which Bell System operating companies are to be assigned after divestiture. Zane Barnes, Southwestern Bell president and chief executive officer, also will serve as board

chairman, president and CEO of the new organization.

Southwestern Bell Corporation will, initially, have four subsidiaries: Southwestern Bell Telephone Company; Southwestern Bell Publications, Inc., the directory subsidiary; Southwestern Bell Mobile Systems, Inc., to provided advanced mobile phone service; and Southwestern Bell Telecommunications, Inc., to sell customer equipment to business markets.

August 5—U.S. District Judge Harold H. Greene accepts plan of reorganization after numerous modifications to the original Consent Decree. He rules that operating companies like Southwestern Bell are entitled to continue using the name "Bell" and its symbol, whereas AT&T and some of its subsidiaries are not.

September 1—Formation of Southwestern Bell Publications, Inc., is announced.

September 19—Formation of Southwestern Bell Mobile Systems, Inc., is announced.

October 5—A certificate of incorporation is filed in Dover, Del., to officially create Southwestern Bell Corporation.

October 17—Board of directors meets officially for the first time as the board of Southwestern Bell Corporation.

November 9—Formation of Southwestern Bell Telecommunications, Inc., is announced.

November 21—Southwestern Bell Corporation stock begins trading on a "when-issued" basis on the New York Stock Exchange. The stock symbol is "SBC."

1984
January 1—Southwestern Bell begins its new life as a stand-alone company, totally independent of AT&T.

MY, HOW YOU'VE GROWN!

SINCE 1912, when this company first came into being in the guise of the "Southwestern Bell System," the number of telephones served by Southwestern Bell climbed year by year, almost without interruption, until 1981. This pattern of steady growth has been obscured by recent regulatory decisions, which permitted customers to replace company-provided equipment with instruments purchased on the open market . . . and consequently, not on company records.

Only in the Depression of the 1930s had there been a decline in the number of telephones served, until quite recently. Since the end of World War II the company has been adding another million telephones, on the average, every 30 months. These are the year-end figures:

One million telephones	1926
Two million	1944
Three million	1948
Four million	1952
Five million	1956
Six million	1960
Seven million	1963
Eight million	1966
Nine million	1968
Ten million	1969
Eleven million	1972
Twelve million	1973
Thirteen million	1975
Fourteen million	1977
Fifteen million	1978
Sixteen million	1979
Seventeen million	1981

The 17-million figure was attained in August 1981. Then the growth curve flattened out and began to decline. By May 1983, the figure had dropped to 16 million. This did not mean that fewer telephones were being

The 100 millionth telephone in the United States was installed in Texas in 1967. Gov. John B. Connally was given a plaque and a gold telephone to commemorate the occasion.

used by Southwestern Bell customers, but that many of the new instruments bore trademarks other than the familiar "Western Electric" insignia—and those in service were being displaced, too.

As a result, company records are no longer maintained on a "telephones in service" basis. Instead, the extent of customer usage is now measured in "exchange access arrangements" (EAAs)—roughly, but not precisely, equal to *main lines* from central offices to residence and some business customers, and *trunks* from central offices to business PBXs. These EAAs continue to increase, although the rate of growth was slowed somewhat during the business recession of the early 1980s.

Here's how access lines have increased through the years:

1920	488,000
1930	1,000,000
1940	1,210,000
1950	2,750,000
1960	4,150,000
1970	5,830,000
1980	9,370,000
October 1983	10,289,000

ACKNOWLEDGMENTS

MUCH OF THIS BOOK is based on "oral history"—interviews either face-to-face or by telephone, with Southwestern Bell people who were employed during as much as half of the century the book covers.

Some of these people have been quoted at length, others only in passing; and there are many who helped round out the picture of telephony's early days but are not quoted directly. At the risk of slighting one or two individuals, the author would like to recognize the following:

E. S. Bridges, Robert Cornielson, E. M. Cummings, Harry Cradduck, Silas Dietz, Al Dunsing, Jim Fidler, Joe Flath, Bob Fleming, Martin Gardner, Harlan Gould, Laura Hardesty, Bob Hollocher, Thelma Kreeger, L. A. Lewis, Ralph Louis, Elsa McGary, Harold Miller, Carl Nelson, Faye Landis Oldham, K. G. Shell, W. B. Stephenson, Earl Toepperwein, Drexyle Turner, William Wimsatt and M. L. Zeiders.

These interviews were further supplemented by written contributions from the following, among others: Ray Blain, Carrie Bowlin, H. P. Bridges, H. R. Brunner, Velma Dahl, Fay Davis, Rosemary Enderle, Wilma Farris, Forrest Gilliland, Mittie Glayzer, K. D. Hammond, Mildred Holley, Diane Hussey, Frank Marlow, Charles Mooney, Frances Neidholt, Goah Ragsdale, Lillie Richards, Sibyl Rushing, Charles

Snyder, Billie Tunnell, Jess Villareal, Faye Williams and Bill Wright.

Special mention is due Henry Altepeter and J. Raymond Peterson, retirees who responded to the appeal for contributions by volunteering their extensive memoirs. These provided a wealth of anecdotes which have been included, often without attribution, at various places in the text. Other individuals are usually named where their offerings appear.

Alongside the writings of Altepeter and Peterson one must mention several older memoirs, some going back to the very beginning of telephony. Extensive reliance has been placed on four volumes, two by George W. Foster—*History of the Telephone in Texas* and *History of the Southwestern Telegraph & Telephone Company, 1881-1912*—and the other two by C. W. McDaniel—*History of Exchanges of the Missouri & Kansas Telephone Company* and *Telephone Reminiscences*.

Other authors who should be mentioned are the following: Huffman Baines, *Pioneering the Telephone in Texas;* J. E. Farnsworth, *A Tenderfoot in Texas in the Early Eighties;* and Raymond Garrett, *History of Telephone Service in Bowie, Tex., 1896-1971.* Several other writers, who chose to be anonymous, compiled various histories to which reference has been made; most of

these endeavors exist only as manuscripts in telephone company files. The Oklahoma City files provided a treasure trove of traffic stories—Chief Operator Mima Blanchard's narrative of her telephone career.

Comptrollers and Personnel department records have been indispensable in providing facts and figures for the more formal historical portions of this book, especially the appendix. In some cases information not found in Southwestern Bell records was provided by public relations staffs of the AT&T or Bell operating companies.

The files of SCENE magazine and its predecessor, *Southwestern Telephone News,* as well as the state editions of the biweekly employee newspaper, *Telephone Times,* were invaluable sources of information.

Thanks are here expressed to Jim Rippey and Cindy Hadsell, who worked as a team in compiling Northwestern Bell's history, and who were delighted to pass on the expertise they had acquired the hard way; to John Ripley, Topeka historian, who provided helpful insights into early telephone history in Kansas; and to Kenneth Todd, who may be surprised to encounter his name here. Todd, of the AT&T Public Relations Department, compiled *A Capsule History of the Bell System,* and by his excellent example provided inspiration and encouragement for all regional telephone historians.

The list of credits would be woefully incomplete without recognizing the conscientious help provided by Carole Becherer and Judy Hammer of the Southwestern Bell headquarters Public Relations Department.

Nor can we fail to acknowledge the cooperation of the Southwestern Bell public relations organizations in St. Louis, Kansas City, Topeka, Little Rock, Oklahoma City, Dallas, Houston, and San Antonio. Their files, besides preserving records of local company activities, also contain newspaper clippings which provide an "outsider's" view of what went on in telephony during those first hundred years.

But beyond all these people and publications that can be clearly identified as sources for this book, there is another group whose names are not so easy to come by. They are the members of the Telephone Pioneers who in the early 1930s undertook the compilation of "exchange histories." Their often anonymous labors, typed and assembled in binders, captured names, facts and viewpoints that otherwise would have been lost forever.

Dozens of public relations people over the years have used these records to prepare news releases, feature stories, booklets and magazine articles. This writer, too, should be added to the list of those grateful to the Telephone Pioneers. ∎

— Dave Park
(Dave Park, author of "Good Connections," retired from Southwestern Bell Telephone Company in 1978. Most of his telephone company career was spent as a writer for SCENE magazine. Before joining the company, he was a writer for International News Service.)

A NOTE ON THE TYPE

The text of this book was set in 11-point Berkeley Oldstyle. The typeface was created by Tony Stan. It is based on a face drawn by Frederic Goudy in 1938 for the University of California Press at Berkeley, Calif. The typeface has remained the property of the University Press since it was released and thus has seen little use elsewhere.

The face was drawn free of ruling pen and straight edge. Natural nuances that result from the pen strokes are seen in each letter. There are slight differences in the serifs and heavy strokes because it is old-style hand lettering.

The book was designed by Charles H. Wallis, district staff manager-graphic arts for Southwestern Bell Telephone Company. The book was illustrated by James J. Cummins.

Kansas City, Mo., 1915.
An operating room.